Le Corbus

Architect and Feminist

Published in Great Britain in 2004 by Wiley-Academy, a division of John Wiley & Sons Ltd

Copyright © 2004   John Wiley & Sons Ltd,
                    The Atrium, Southern Gate,
                    Chichester, West Sussex PO19 8SQ,
                    England
                    Telephone (+44) 1243 779777

Email (for orders and customer service enquiries): cs-books@wiley.co.uk
Visit our Home Page on www.wileyeurope.com or www.wiley.com

This publication is designed to provide accurate and authoritative information in regard to the
subject matter covered. It is sold on the understanding that the Publisher is not engaged in rendering
professional services. If professional advice or other expert assistance is required, the services of a
competent professional should be sought.

Other Wiley Editorial Offices

John Wiley & Sons Inc., 111 River Street, Hoboken, NJ 07030, USA

Jossey-Bass, 989 Market Street, San Francisco, CA 94103–1741, USA

Wiley-VCH Verlag GmbH, Boschstr. 12, D-69469 Weinheim, Germany

John Wiley & Sons Australia Ltd, 33 Park Road, Milton, Queensland 4064, Australia

John Wiley & Sons (Asia) Pte Ltd, 2 Clementi Loop #02–01, Jin Xing Distripark, Singapore 129809

John Wiley & Sons Canada Ltd, 22 Worcester Road, Etobicoke, Ontario, Canada M9W 1L1

ISBN 0470 847476

Front cover: *Taureau* # 1,162 × 114 cm, oil on cavas, 1952 © FLC/ADAGP, Paris and DACS, London 2004.
Back cover: 'Le Corbusier and his wife Yvonne' © FLC/ADAGP, Paris and DACS, London 2004.
Cover design: Artmedia Press Ltd, London
Typeset by Florence Production Ltd, Stoodleigh, Devon, UK, based on a text design by Liz Brown
Printed and bound in Italy by Conti Tipocolor

Le Corbusier
Architect and Feminist

Flora Samuel

WILEY-ACADEMY

Contents

Acknowledgements

Many people have assisted with this project. Firstly I have to thank Maggie Toy and Abigail Grater at Wiley for their belief in this book. Charles Jencks and Karen Franck provided their thoughts on my proposal in its early stages. Heidi Weber, Henriette Trouin and the late Jane Drew were kind enough to give their time to my research. Mary McLeod and Russell Walden have provided both inspiration and practical assistance. Gisela Loehlein and Thomas Emig generously went to Switzerland to interview Heidi Weber for me. I am indebted to Evelyne Trehin, Isabelle Godineau and the staff at the Fondation Le Corbusier as well as Gwenaelle Fossard at DACS. I have received much help in translation from both Marie Gastinel Jones and Elizabeth Warman, but any mistakes are all mine. Prue Chiles, Jude Harris and Guy Pitt have contributed to the illustrations.

Amongst my colleagues Mary Brice, Phil Jones, Ian Knight, Judi Loach, Juliet Odgers, Chris Powell, Paola Sassi, Simon Unwin, Richard Weston and Kathryn Wilkinson have all assisted me in a number of important ways. I am particularly indebted to Adam Sharr for reading early drafts and providing invaluable commentary. Sylvia Harris and her staff at the library in the Welsh School of Architecture have been unceasingly helpful. Of the students with whom I have worked David Miles, Kwan Phil Cho, Robin Keates and Hannah Yoell have helped me particularly with thoughts, images and an enthusiasm for Le Corbusier.

This book provides me with the welcome opportunity to thank my parents for introducing me to Le Corbusier. Lastly and most importantly I have to thank my husband Alejandro Ojeda-Marin and my daughters Alicia and Otilia for their constant support and enthusiasm.

The research for this book was completed with the assistance of a British Academy Grant.

List of Illustrations

Illustration Credits

The author and publisher gratefully acknowledge the following for permission to reproduce material in the book. While every effort has been made to contact copyright holders for their permission to reprint material in this book the publishers would be grateful to hear from any copyright holder who is not acknowledged here and will undertake to rectify any errors or omissions in future editions.

Front Cover, Back Cover, Figures I.1, I.2, I.3, I.4, I.5, 1.1, 1.2, 1.3, 1.4, 1.5, 1.6, 1.7, 1.9, 1.10, 1.11, 1.12, 1.12, 2.1, 2.2, 2.3, 2.4, 2.5, 2.6, 2.7, 2.8, 2.9, 2.10, 2.11, 2.12, 2.13, 2.14, 3.1, 3.2, 3.3, 3.4, 4.1, 4.2, 5.1, 5.2, 5.3, 5.4, 5.5, 5.6, 5.7, 5.8, 5.9, 5.10, 5.11, 5.12, 5.13, 5.14, 5.15, 5.16, 5.17, 5.18, 5.19, 5.20, 5.21, 5.22, 5.23, 5.24, 5.25, 5.26, 5.27, 5.28, 5.29, 5.30, 5.31, 5.32, 5.33, 5.34, 5.36, 5.37, 5.38, 5.39, 5.40, 5.41, 5.42, 5.43, 5.45, 5.46, 5.47, 6.1, 6.2, 6.3, 6.4, 6.5, 6.6, 6.7, 6.8, 6.9, 6.10, 6.11, 6.12, 6.13, 6.14, 6.15, 6.16, 6.17, 6.18, 6.19, 6.20, 6.21, 6.22, 6.23, 6.24, 6.25, 6.26, 6.27, 6.28, 6.29, 6.30, 7.1, 7.2, 7.3, 7.4, 7.5, 7.6, 7.7, 7.8, 7.10, 7.11, 7.12, 7.13, 7.14, 7.15, 7.16, 7.17, 7.18, 7.19, 7.21, 7.22, 7.23, 7.24 © FLC/ADAGP, Paris and DACS, London 2004; 1.13 Collection Centre Canadien d'Architecture/Canadian Centre for Architecture, Montréal; 4.3 by permission of the British Library, shelfmark 89.e.24; 5.44, C.G. Jung collection. 6.1 © Galleria dell 'Accademia, Florence; 6.2 © Unterlinden Museum, Colmar; 6.18 by permission of Harvard University Press; 7.9, Galleria Nazionale delle Marche, Urbino.

Photographs 1.1, 2.4, 6.29, 6.30 © René Burri/ Magnum Photos; 1.9, 5.17, 6.23, 6.24 © Lucien Hervé, Research Library, The Getty Research Institute, Los Angeles (2002.R.41); I.1, 5.7, 6.11, 7.3 © Flora Samuel; 2.9, 6.28 © Thomas Emig; 6.12, 6.15 © Jude Harris.

Preface

The idea for this book came to me over ten years ago whilst teaching history to access students on the Women into Architecture and Building Course at South Bank University in London. I then realised that the standard texts on architectural history had little to offer my students – mature women, many with children, often from ethnic minority groups, none of whom were easily fooled. Indeed, it quickly became clear that such texts very often perpetuated the very myths that worked against such women embarking upon architectural careers. It seemed to me that there was a real need to make history relevant to those students by showing where they fitted into it, the presence of women being noticeably lacking in most versions of architectural history.

As I travelled with the students through the standard myth of Modernism that I myself had been taught (I was at that time a very novice teacher), it became apparent to me that one architect, above all others, did actually give consideration to women and their needs. This was Le Corbusier. I was however perplexed by the way in which the female sex was represented in his paintings. I could not understand why, if in his opinion women were solely creatures of the flesh, he spoke so highly of them in his writings and worked closely with a number of them on a professional basis. Further investigation led me to a vein of feminist writing on the subject of Le Corbusier in which he was vilified in the most extreme terms. Such a perspective seemed too simplistic to be useful.

Writing in the late 1980s Adrian Forty noted the way in which Le Corbusier came to embody Modernism for the architects of Britain during the postwar period.

To a large extent, the history of Le Corbusier in Britain is the history of modern architecture in this country. In a way that has happened to no other architect, he has been used to personify the ideas, ideals and the architecture of Modernism; as a result his name has been used, sometimes as a talisman, sometimes in the place of Lucifer himself, in arguments that may only be related distantly to the man. That he has attracted so much controversy is not only on account of his own talents, or failings, but because of what he has been taken to represent in the debate about modern architecture.[1]

I would argue, on the same note, that Le Corbusier's views on women have been taken to represent those of Modernism itself. Consistently misrepresented, it is my aim to find out what they may have been.

Cardiff, May 2003

Note

1   A. Forty, 'Le Corbusier's British Reputation' in T. Benton (ed.), *Le Corbusier Architect of the Century* (London: Arts Council, 1987), p.35.

Introduction

In the *Pilgrims Manual* for Ronchamp Le Corbusier annotated the words 'cult of Mary' with the word 'feminism'.[1] What follows is an examination of Le Corbusier's interest in this subject, defined in the *Oxford English Dictionary* as the 'advocacy of extended recognition of claims and achievements of women'. Le Corbusier saw the world as an ordered whole, governed by the laws of nature in a union of opposites. This would include male and female who, according to his ideal vision, would exist in equal balance. It is my suggestion that he tried to raise the status of woman so that this state of equilibrium, so evidently lacking in France at that time, could be achieved. What he perceived as the damaging 'imbalance' of the machine age was in part caused by her subjugation.

The scope of the book comes from Le Corbusier himself, from his implied definition of women's sphere, which, it will be seen, has few limitations. Whilst its main focus is Le Corbusier's attitude to women, a number of other related areas will be covered: the relationship between the sexes; the attributes and definitions of each sex; the use of sexual imagery in architecture and art; sensual response to objects and buildings; the harnessing of the libido in creative activity; love in its different forms and its relationship with the sexual act.

Le Corbusier believed himself to be something of an expert on what he called 'the sexual equilibrium' of various countries, immodestly acknowledging his possession of 'the touchstone of comparison, liberty and clarity of judgement'.[2] He wrote:

What is a prophet? He who, in the heart of a whirlwind, can see events, can read them. He who perceives relationships, who denounces relationships, who points out relationships, who classifies them, who foresees them.

The poet is he who shows a new truth.[3]

Ever eager to classify what he saw, positioning each thing within his well ordered world view, Le Corbusier was to ascribe a very particular and perhaps surprising role to woman. She would play a fundamental part in bringing about the radiant world that he so desired.[4]

The study of Le Corbusier is almost an industry in itself. Multitudes of scholars have launched their careers using the work of this one man as a springboard into academia – ironic because of his own loathing for the 'academies', in his eyes places of stultification of the spirit. Russell Walden notes that although so much has been written about him we are still barely scraping at the surface.[5] Le Corbusier's particular interest in the subject of woman is one of fundamental importance to his work as a whole, but one that has been very largely ignored, first by historians contemporary with the architect, for example Nikolaus Pevsner, and latterly by writers such as William Curtis, Stanislaus von Moos, Geoffrey Baker and H. Allen Brookes. Perhaps more than any other writer Mogens Krustrup has brought to light the symbolic meaning of Le Corbusier's late work, but he has spent less time exploring the significance of his discoveries. Charles Jencks, Mary Wigley, Mary McLeod and Walden have done much to prepare the ground for this book in identifying the important role played by women in Le Corbusier's life. McLeod observes:

We've now passed the point of needing to brand all heroes of the Modern Movement as 'sexist pigs'. We must begin to examine historically what was progressive and what was regressive in their attitudes and practices . . . of course, there were voyeuristic dimensions to Le Corbusier's attitude to women, but he also praised them as actors/ creators who were often at the forefront of modern life. I just feel we're at a stage in feminist scholarship where we can go beyond earlier reductive readings, and try to figure out to what extent modern architecture both embodied and challenged traditional gender constructions. Besides considering its oppressive dimensions, we need to ask how modern architecture contributed to more emancipatory ideas of domestic life and of the design profession itself.[6]

In doing so she summarises the primary purpose of this book. It is my aim to open up for discussion the possibility that Le Corbusier may have liked and admired women and, indeed, may have taken an interest in their wellbeing.

Born in 1887 in La Chaux de Fonds in the Swiss Jura as Charles Edouard Jeanneret, Le Corbusier's career can be roughly divided into three phases. The first, his early life and education, will be described in some detail in Chapter 4.[7] The second phase, brief but very active (the 1920s), was when he moved to Paris and began his collaboration with Paul Dermée and the painter Amedée Ozenfant to produce the journal *L'Esprit Nouveau* which ran for twenty-eight editions. In it Le Corbusier published some of his earliest polemical statements on architecture and city planning, including those that were later published as his first highly influential book *Towards a New Architecture* in 1923. It was at around this time that he changed his name to Le Corbusier and began his prolific output of writings, paintings and stark modern buildings, such as the Villa Savoye (Fig. I.1, 1929), built according to his 'Five Points for New Architecture', with a free plan, free facade, horizontal windows, roof garden and pilotis, each planned around a route or promenade.

Towards the end of the 1920s Le Corbusier entered into a third phase. His architecture began to change in character from his trade mark crisp white boxes with muted coloured interiors into something far more sensuous and tactile, anchored to the ground, both physically and metaphorically, buildings such as the Pavillon Suisse, with a rubble side wall, and his own home at 24 Rue Nungesser et Coli, with a raw unrendered brick party wall and coffered ceiling, being hybrids of the two. Ideas developed for such vaulted rough cast houses as the Maison du Petite Weekend (Fig. I.2, 1935) were sustained in his work for the rest of his life, *beton brut*, exposed brickwork, chunky timber, strong colours, symbolism and geometry being characteristics of Le Corbusier's late work. Possible reasons for the transformation in his architecture may lie in the disillusionment he began to feel at the soulless way Modernism was progressing (typified by his altercations with the functionalist Hannes Meyer over the League of Nations competition), in his marriage to Yvonne Gallis and in the introduction of women into his paintings. It was at this point that he became involved in the left wing Regional Syndicalist movement, publishing in its journals a number of the essays that were eventually compiled into his book *The Radiant City*.

Le Corbusier moved without compunction from left wing to right wing circles in pursuit of work, attempting to find it by currying favour with Vichy, but his associations with that regime left him out of favour when it came to finding architects to assist with the reconstruction after the war.[8] The period of reflection provided by world events was, for Le

Figure I.1 Villa Savoye, 1929.

Figure I.2 Maison du Petite Weekend, 1935.

Corbusier, followed by a period of enormous creativity, arguably the most significant schemes being the Chapel at Ronchamp (consecrated 1955) and the Monastery at La Tourette, the Unité housing blocks and his work on the city of Chandigarh, new capital of the Punjab. Le Corbusier used these schemes as an opportunity to develop further his ever-evolving philosophy of life, Orphism, to be explored in Chapter 4.

Slowly a more human Le Corbusier is starting to enter the public domain. He is usually portrayed as a rigid figure in heavy glasses and bow tie and is famous for being brusque and domineering, but there was evidently far more to him than this.[9] He was just as likely to be found flirting (Fig. I.3), playfully picking sequins off the dress of a glamorous student or making sand sculptures with his friend Nivola's children (Fig. I.4) as he was to be found spending hours in earnest discussion with architectural luminaries, perhaps more so. His friend Maurice Jardot observed that

> His honour, if hypersensitive, is beyond question and his rectitude inflexible, while his actions, although occasionally maladroit, are never guided by deception or intrigue.
> And he loves good food and good stories.[10]

In this book I will focus upon the private as well as the public Le Corbusier in the belief that the former had a direct effect on his work as an architect. Unlike certain writers, I do not believe that his evident enjoy-

Figure I.4 Le Corbusier playing with the children of his friend Nivola, making sand cast plaster sculptures, 1950.

ment of sex and appreciation of the female body necessarily prevented him from having women's best interests at heart.

Whilst he has frequently been reviled by feminists of our generation,[11] I will be examining the ways in which his arguments actually coincided with those of French feminists during the first half of the twentieth century. It is my opinion that Le Corbusier should actually be credited for having a rather more open attitude to women than many of his contemporaries, but how can I prove this? One way might be to examine the statistics regarding the numbers of women working in architectural practice at that time. Certainly my mother, who went to work as an architect in a Paris office after the Second World War, was seen very much as a novelty by her French colleagues. Was Le Corbusier alone in giving a woman, Charlotte Perriand, a pivotal role in his office (Fig. I.5)? Certainly, McLeod suspects that 'offices such as Le Corbusier's were more open to women architects than more traditional firms in France'.[12] Another way to find out whether Le Corbusier was unusual in this regard might be to compare him with one or a number of his contemporaries, to find out how many women they had working for them. This would seem to be problematic, as there is no other architect with a career comparable to his in scope. Certainly there

Figure I.3 Le Corbusier with Minette De Silva at Hoddeston.

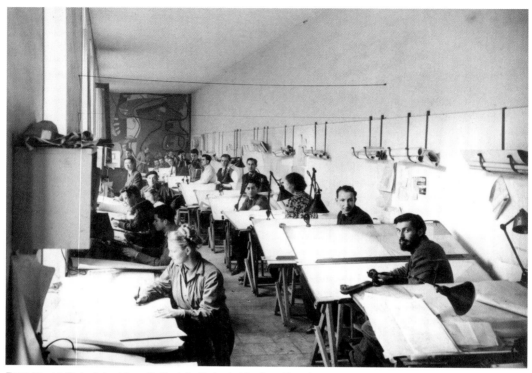

Figure I.5 Le Corbusier's atelier with Charlotte Perriand at the front. Note the presence of other women at drafting tables.

are no such famous working partnerships as that between Le Corbusier and Perriand, a significant point in itself. I believe that the only way to gain a sense of the real nature of Le Corbusier's interest in women is through a study of the cultural norms prevailing in Paris during the first half of the twentieth century. I use as my guide Claudine Mitchell's study of Jane Poupelet[13] in which she examines the sculptress' work against the background of feminist discourse in France at that time. In a similar way I hope to shed light upon Le Corbusier's own attitude to women by examining his work in the context of contemporary French attitudes to women, both inside and outside his immediate circle. Only then does it become possible to discern whether he was in any way out of the ordinary.

Sexuality, like gender, is a burgeoning theoretical area on to which any number of theories could be brought to bear. An excellent introduction to this field is provided by Joseph Bristow in his book *Sexuality* in which he clearly delineates the theories of Sigmund

Freud, Jacques Lacan (1901–1981) and, of course, Michel Foucault (1926–1984).[14] For Freud and Lacan, sexuality was a repressed force bubbling beneath the surface of Western culture, an opinion with which it seems Le Corbusier would have agreed:

> The products of the first machine age have reached their sexuality. It is a song of hidden, prohibited, forbidden sex. It's the world's great torment, Sexuality has been tamed (2,000 years of Christianity priests and pastors): civilisation. One is right back at the starting point; nature pleads together with the negro, implores, begs, desires, aspires: man, woman. The profound origin of worlds,[15] final accounting, the reckoning.[16]

Foucault is more matter of fact, seeing sexuality as 'an especially dense transfer point for relations of power'.[17] Le Corbusier might also have had some sympathy with this viewpoint as he enthusiastically underlined passages in his friend, Rene Allendy's book, *Capitalism et Sexualité*, which refer to the links between money and sex.[18] Whilst I will not be applying the ideas of any one theorist to the ideas of Le Corbusier, it is important to remain aware that such theories exist. This is one specific reading of a subject for which many different readings are possible.

This book pullulates with terms that, in the jargon of feminism, are 'gendered'. They are not value neutral, one clear example being the term 'Modernism'.[19] Over the last few years certain writers have commented on the fact that such old fashioned binary constructions as male and female had no relevance for contemporary architectural debate.[20] I would argue, along with Sarah Wigglesworth that:

> At a practical level, we have to start by acknowledging that our society is structured, at a symbolic level, around a binary whose foundational difference is sexual (the biological and symbolic possession/lack of phallus). Although the challenge to this symbolic framework is an essential project because it is of crucial significance for the fundamental shift in society's order, there is an urgent need for political and social strategies for action while we await the dismantling of existing structures. I argue that such structures must employ the binary, so as to demonstrate the injustices and inconsistencies which lie behind the 'truth' of patriarchal culture. We must use the binary against itself.[21]

It is my hope that, in exploring meaning and significance of the binary, male and female in the work of Le Corbusier, I can arrive at a better understanding of what it means for architecture in general.

Ironically the word feminine is itself a masculine construct and should perhaps be gendered masculine. It has to do with expectations of female behaviour, but may bear little relation to what it is to be female. It is therefore a word that needs to be used with caution. Where the words feminine and female are used in quotes they have been left intact. Having said this, as Shari Benstock writes, 'Neither the biologically determined categories "male" and "female" nor the socially produced categories "masculine" and "feminine" are absolute – entirely consistent, even

monolithic, within themselves. Each inhabits and is inhabited by its opposite'.[22]

The first part of the book focuses on the reality of Le Corbusier's dealings with women and to the situation for women in France during the first half of the twentieth century. Given that Le Corbusier seems to have been open to the ideas of feminism, a necessary stage in this investigation is to find out if he really put any of his theories into practice, working and living with women as equals. For this reason Chapters 1 and 2 will be devoted to an examination of his actual relationships with women, the aim being to gain an insight into his real feelings about women and their worth. In their book *Significant Others*, Whitney Chadwick and Isabelle de Courtivron write that 'a new wave of writings has focused on groups, interactions, friendships and mutually enriching influences, which blur our existing notions of heroic individuality'.[23] It is my belief that Le Corbusier was not a lone genius; he relied heavily on the help of others, many of them female. In Chapter 3 'Feminism, Fashion and Physical Culture' I will set Le Corbusier's ideas into a cultural context, showing that certain of his ideas lend themselves to a feminist interpretation.

In contrast to Part 1 of this book, Part 2 is focused on Le Corbusier's ideal vision of society and of women in particular. Chapter 4 is devoted to a discussion of the theoretical ideas underpinning his work. Here a number of key themes will be identified, most importantly Orphism: a world view based on the ideas of Pythagoras, its central aim being harmony with nature, a harmony that, for Le Corbusier, could only be achieved through a balanced relationship between male and female. Then in Chapter 5 I will move on to a discussion of the way in which Le Corbusier chose to represent woman in his work as an artist. It is evident from an examination of his paintings, murals and drawings that he saw women as an ideal, conforming to a fixed image derived from his personal doctrine of Orphism. It will become apparent that this idealised view of women was somewhat at odds with the reality of those whom he encountered in his day-to-day life.

The ideal and the real meet in poignant juxtaposition in the final part of the book which is devoted to an investigation into the way in which Le Corbusier built his ideas about women and femininity into his architecture. In Chapter 6 I will look at the ways in which the idealised view of femininity expressed in his art was translated into his designs for the scheme for the Basilica, City, Museum and Park at La Sainte Baume (1946–1960). Although this scheme was never built, it provides important background for my subsequent investigation into the role of women in the iconography of the chapel at Ronchamp.

Late in life, when he became acutely conscious that his time in this world was running out, Le Corbusier decided to devote what remained of his energies to housing. It was through this medium that he felt best able to convey his particular message. In Chapter 7 I will examine the fundamental role of women and the feminine in Le Corbusier's theories of urbanism, within which they played a pivotal part. Central to the discussion will be his scheme for the Unité in Marseilles, perhaps the most influential housing block ever built.

Notes

1   In Le Corbusier's collection of books in the Fondation Le Corbusier (hereafer referred to as FLC). M. Le Chanoine Belot, Curé de Ronchamp, *Manuel du Pèlerin* (Lyons: Editions Lescuyer, 1930), p.22.

2   Le Corbusier, *Sketchbooks Volume 3* (Cambridge, MA: MIT Press, 1982), sketch 129. His pseudonym Le Corbusier appears to be derived from the alchemical crow that flies over the world, witness to its destruction during the process known as *nigredo*.

3   Le Corbusier, *Precisions* (Cambridge, MA: MIT Press, 1990), p.31.

4   Significantly, evidence is emerging that Frank Lloyd Wright also took more than a passing interest in feminism. A.T. Friedman, 'Frank Lloyd Wright and Feminism: Mamah Borthwick's Letters to Ellen Key', *Journal of the Society of Architectural Historians* 61, 2 (2002), pp.140–151.

5   R. Walden (ed), *The Open Hand* (Cambridge, MA: MIT Press, 1982).

6   McLeod quoted in K. Ven Herck (ed.) 'First Interlude: on the nuances of historical emancipation', *Journal of Architecture* 7 (2002), p.245.

7   See H. A. Brookes, *Le Corbusier's Formative Years* (London: University of Chicago Press, 1997) for a summary of his early years.

8   His old employer Auguste Perret would suffer no such problems. Having also flirted with Vichy he went on to join the Resistance, an act that made up for his previous sins.

9   Jenger writes that Le Corbusier's letters reveal that the image that is often presented of him is horribly over-simplified. J. Jenger, *Le Corbusier Choix de Lettres* (Basel: Birkhauser, 2002), p.29.

10   Maurice Jardot quoted in Le Corbusier, *My Work* (London: Architectural Press, 1960), p.11.

11   For example see B. Colomina, 'The split wall: Domestic Voyeurism' in B. Colomina (ed.) *Sexuality and Space* (New York: Princeton University Press, 1992), p.104.

12   McLeod quoted in Ven Herck (ed.) 'First Interlude: on the nuances of historical emancipation', p.245.

13   C. Mitchell, 'Style/Ecriture. On the classical ethos, women's sculptural practice and pre-First-World-War feminism', *Art History* 4 (5), 2002, pp.6–7.

14   J. Bristow, *Sexuality: the New Critical Idiom* (London: Routledge, 1997).

15   Possibly a reference to Gustave Courbet's scandalous close up painting of female genitalia, *L'Origine du monde*, 1866.

16   Le Corbusier, *Sketchbooks Volume 1* (London: Thames and Hudson, 1981), sketches 616–620.

17   M. Foucault, *The History of Sexuality, Volume 1: An Introduction* (New York: Random House, 1987), p.103.

18   R. Allendy, *Capitalisme et Sexualité: le conflits des instincts et les problèmes actuels* (Paris: Denoel, 1931), FLC, p.14.

19   Kime Scott observes that this word 'as we were taught it at midcentury was perhaps half way to truth. It was unconsciously gendered masculine.' Bonnie Kime Scott (ed), *The Gender of Modernism* (Bloomington: Indiana University Press, 1990), p.2.

20   See for example, N. Lahiji, 'The Gift of the Open Hand: Le Corbusier's reading of Georges Bataille's La Part Maudite', *Journal of Architectural Education* 50/1 (1996), pp.50–67.

21   S. Wigglesworth, 'Practice: the significant others', in D. McCorquodale, K. Ruedi and S. Wigglesworth (eds), *Desiring Practices: Architecture, Gender and the Interdisciplinary* (London: Black Dog, 1996), p.280.

22   S. Benstock, *Women of the Left Bank* (London: Virago, 1994), p.8.

23   W. Chadwick and I. de Courtivron, *Significant Others: Creativity and Intimate Partnership* (London: Thames and Hudson, 1993).

Part One

REAL

1 Intimate Relationships

Before moving on to a discussion of the idealised view of womanhood represented in Le Corbusier's art and architecture it is necessary to gain a picture of his dealings with real women: women whom he saw in the crowd; his clients; those friends, colleagues and lovers with whom he surrounded himself. Only then will it be possible to ascertain whether he really was interested in promoting women and what they stood for.

Photographs taken by Rene Burri of Le Corbusier's apartment in 24 Rue Nungesser et Coli show a pin board on the wall covered in images of his wife and mother, both of whom he loved dearly (Fig. 1.1). Le Corbusier wrote to his mother that he was an 'infinitely sentimental being (contrary to appearances)'.[1] He was also a very private man. Little is known of his personal life though more and more is seeping into the public realm.[2] The focus of this chapter is Le Corbusier's evident love for women and the pleasure he seems to have derived from their company.[3] His relationships with women would have a direct influence upon his work.

Marie Charlotte Amélie Jeanneret-Perret: his mother

According to Jane Drew, Le Corbusier's love for his mother Marie Charlotte Amélie Jeanneret-Perret (Fig. 1.2) 'was a very great force in his life'.[4] At the inauguration of the chapel at Ronchamp the presiding bishop drew attention to Le Corbusier's dedication to his mother – a 'woman of courage and faith' – at the beginning of Le Corbusier's book *When the Cathedrals were White*, suggesting that she occupied some primary role in his creativity.[5] Le Corbusier wrote, in response

Figure 1.1 Pinboard in Le Corbusier's penthouse, 24 Rue Nungesser et Coli.

Figure 1.2 Le Corbusier and his family.

to his friend Jean Petit's suggestion that his mother was Le Corbusier's major source of inspiration, 'it is the music of Mme Jeanneret-Perret which explains the art of Le Corbusier'.[6] Evidently her role in his creativity cannot be stated too strongly. As a dedicated musician it was she who imparted to Le Corbusier an understanding of music and hence Pythagorean harmony.

By all accounts Madame Jeanneret was a strong woman.[7] Charles Jencks writes that Drew, amongst others, believed that Le Corbusier's love for his mother was 'tinged with a certain awe and fear of her determination'.[8] Le Corbusier described her as being diligent and a 'model of moral force': an example to both him and his brother, instilling in the two boys a sense of independent judgement.[9] Her motto, 'whatever you do, see that you do it' (taken from

Rabelais) was to appear at the foot of the card announcing her death.[10] Le Corbusier wrote of the way his mother would read the Bible looking for something other than the Protestant point of view, something more profound: 'The choices in life, the important things above all others'. He wrote to her 'you, your life, your effigy, that which others look for in you, your artistic strength, your liberty of spirit, your individual response, personal. Life, life, life. It is that that we all love'.[11] In his mind she seems to have been a symbol of wisdom and discernment, a supposition that is corroborated by a sketch of her as an old woman in which she evokes an enigmatic and all knowing sphinx (Fig. 1.3). It may be no coincidence that he described the house that he designed for her at Vevey as 'an antique temple by the side of the water', fitting for the goddess within.[12]

As Jean Jenger observes, Le Corbusier's ability to freely express affection for his mother is striking, for example: 'Your letters are fresh like a bouquet of flowers. The sun is in you. You show us the light side of life'.[13] In a further communication, that is by no means unusual, he wrote, 'understand our profound respect, our admiration, our affection. And above all our gratitude. You are somebody'.[14]

In *Nature and Space: Aalto and Le Corbusier*, which I co-authored with Sarah Menin, we developed the argument that Le Corbusier had an unsatisfactory relationship with his mother[15] during his early years beginning, it seems, with her inability or refusal to

Figure 1.3
Drawing by Le Corbusier of Marie Charlotte Amélie Jeanneret-Perret as a sphinx.

breastfeed him.[16] Utilising the theories of Donald Winnicott and Edith Cobb we suggested that Le Corbusier turned to nature to create a holding environment, a place of security in an otherwise uncertain world, a role more usually occupied by the mother. Certainly he seems to have spent much of his life trying to seek her approval since she favoured his younger brother Albert, like her a musician.[17] Le Corbusier observed that his brother 'was destined for music . . . The entire activity of the family concentrated on him. In the meantime I was left on my own.'[18] With surprising frankness Le Corbusier actually wrote to his mother about an encounter that he had with an American psychiatrist who told him that, judging from his paintings, Le Corbusier evidently had some complex about her that he had not managed to resolve.[19] Significantly, Le Corbusier made a number of annotations to a discussion of Freud's Oedipus complex in Allendy's *Capitalisme et Sexualité*, suggesting that he may have recognised his own jealousy of his father and attraction to his mother.[20]

In contrast to his mother, Le Corbusier's father, Georges-Edouard Jeanneret Gris seems to have been a slightly low-key figure. As president of the local Swiss Alpine club, his main gift to his son seems to have been an appreciation of nature and the 'unity' of its laws.[21] He died in 1926, leaving Le Corbusier's mother very much the decisive parental influence in his life.

Jenger writes that Le Corbusier never seems to have felt relaxed about the way his parents received the news of his successes. He did not feel confident of their esteem.[22] Le Corbusier wrote in a letter to his friend William Ritter that his mother often told him that he was not good, *bon*, and that she knew him well.[23] This situation polarised after his father's death, which transformed his relationship with both his mother and his brother when he adopted a new role as her 'protector'.[24] In Jenger's opinion Le Corbusier's situation was paradoxical: on the one hand he was the rock, the solid son and active protector of his mother, on the other hand he was insecure, always trying to prove to her the importance of his work.[25]

Le Corbusier helped his mother in a number of different ways: he provided her with financial support, sent her presents and gave advice on all sorts of daily decisions, such as what type of dog to have,

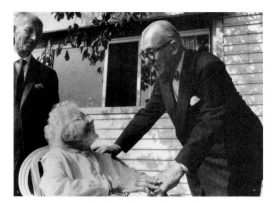

Figure 1.4 Le Corbusier and his mother on her 100th birthday, 1959.

what food to eat and so on.[26] She lived to be 100 years old, her birthday falling on 10 September 1959 (Fig.1.4). In Switzerland the government sends a certificate to those citizens who reach the age of 100, but it was Le Corbusier's opinion that she did not need a certificate: 'just give her a good chair' which his friend Heidi Weber accordingly did.[27] It seems that her longevity was proof of her extraordinary powers. When she died in February 1960, her 101st year, Le Corbusier was devastated.[28]

Yvonne Gallis: his wife

Le Corbusier himself acknowledged that he would not be who he was without the assistance of his wife Yvonne,[29] emphasising the help and support that she gave him in keeping up his spirits (Fig. 1.5).[30] Le Corbusier told Jane Drew that Yvonne was his closest confidante, a friend, companion, and wife, but that he 'felt he had wronged her' by 'keeping her in a drawer'.[31]

Le Corbusier had known Yvonne since about 1920 when he had met her as a model in the fashion house that was directed by Ozenfant.[32] In a 1962 sketchbook Le Corbusier noted:

'Grandeur:
VON = And that time when I came down on foot from Montmartre all the way to the rue Jacob?
Corbu: But why did you come down on foot?
Von: Because I didn't have the money to pay my way on the Metro (The incident recalled here takes place around 1921–22).'[33]

Figure 1.5 A youthful Yvonne on the beach.

Curiously he also made a note of this incident on the inside cover of his copy of Nietszche's *Thus Spake Zarathustra*. Clearly he was touched by the degree of love that she seemed to hold for him at this early stage in their relationship. Le Corbusier underlined a passage in René Allendy's book *Capitalisme et Sexualité* referring to men who pursued women with money. Evidently he felt he did not belong to this category. He pursued Yvonne for entirely different reasons.[34]

Von Moos writes that she was 'daughter of a concierge, native of a little village on the Côte d'Azur'; Yvonne Le Corbusier was something of a 'gypsy'.[35] Jencks writes that 'it took her a few years to break his monkish habits and establish a stable relationship, but this occurred by 1927, and she stopped seeing other men' (Fig. 1.6).[36] He married her in December 1930, three months after being naturalised as a Frenchman. Together, in 1934, they moved from his old bohemian apartment at 20 Rue Jacob to the penthouse apartment that he built at 24 Rue Nungesser et Coli. Her presence in his life heralded the introduction of women into his painted work. As Françoise de Franclieu observes, Le Corbusier's sketches of women during this period are 'massive and powerful, drawn with a vigorous pencil line that reflects the artist's emotion'.[37]

In a letter to Marguerite Tjader Harris, Le Corbusier wrote of his admiration for his wife, that she was 'always strong, clean, pure, entirely clear. Daughter of a peasant, she is for me a perfect companion'.[38] Jenger writes that Yvonne gave Le Corbusier great stability. A good cook – her Bouillabaisse was famous – she entertained their friends and supported him through the

Figure 1.7 Le Corbusier, Yvonne Le Corbusier and Father Couturier at dinner in Le Corbusier's penthouse apartment, 24 Rue Nungesser et Coli.

difficult times with her cutting wit and evident sense of fun. To his friends and family he would often express admiration for her character, describing her rather paternalistically as his 'devoted child, loving, faithful and dignified, but pathologically wild'.[39] Jencks writes that 'Yvonne, from all accounts, was the kind of woman to which Le Corbusier was occasionally attracted: not an intellectual, a good cook with an earthy humour – interested in bawdy jokes and not at all in architecture. She was someone who could be counted on to break up solemn meetings of architectural luminaries, such as those of CIAM,[40] by pointing out some hidden virtues of female anatomy. She had a sharp wit and, like Le Corbusier, loved to shock . . .'[41] In a 1951 letter Le Corbusier wrote to Yvonne of his luck at having such a wife, one who 'protected' his 'soul from banality'.[42]

Von Moos writes that according to friends of the couple she evoked a character out of Rabelais, making jokes worthy of his book *Gargantua and Pantagruel* to embarrass dignified people.[43] One such incident is described in a letter by Edouard Trouin. He was sitting at dinner at 24 Rue Nungesser et Coli with Le Corbusier, his wife and Father Marie-Alain Couturier of the influential journal *L'Art Sacré* (Fig. 1.7). Yvonne passed a mustard pot to the unsuspecting Jesuit which opened up to reveal a miniature phallus, causing much laughter all round.[44] Whilst the term 'Rabelaisian' has become a part of common usage, even in the English language, it seems significant that

Figure 1.6 Photograph of Pierre Jeanneret, André Bauchant, Yvonne Gallis and Le Corbusier with a Bauchant painting of Le Corbusier and his cousin wooing Yvonne, 1927.

Yvonne, like Le Corbusier's mother, was linked by her friends to *Gargantua and Pantagruel*, especially since Le Corbusier's own fascination with the book must have been widely known. Trouin, who was evidently a great friend of the pair, wrote crude jokes as an addendum to his letters, especially for Yvonne. Indeed many of his letters were addressed to the pair suggesting that she too would cast her eye over them.

From the letters we gain a picture of Yvonne as somebody who could not be trusted to look after herself, a view rather at odds with Le Corbusier's graphic images of her as mysterious siren. Evidently she was tempestuous and unpredictable, preventing Le Corbusier from becoming complacent. Jenger observes that while Le Corbusier was away on his extended trips he wrote her frequent letters in which he took a tone that was 'protective, vigilant, almost paternal', full of advice and words of caution for her health, her eating habits and smoking.[45] One letter from Le Corbusier to Yvonne, dated 1926, provides a specific example. In it he informed her that he had opened a bank account for her but that she should only use the money it contained on useful things, not frivolities.[46] Yvonne similarly called Le Corbusier 'baby', her pet name for him being 'Dou Dou', the French word for a child's comfort blanket or toy, and reminded him to take care of things such as his passport.[47] Each was highly solicitous of the other.

Whilst it seems that Le Corbusier did not marry Yvonne for her intellectual prowess, she does seem to have provided a source of outside inspiration, bringing new music and books into the house. In a note in his sketchbook Le Corbusier writes of slitting the pages of a book *La Vie Sensible de Louis XIV* by Lady Clemenceau-Jaquemaire, 'bought by Von from her student friend [the] sidewalk bookseller'.[48]

Le Corbusier is quoted as having said, 'When I was married, I said to my wife "no children" because I feared at that time that my life would be very hard as an architect'.[49] Drew records that this was a decision that he came to regret.[50] In accepting this dictum it is likely that Yvonne was forced to make a great sacrifice, especially at a time when the Church and government were placing such an emphasis on the importance of childbirth to women. Instead she had to take solace in the company of their dog Pinceau (Paintbrush) while Le Corbusier was on his long journeys away from Paris. A brief survey of letters to her husband suggests that she was not happy with his long periods of absence.[51]

A spirited woman, she was quick to make her feelings clear to Le Corbusier when crossed, an example being cited in a letter to Jean Badovici in which Le Corbusier ruefully complained about Yvonne's noisy refusal to spend winter in Ozon during the war.[52] Evidently Yvonne had quite a temper.[53] In the opinion of Mogens Krustrup, Le Corbusier based the image of an angry Hera in one of his annotations to the *Illiade* drawings on his wife. Krustrup mentions a letter in the personal correspondence of Le Corbusier and Yvonne in which he tried to justify the presence of lipstick on his underwear, an archetypal predicament.[54] Late in life, long after Yvonne's death, Le Corbusier, whilst musing upon the best position for his new television set, commented that the introduction of television into the family, its position within the home, would cause the break up of marriages the world over, suggesting that he was used to this type of domestic struggle.[55] Von Moos observes that it is hard to imagine that the two represented an image of matrimonial peace, but that they seem to have been more attached to one another than either would have admitted (Fig. 1.8).[56]

Together the two rode out periods of great financial difficulty, Le Corbusier being forced to borrow money from his 'employee' Jerzy Soltan, and Yvonne making her own clothes.[57] For Le Corbusier, Yvonne seems to have symbolised both hearth and home.[58] In a letter to his wife dated 1928 Le Corbusier expressed his pain at being so far away from her 'petit foyer', her little hearth.[59] In another letter, written nearly a quarter of a century later, he wrote to her of the fact that she inhabited 'the bottom' of his 'heart', for so many years his 'guardian angel'. He thought of her all the time; beautiful, in spite of age, she had in her 'face something extraordinary' her 'smile, rare but magnificent'.[60]

It is evident from Le Corbusier's letters to his wife that he began to grow increasingly worried about her health, her smoking and her drinking as she entered into old age. On one occasion he drew a diagram for her showing the ways in which her smoking was poisoning her body, but apparently to no avail. Le Corbusier wrote to Yvonne of his torment worrying about her health, enquiring whether it was possible that she was simply depressed.[61]

Apparently Yvonne became an alcoholic and near cripple in later life and Le Corbusier looked after her much as a nurse would. It was for her that he built, in 1952, the Cabanon at Cap Martin, which he hoped would provide her with 'a casket of happiness' (Fig 1.9).[62] Indeed, it seems that Le Corbusier genuinely believed that the one way he could cure his wife of her ills was by creating for her such a retreat.[63]

Jacques Hindermeyer, her doctor, observed that Yvonne had a problem with drink and was afflicted by chronic gastritis. Suffering greatly from what seems to have been osteoporosis, she had great difficult in walking which led to a reclusive lifestyle during her final years.[64] Zacnic observes that Le Corbusier claimed that Yvonne's reclusiveness allowed him to immerse himself in his work. Apparently only a few close friends actually knew about her situation, about which they kept very quiet.[65]

In May 1957, when she only had a few months left to live, Le Corbusier was to write to her desperately complaining at her inability to reply to his letters at all.[66] A very moving account of her last hours is recorded in Le Corbusier's sketchbooks:

> Yvonne died yesterday morning at four o'clock, her hand in mine, in silence and complete serenity. I was with her at the clinic for eight hours, watching over her, she was the opposite of a suckling baby, leaving life with spasms and mutterings in a *tête-à-tête*, the whole of the long night. She finally died just before dawn. She was a highly spirited woman with a strong will, integrity and tidiness. Guardian angel of the home, my home, for thirty-six years. Liked by all, adored and loved

Figure 1.8   Le Corbusier and Yvonne.

Figure 1.9   Le Corbusier's Cabanon at Cap Martin.

by the simple and rich, the rich of heart only. She took the measure of people and things in scale. Queen of a little fervent world. An example for many and yet without any pretence. For my 'poem to the right Angle,' she occupies the central place: character E3. She is on her bed in the guestroom, stretched our, with her masque of magisterial and Provençal structure. During that calm day, I discovered that death is not a horror . . . in gratitude to my wife for thirty-five years of wonderful devotion, for surrounding me with the blessings of quiet, affection and happiness.[67]

Her death on 5 October 1957, his 70th birthday, was a great blow to Le Corbusier. Jencks writes that 'according to Walter Gropius and others Le Corbusier suffered some kind of breakdown' at this point. He had experienced 'thirty-seven years of perfect happiness, thanks to her'.[68]

Le Corbusier's sketchbooks provide ample evidence of her continued presence in his thoughts. He made notes to himself to give away many of her possessions, jewellery and trinkets, to close friends.[69] He continued to send messages and gifts 'in the name of Yvonne or in her memory'.[70] He wrote of the way in which, had she been alive, she would have been able to make his friends smile.[71] In addition to this he spent a great deal of time perfecting the details of the tomb he would share with her in the cemetery above Cap Martin,[72] a triangle and a circle, its sculptural forms delineating a veritable marriage of opposites, his own with his wife.

Intimate relations

Recently much has been written about Le Corbusier's affairs with other women, though Heidi Weber, for one, finds this hard to believe, given his preoccupation with his work.[73] Jencks observes that 'if he was the mythical French husband whenever he travelled, at least he was faithful and considerate to Yvonne in Paris'.[74] Jencks describes a conversation about Le Corbusier's 'sexual ethics' that he had with one of Le Corbusier's female acquaintances:

She described how he said to her 'women are good for bed' and made a few rude remarks, after he received the Gold Medal of the Royal Institute of British Architects in 1953, he and others had a lot to drink when they returned to the home of the British modernist Wells Coates. Characteristically, LC was elated by the reception, being abroad and of course having received the Gold Medal, and he produced lots of sketches showing himself as a cab donkey, genius and ass, which he dashed off for the women present. It was all very intoxicating, and by the end of the evening he was under the table with a famous British beauty, enjoying an amorous bout. But, my friend continued, in spite of such indiscretions 'he was not unfaithful to his wife'. 'How do you mean that' I inquired, 'in the French sense?' 'No, these were just one-night stands, sleeping with other women is not being unfaithful.'[75]

Certainly, anecdotes abound on the subject of Le Corbusier's interest in pretty girls.

Evidently proud of his own sexual prowess, he referred to himself as a 'gigolo' at the age of 63.[76] Annotations to Allendy's *Capitalisme et Sexualité* suggest that he believed a passionate nature to be a necessary qualification for an artist.[77] Jencks sees in Le Corbusier 'the discovery, rather late in life, of sexual delight seen as a cosmic pleasure, something to be celebrated in poetry, drawing, and architecture'.[78] Certainly Le Corbusier felt that people were being educated to be frightened of sex and that this was very wrong.[79] He wrote to Tjader Harris that he felt a real need for 'communion in a few seconds of harmony: man and woman'.[80] In another postcard he appears to use the word harmony as a euphemism for sex.[81]

Whilst there is perhaps no justification for Le Corbusier's infidelities, it should be noted that he was often away from Yvonne for very long periods, something that must have placed further strain on their relationship. Le Corbusier was often the recipient of adoring fan mail. In spite of his age, temptation must have been omnipresent. It was also common for married men in France to make use of brothels, places that continued to be sanctioned by the state until 1946.[82] Drew records that his cousin Pierre Jeanneret liked going to brothels, as did Le Corbusier,[83] who put a large question mark next to a statement made by Allendy, in his book *Capitalism and Sexuality*, to the effect that all prostitutes are frigid.[84]

Taya Zinkin, an Indian woman whom Le Corbusier had apparently tried to seduce without success in the 1950s, wrote of a conversation she had with the architect. Her account sounds depressingly typical of that of a middle-aged married man bent on seduction:

> He spent the evening discussing women, prostitution, the importance of Indian males and his own wife. 'I absolutely fail to understand her. Of course she is pretty stupid, mais quand même. I give her all the money she wants but that is not enough for her. No, Madame wants children! I hate children. She already has a little dog, that should be good enough. Take another dog, have two dogs by all means, but leave me alone is what I say to her. Children are the curse of society. They make noise, they are messy, they should be abolished.'[85]

Whilst it is evident that there were frictions in his relationship with Yvonne, it is hard to imagine that he was really so vindictive about her, given the loyal way that he consistently praised her elsewhere. One suspects a certain amount of journalistic licence at work here. Zinkin continued:

> As we were getting off the plane he asked me what I was doing that evening: 'catching a train, I am afraid,' I said. 'Pity. You are fat and I like my women fat. We could have spent a pleasant night together.' He said this quite casually. He was not being offensive, he was being factual. He took such a functional view of sex that it never occurred to him that the act would not carry its own reward for both of us . . . By the time he had had a few drinks he was paying me the sort of compliments Rubens must have paid to Hélène Fourmont when she was far gone with child. Had I not studied medicine I would have found his anatomical precision embarrassing. I had always known that I was fat, but I had not realized before that I looked as fat as all that.[86]

Although it seems very likely that Zinkin wrote her article as a form of revenge, Drew also spoke of Le Corbusier's graphic attitude to sex. She observed that 'the way he talked over this and that was very derogatory in some funny way'. Further, he had a 'very French' view of sex that she did not 'like'.[87] 'Perhaps I am too English' she mused, but it was 'something coarse'.

In the opinion of Drew, Le Corbusier 'gave his life to his work' adding that 'he did however, value affection and women – not in an English way'. She observed that 'although he recognised sex as the force it is and was not respectful of man-made laws, he did respect the women he loved'.[88] Certainly Le Corbusier did have a number of close female friendships outside his marriage, with women such as Marguerite Tjader Harris, Drew herself, Josephine Baker and Minette De Silva. While this list is not exhaustive, a brief examination of his relationship with each of these women will serve to prove the enjoyment and inspiration he derived from their company.

Josephine Baker

According to Heidi Weber, Le Corbusier described the celebrated singer Josephine Baker as the most 'erotic' women he had ever known.[89] Drew likewise reflected that he 'adored Josephine Baker'[90] – hence, it would appear, the spell she seems to have cast over him during the period that he was beginning married life with Yvonne. Recourse to one of her many biographies reveals that Baker was indeed an extraordinary woman, breaking established modes of behaviour, starting life as a clown, singer and dancer and then moving on to devote herself to philanthropic work experimenting with creating a 'rainbow tribe' of adopted children in an ideal community.[91]

Le Corbusier met Baker while travelling to South America in 1929 on the ocean liner, Giulio Cesare (Fig. 1.10). Jean Claude Baker, one of her 'adopted' sons, quotes his mother describing Le Corbusier as 'a modest, fun-loving man' with whom she 'quickly struck up a friendship,' a euphemism for a love affair, in the opinion of her son.[92] She was already a well-known and glamorous figure amongst the intellectual and artistic circles in which Le Corbusier moved (Adolf Loos had designed a villa for her in 1928) and Le Corbusier was to encounter her a number of times as they criss-crossed the continent, spending the last days of their respective tours together in Brazil.[93]

Figure 1.10 Le Corbusier and Josephine Baker (right hand side front) on board ship. Note that he is conspicuously not wearing evening dress.

Figure 1.11 Le Corbusier self portrait with Josephine Baker.

In remembrance of their days spent together in Rio, Le Corbusier made a drawing of the two as a stylish couple, true representatives of the jazz age, posing in front of the city's dramatic skyline (Fig. 1.11). In December they embarked for the return journey to Paris. At a costume party held on the night that they crossed the equator, Le Corbusier appeared as Josephine,[94] a significant gesture by a man so interested in the way in which the masculine and feminine intermingled within a relationship.

During the two voyages their cabins provided the venue for their deepening friendship. There exist a number of touching sketches of Baker, testament to their intimacy, including one of her sleeping (Fig. 1.12). In Jencks' opinion the experience of sketching Josephine revived Le Corbusier's interest 'in the female body as a cosmic force'.[95] It will be seen in Chapter 5 that, like all the women whom he cared for deeply, Baker would gain a mythic dimension in Le Corbusier's painted work.

Le Corbusier wrote that when Baker crooned 'Baby' in a music hall show in Sao Paulo in November 1929, she sang it with 'such an intense and dramatic sensitivity' that tears rushed to his eyes.[96] He writes of how she entertained him in her steamship cabin singing 'I'm a little blackbird looking for a white bird; I want a little nest for the two of us . . .' and other popular songs, an event that obviously made a deep impression on him.[97] In this way, he wrote with admiration, 'she lives all over the world. She moves immense crowds'. She brings music to 'man', in Le Corbusier's terms a

calling of the highest importance. She, in a very literal way, acted as a muse.

Such was Le Corbusier's fascination with the singer that he planned a ballet in which she would play the central role. Contemporary Hollywood depictions of tropical life, often stereotypical in the extreme, must be borne in mind when considering the scene which he evokes:

1 entrance
2 Showgirls made up with tatoos sound: one step or pure negro tamtam without music only one negro on stage
3 1 negro wearing a banana tree
4 A modern man and woman and New York dancing only 1 step holding each other and slowly the cylinder is lowered Josephine descends dressed as a monkey
5 she puts on a modern dress
6 goes forward on a podium, sings
7 steps off the podium, sings
8 last solemn song: the gods rise
9 background meandering sea of santos and at the end a big ocean liner[98]

For Le Corbusier oval and curved forms were associated with woman. Here he draws attention to the links between the modern and primitive as exemplified so potently by Baker herself.

Never one to miss a business opportunity, Baker was for Le Corbusier a prospective client as well as a

Figure 1.12   Le Corbusier sketch of
Josephine Baker asleep,
1929.

Figure 1.13   Le Corbusier, 'Au revoir, amie!': sketched standing, portrait of Marguerite
Tjader-Harris, with New York skyline in background. Pen and Ink on
woven paper (with hotel letterhead on the verso) 21.6 × 27.7cm.
Collection Centre Canadien d'Architecture/ Canadian Centre for
Architecture, Montréal.

muse. In letters to the singer both before and after his tour of the United States, early in 1935 he had heard through friends that she was about to build a series of houses, in effect a village for children. He reminded her of their travels together 'when you asked me so sweetly to collaborate with you in your building projects on returning to Europe.'[99] These overtures, which may in fact have spoiled the relationship, came to nothing.

Marguerite Tjader Harris

In *When the Cathedrals were White* Le Corbusier wrote of 'a woman' who had said to him on his last night in New York, 'Come back to America, my friend. America is a great country'. At this point his 'heart was a little torn by the imminent departure, a heart which had been torn every day for two months by hate and love of this new world which must be seen to be really known as it is'. Here he couched his feelings for Tjader Harris in the impersonal terms of his love for America.[100] A similar impression is given by a sketch made by Le Corbusier as he left New York on 14 December 1935. In it Marguerite stands tall against the skyline of New York (Fig. 1.13.). Not for the first time does Le Corbusier make a woman into a symbol of a place. In a letter of farewell that accompanies the drawing he wrote:

Everything was beautiful and good and clean, worthy and loving. Why shouldn't the heart have the right to love, there where things make it open up, discover itself, and receive a full measure of joy and benefit? . . . You are strong, right-minded, fair and good. You are loving and open. Not closed up. Around you are gathered many affections . . . I can't imagine – because I can't imagine the unknown – what would have been my New York and my USA without you, without the sea, without your mother, without Toutou and booby, without the cabin and without the colonial house, without the roadways of Connecticut and the red haired amazon who drives. It would have been something, but what? Risqué adventures on Broadway, or some other escape along Park Avenue or wherever. You were the peasant woman of New York, Corbu's little Jeanne d'Arc facing clumsily in the void. A support. The peasant woman, in opposition to the other of Chicago and who is the woman of the skyscrapers, courageous but fearful, reckless but irrational, another Jeanne d'Arc without possible victory, because artifice leads to defeat, whereas health and goodness go toward the light. Blonde sweet light . . . Let us imagine instead of the cold, the heat of summer, or the mildness of spring. The seas gentle, the water near at hand and soon deep. Nights in the water and on the sand. Frolics. Honest joy and tender gestures. Tenderness! What a rare event, thing, word. Tenderness in the country of skyscrapers, so close to New York. The future does not belong to us. The years pass, will continue to pass. Poor old Corbu, so near the autumn of his life, and whose heart is that of a child.[101]

Mardges Bacon must be credited for bringing this affair, lasting some five or six years but continuing as a friendship into the 1950s, to light. In her opinion Le Corbusier kept the relationship hidden, worried that news of it might reach his wife or that it would jeopardise his chance of gaining work in the USA. Bacon records that 'It is only through the letters that Marguerite kept, her unpublished "portrait" of him, and the recollections of her son Hilary that her significance as guide and muse emerges'.[102]

Le Corbusier had met the writer Tjader Harris, 'the radiant one',[103] in Vevey early in March 1932 when she had offered to act as his guide in New York. A handsome young woman with an athletic physique she had, with her young son, escaped to Switzerland from America and a miserable marriage. In her unpublished 'Portrait of Le Corbusier', she recalled how she had boldly introduced herself to Madame Jeanneret at Le Lac, the villa Le Corbusier designed for his parents on the shores of Lac Leman.[104] She was soon to become a firm friend of the family.

Whilst Le Corbusier would, during his time in America, have flirtations with other women, his allegiance remained firmly with Tjader Harris. In one letter, unfortunately undated, he complained bitterly that he has not had sex since 13 December,[105] his apparent need for regular physical release[106] causing him to hire a prostitute for a night.[107] He wrote her a multitude of swift notes listing his engagements, indicating 'minutes of liberty worthy of employment'.[108]

In Bacon's opinion Tjader Harris 'accepted and embraced Le Corbusier's need to dominate a woman, but she also appreciated in him such "female" elements as "his faith and his emotions".' She observes:

A feminist critique might conclude that without Marguerite's worship, sexual desire, and submis-

sion Le Corbusier would have left America having failed to get commissions and with his male ego irrevocably wounded. But Marguerite's importance transcended the personal because she encouraged the continuing transformation in Le Corbusier's architecture during the early 1930s, characterised by the difference between the Villa Stein-de Monzie (1926–1928) and the de Mandrot House. In Nietzschean terms the free spirited divorcée symbolised (as did Yvonne) the Dionysian attributes of nature, the body, passions, and emotions. These countered the Apollonian male virtues of culture, intellect, soul, order, reason, authority, elitism, and supremacy with which Le Corbusier identified and which he projected onto his architecture and urbanism before 1930. Marguerite's unfettered temperament, her sensuality, her embrace of nature, and her appreciation of Le Corbusier's paintings with its own Dionysian associations of the female and the feminine, the cosmic and the cyclical, served as a catalyst for his artistic creativity.[109]

In Jencks' opinion she was for Le Corbusier 'his spiritual guide, his Beatrice'.[110] This statement would seem to need some qualification as Tjader Harris occupies the role of one of a number of different muses. Her particular realm for Le Corbusier seems to be that of the intellectual. Le Corbusier was an admirer of her intellect, writing, for example, of her 'skilful and intelligent translation' of *When the Cathedrals were White*.[111] She, the 'red haired amazon', occupied a rather different territory to that of Yvonne.

Jencks observes that from 1932 to 1937 women, and particularly the subject of two women, dominate his paintings. In his view it would be 'simplistic to see these as Yvonne and Marguerite, especially since the presence of Josephine can be felt in many of the drawings and the theme of two women making love was an old one for him, but there is no doubt that the feminine presence was abstracted as such during this time, perhaps becoming an earth goddess, mother figure, and object of sexual desire'.[112] Le Corbusier seems to have assimilated the Symbolist tendency to categorise women into archetypes, discussed more extensively in Chapter 5, into the very fabric of his life.

Minette De Silva

In 1946 André Bouxin, editor of *Architecture et Techniques* and secretary general of ASCORAL, introduced Le Corbusier to Minette De Silva, a beautiful and elegant student at the Architectural Association in London who came from Ceylon, now Sri Lanka. Le Corbusier was taken with her beauty and they began a friendship that lasted until his death (Fig. I.3). Jencks writes that it is not known whether their relationship was sexual. As ever categorising women as archetypes, it seems that Le Corbusier erroneously identified her with India. De Silva observed that

> He was greatly attracted by his first live contact with *L'Inde*. I think he romanticized our meeting. I became the symbolic link with L'inde, the idealized symbol. Since then I have been deeply touched by his sympathy and interest in me and my work.[113]

Le Corbusier was to write to her: 'Your image is always in front of me – you who carry two thousand years of beauty and traditional wisdom in a bearing that really moves me.'[114]

Early letters from De Silva to Le Corbusier are full of affection. She wrote of Le Corbusier being 'so sympathetic . . .' but bemoaned the fact that Paris was so far away, as she felt 'hungry' for his 'sympathy'.[115] Le Corbusier wrote her a glowing reference for a job at UNESCO describing her 'building in Ceylon' as 'excellent'.[116] He also attempted to pull strings for her with his connections at Harvard. An increasingly needy correspondent, she remained devoted to him until the end, writing in a postcard of 1964 from Mykonos, 'I think of your eyes all the days I am here'.[117]

Conclusion

From this brief account of the most significant of Le Corbusier's relationships with women, a number of themes become apparent. Firstly, that he valued and enjoyed the company of women, appreciating on occasion their intellectual as well as physical attributes. The fact that a woman was a professional in her work made her no less attractive to Le Corbusier.

Secondly, in line with his rather Symbolist tendencies, Le Corbusier often tried to conceptualise the women whom he loved as countries: Tjader Harris as America, Baker as Africa, De Silva as India; or as archetypes, his mother and Yvonne being feminine divinities. This tendency to idealise, a manifestation of his obsession with seeing small things as part of a larger pattern, may have prevented him from communicating fully with the women in question, causing him to block out those things that did not conform to his own vision. Then again it is possible that it added something to the relationship: something much grander was at stake than a simple relationship between two people.

Notes

1 Letter Le Corbusier to his mother, 28.11.1928, in J. Jenger, *Le Corbusier Choix de Lettres* (Basel: Birkhauser, 2002), p.200.
2 See for example Nicholas Weber's biography of the architect due for publication in 2004.
3 Edouard Trouin wrote of a little group of women, the 'saintes femmes', that revolved around Le Corbusier, amongst them 'Mad.', an old friend of Jean Badovici and Consuelo de Saint Exupéry. Montalte, L. (E. Trouin pseud.), *Fallait-il Bâtir Le Mont-Saint-Michel?* (St Zachaire: Montalte, 1979), p.148.
4 J. Drew, 'Le Corbusier as I knew him' in R. Walden (ed), *The Open Hand* (Cambridge, MA: MIT Press, 1982), p.369.
5 Le Corbusier, *When the Cathedrals were White: A Journey to the Country of the Timid People* (New York: Reynal and Hitchcock, 1947), frontispiece.
6 Letter Le Corbusier to his mother, 15.10.1952 in Jenger, *Le Corbusier Choix de Lettres*, p.254.
7 Conversation Heidi Weber and Gisela Loehlein, Zurich, June 2002.
8 C. Jencks, *Le Corbusier and the Continual Revolution in Architecture* (New York: Monacelli Press, 2000), p.193.
9 Letter Le Corbusier to his mother, 28.09.1930, in Jenger, *Le Corbusier Choix de Lettres*, p.209.
10 Le Corbusier, *My Work* (London: Architectural Press, 1960), p.20. Albert Jeanneret stressed the importance of this saying to his mother. Interview Lowman and Albert Jeanneret, Vevey, June 1972. J. Lowman, 'Le Corbusier 1900–1925: The Years of Transition.' Unpublished doctoral dissertation, University of London (1979), p.251.
11 Letter Le Corbusier to his mother, 10.11.1931, in Jenger, *Le Corbusier Choix de Lettres*, p.215.
12 Letter Le Corbusier to Yvonne, 11.09.1924, FLC R1.12.13.

13 Letter Le Corbusier to his mother, 03.11.1934, FLC R2.1.191.

14 Letter Le Corbusier to his mother, 11.11.1945, FLC R2.4.129.

15 S. Menin & F. Samuel, *Nature and Space: Aalto and Le Corbusier* (London: Routledge, 2003).

16 H. Allen Brookes, *Le Corbusier's Formative Years* (Chicago: University of Chicago Press, 1997), p.9.

17 Apparently she was not impressed by Le Corbusier's achievements as an architect though Marguerite Tjader Harris commented on her pride in her own home at Vevey. 'Portrait of Le Corbusier', unpublished manuscript, 1984 (Harris family papers) reproduced in M. Bacon, *Le Corbusier in America* (Cambridge, MA: MIT Press 2001), p.50.

18 J. Peter, *The Oral History of Modern Architecture* (New York: Harry N. Abrams, 1994), p.138.

19 Letter Le Corbusier to his mother, 19.02.1937, FLC R2.1.149.

20 R. Allendy, *Capitalisme et Sexualité: le conflits des instincts et les problèmes actuels* (Paris: Denoel), pp. 61 and 64 in FLC.

21 Le Corbusier, Modulor 2 (London: Faber, 1955), p.297.

22 Jenger, *Le Corbusier Choix de Lettres*, p.26.

23 Letter Le Corbusier to Ritter, 22.03.1916, FLC R3.19.18.

24 Letter Le Corbusier to Ritter, 18.01.1926, FLC R3.19.408.

25 Jenger, *Le Corbusier Choix de Lettres*, p.26.

26 Ibid.

27 Weber remembers that her own mother knitted a pair of socks for Le Corbusier which she did not really want to give to him, but had to because they were from her mother. He was very grateful and wrote a warm thank you card to Weber's mother personally. Conversation Heidi Weber and Gisela Loehlein, Zurich, June 2002.

28 Letter Le Corbusier to his brother, 30.15.1960, FLC R1.10.448.

29 Tjader Harris said that Le Corbusier described Yvonne as his 'beautiful Mediterranean wife ... without whom I would not be what I am'. Bacon, *Le Corbusier in America*, p.383.

30 Jenger, *Le Corbusier Choix de Lettres*, p.22.

31 J. Drew quoted in C. Jencks, *Le Corbusier and the Continual Revolution in Architecture* (New York: Monacelli Press, 2000), p.193.

32 S. Von Moos, *Le Corbusier: L'architecte et son mythe* (Paris: Horizons de France, 1971), p.302.

33 Le Corbusier, *Sketchbooks Volume 4*, sketch 1011.

34 Allendy, *Capitalisme et Sexualité*, p.39 in FLC.

35 Von Moos, *Le Corbusier: L'architecte et son mythe*, p.302.

36 Jencks, *Le Corbusier and the Continual Revolution in Architecture*, p.191.

37 Le Corbusier, *Sketchbooks Volume 1* (London: Thames and Hudson, 1981), p.13.

38 Letter Le Corbusier to M. Tjader Harris, 22.11.1939, FLC E3.10.37.

39 Letter Le Corbusier to his mother, 08.1931, FLC R2.1.130.

40 Congrès Internationaux d'Architecture Moderne.

41 Jencks, *Le Corbusier and the Continual Revolution in Architecture*, p.191.

42 Letter Le Corbusier to Yvonne, 25.02.1951, FLC R1.12.96.

43 Von Moos, *Le Corbusier: L'architecte et son mythe*, p.302.

44 Letter Edouard Trouin to Picasso, 23.02.1956, FLC P5 2 37.

45 Jenger, *Le Corbusier Choix de Lettres*, p.22.

46 Letter Le Corbusier to Yvonne, 31.03.1926, in Jenger, *Le Corbusier Choix de Lettres*, p.177.

47 Letter Yvonne to Le Corbusier, 11.05.1942, FLC R1.12.198.

48 Le Corbusier, *Sketchbooks Volume 3, 1954–1957* (Cambridge, MA: MIT Press, 1982), sketch 881.

49 Quoted from memory by Kunio Maekawa, who worked with Le Corbusier, in *Aujourd'hui Art et Architecture*, November 1965, p.109 cited in Jencks, *Le Corbusier and the Continual Revolution in Architecture*, p.191.

50 J. Drew interview with M. Garlake, 20–21 May 1995, National Life Story Collection, British Library, F823.

51 See for example letters Yvonne to Le Corbusier, 11.06.1940, FLC R1.12.151 and 11.05.1942, FLC R1.12.198.

52 Letter Le Corbusier to Jean Badovici, 18.08.1940 in Jenger, *Le Corbusier Choix de Lettres*, p.267.

53 Letter Le Corbusier to his mother, 13.1.1956 in ibid., p.396.

54 M. Krustrup, 'Les Illustrations de Le Corbusier pour l'*Illiade*' in Viatte, G. (ed), *Le Corbusier et la Méditerranée* (Marseilles: L'Université de Provence, 1991), p.111.

55 Letter Le Corbusier to L.C. Kalff, 20.06.1957 in Jenger, *Le Corbusier Choix de Lettres*, p.410.

56 Von Moos, S., *Le Corbusier: L'architecte et son mythe*, p.302.

57 Le Corbusier, *Sketchbooks Volume 4*, sketch 853.

58 The image of woman the 'foyer', the hearth, was not unique to Le Corbusier but was omnipresent in French culture at that time. Le Corbusier was to write to Yvonne of the way that the nomadic women of Chandigarh had no foyer. Letter Le Corbusier to Yvonne, 26.11.1952, FLC.

59 Letter Le Corbusier to Yvonne, 24.10.1928, in Jenger, *Le Corbusier Choix de Lettres*, p.199.

60 Letter Le Corbusier to Yvonne, 18.07.1952 in Jenger, *Le Corbusier Choix de Lettres*, p.254.

61 Letter Le Corbusier to Yvonne, 18.09.1940 in Jenger, *Le Corbusier Choix de Lettres*, p.254.

62 Letter Le Corbusier to Yvonne, 18.07.1952 in Jenger, *Le Corbusier Choix de Lettres*, p.360.

63 Menin & Samuel, *Nature and Space*, p.91.

64 Le Corbusier, *The Final Testament of Père Corbu: a Translation and Interpretation of Mise au Point by Ivan Zaknic* (New Haven: Yale University Press, 1997), p.61.

65 Dr Jacques Hindermeyer taped interview with Ivan Zacnic, Paris, 8 and 23 July 1994. Ibid.

66 Letter Le Corbusier to Yvonne, 03.05.1957, FLC R1.12.361.

67 Petit, J., *Le Corbusier Lui-même* (Paris: Editions Forces Vives, 1970), p.121 and Le Corbusier, *My Work*, p.199.

68 Petit, *Le Corbusier Parle* (Geneva: Editions Forces Vives, 1967), p.20.

69 Le Corbusier, *Sketchbooks Volume 4*, sketch 449.

70 Jenger, *Le Corbusier Choix de Lettres*, p.22.

71 Letter Le Corbusier to Henri Bruaux, 14.02.1962 in Jenger, *Le Corbusier Choix de Lettres*, p.478.

72 Le Corbusier, *Sketchbooks Volume 4*, sketch 927.

73 Conversation Heidi Weber and Gisela Loehlein, Zurich, June 2002.

74 Jencks, *Le Corbusier and the Continual Revolution in Architecture*, p.194.

75 Ibid., p.195.

76 Le Corbusier, *Sketchbooks Volume 2* (London: Thames and Hudson, 1981), sketch 240.

77 Allendy, *Capitalisme et Sexualité*, p.31 in FLC.

78 Jencks, *Le Corbusier and the Continual Revolution in Architecture*, p.198.

79 See annotations to Allendy, *Capitalisme et Sexualité*, p.68 in FLC.

80 Letter Le Corbusier to Marguerite Tjader Harris, 17.05.1946, FLC E3.10.42.

81 Postcard Le Corbusier to Tjader Harris, 07.10.1948, FLC E3.10.47.

82 Neil Philip, *Working Girls: An Illustrated History of the Oldest Profession* (London: Bloomsbury, 1991), p.62.

83 J. Drew interview with M. Garlake, 20–21 May 1995. National Life Story Collection, British Library, F823.

84 Allendy, *Capitalisme et Sexualité*, p.208 in FLC.

85 Taya Zinkin, 'No Compromise with Le Corbusier', *Guardian*, September 11, 1965 cited in Charles Jencks, *Le Corbusier and the Tragic View of Architecture* (London: Allen Lane, 1973), p.100.

86 Ibid., p.104.

87 J. Drew interview with M. Garlake, 20–21 May 1995. National Life Story Collection, British Library, F823.

88 Walden (ed.), *The Open Hand*, p.369.

89 Conversation Heidi Weber and Gisela Loehlein, Zurich, June 2002.

90 J. Drew interview with M. Garlake, 20–21 May 1995. National Life Story Collection, British Library, F823.

91 See for example P. Rose, *Jazz Cleopatra* (New York: Doubleday, 1989).

92 J.C. Baker and C. Chase, *Josephine* (New York: Random House, 1993), p.164.

93 Bacon, *Le Corbusier in America*, p.222.

94 Ibid.

95 Jencks, *Le Corbusier and the Continual Revolution in Architecture*, p.196.

96 Le Corbusier, *Precisions* (Cambridge, MA: MIT Press, 1990), p.12.

97 Ibid.

98 Le Corbusier, *Sketchbooks Volume 1*, sketch 261.

99 Letter Le Corbusier to Josephine Baker, 04.02.1933, FLC E1.5.165.

100 Le Corbusier, *When the Cathedrals were White*, p.40.

101 Letter Le Corbusier to Marguerite Tjader Harris, 14.12.1935, FLC E3.10.12, Translation, Bacon, *Le Corbusier in America*, p.251.

102 Bacon, *Le Corbusier in America*, p.xvi.

103 'La rayonnante'. Letter Le Corbusier to Tjader Harris, October 1954 (date not given), FLC E3.10.52.

104 Bacon, *Le Corbusier in America*, p.48.

105 Letter Le Corbusier to Tjader Harris, FLC E3.10.15.

106 See Le Corbusier's annotations to Allendy, *Capitalisme et Sexualité*, p.203, in FLC. Le Corbusier underlined Allendy's point that coitus brings about a state of 'specific calm' and that 'all the instinctive nature of the male is brought to bear on renewing this type of experience'.

107 Bacon, *Le Corbusier in America*, p.56.

108 Letter Le Corbusier to Tjader Harris, FLC E3.10.8. See also FLC E3.10.7, FLC E3.10.9, FLC E3.10.11.

109 Bacon, *Le Corbusier in America* (Cambridge, MA: MIT Press, 2001), pp.56–7.

110 Jencks, *Le Corbusier and the Continual Revolution in Architecture*, p.212.

111 Le Corbusier, *When the Cathedrals were White*, p.xv.

112 Jencks, *Le Corbusier and the Continual Revolution in Architecture*, p.211.

113 Minette De Silva, *Minette De Silva: The Life and Work of an Asian Architect* (Orugodawatte: Sri Lanka, private press, 1998), p.100. Cited in Jencks, *Le Corbusier and the Continual Revolution in Architecture*, p.280.

114 Ibid., p.282.

115 Letter De Silva to Le Corbusier, 14.12.1948, FLC R3.4.2.

116 Letter Le Corbusier to René Makin, 20.01.1961, FLC R3.4.37.

117 Postcard Minette De Silva to Le Corbusier, 26.01.64, FLC R3.4.510.

2 Professional Relationships

In this chapter I focus on the way Le Corbusier interacted with women in the course of his professional life as he moved about the globe looking for commissions: both the women he worked for and the women he worked with. My aim is to highlight a theme that emerges from his observations of women across the globe: that women would have a particular and important role in bringing about the new civilisation which he so desired.

Women abroad

Le Corbusier's sketchbooks bear testimony to the fact that he constantly took notice of the presence of women around him. Whilst at the monastery of the virgin on Mount Athos that he visited on his 'journey to the East' he complained of their absence: 'Not a single woman is to be seen; thus everything is missing here in the East where only for the sight of her woman is the primordial ingredient'.[1]

Later in his life Jane Drew wrote that 'to go for a walk with Le Corbusier was a revelation, he would notice so much',[2] making her feel as though she had 'another pair of eyes'.[3] For Le Corbusier, women from other cultures seem to have had the added attraction of being in some way doubly Other, both female and foreign, enigmatic recipients of his multiple projections. His sketchbooks are filled with observations about women whom he encountered on his travels. His representation of Eastern women, a particular fascination for Le Corbusier and many of the artists of his time, will be discussed in Chapter 5.

Such was his level of interest in the subject of American women that Le Corbusier was to paint two canvases entitled *Femmes New York* (Fig. 2.1). In the opinion of Mardges Bacon he saw 'signs of hope for American culture' in its 'strong and free-spoken' women.[4] She believes that Le Corbusier identified, in particular, with the rich cultured women whom he met on his trips. Le Corbusier believed that these women had remarkable 'confidence' and 'the liveliest kind of feeling for contemporary life'.[5] He felt sympathy for their inability to communicate with their besuited, cowed and earnest husbands.[6]

During his first tour round the USA in 1935, Le Corbusier visited Vassar, 'a college for girls from well-to-do families'.[7] The fact that he took the trouble to address an audience of females is in itself important evidence of his belief that 'in the society of the USA women play a part through their intellectual efforts.'[8] Certainly it seems likely that he decided to visit Vassar because he felt that the girls there would be particularly receptive to his theories. Le Corbusier wrote of the experience: 'I never had a more responsive audience during my trip. It is a pleasure and I amuse myself by developing the bold theses for which these women will be the best propagandists.'[9] This is a really significant point. Le Corbusier believed that women would spread the word, his word. He saw women as being flexible and open to change: indeed, they had a real interest in change as the old order held few benefits for them. Whilst he was undoubtedly paternalistic, he saw a need and a potential in women. His theories would be to their benefit. Women 'take to' modernity; they 'feel flattered in that frame-

Figure 2.1 Le Corbusier, *Femmes New York* (1947).

work'.[10] Progress was, for Le Corbusier, characterised in feminine terms as an 'imperious goddess' with a 'whip that spares no one'.[11]

The whole episode at Vassar carries the unmistakable tinge of eroticism. 'Spurred on by their enthusiasm' the drawings which he made on that day had a 'particular verve'.[12] Le Corbusier wrote of the questions that he was asked at the buffet:

> Some asked my companion whether I preferred blondes or brunettes, others nearly annihilated me with the weight of their questions. I am dumbfounded by the nature of the questions: sociology, economics, psychology. They are well informed about the serious problems of our days. They speak impeccable French. I have never felt so stupid: 'But I am ignorant of the problems which concern you: I am only a city planner and an architect and perhaps an artist. You overwhelm me, you are too serious, I must be excused. I am going to join the people who are eating cookies!'[13]

Here his ignorance is obviously disingenuous, but there is a serious underlying message. In Jungian terms these girls are 'animus ridden'; they have gone too far to the opposite extreme in allowing themselves to be dominated by their inner masculine side. Le Corbusier would seem to be suggesting something similar. 'American women are dominators and they dominate' wrote Le Corbusier, adding that 'If you envisage a certain kind of society, you can get to the bottom of the import of these remarks', presumably alluding to his idealised society – the radiant city, in which masculine and feminine would exist in harmonious equilibrium.[14]

Significantly, Le Corbusier was particularly concerned at meeting a Vassar girl who was 'absorbed' in the study of Caravaggio, 'well thought of in the intellectual circles of the USA'.[15] He saw their appreciation of this painter of sensuous chiaroscuro paintings as a sign of 'a complex disturbance [sic] and the anxieties of sexual life',[16] the source of which presumably lay in the imbalance which he perceived between the sexes which will be studied more closely in Chapter 7.

For Le Corbusier this 'complex disturbance' was endemic in the affluent white society of America. It does not, in his view, appear to have been an issue for African Americans, either male or female, whom he admired for their particular connection to tribal rhythms and their ability to wear brilliant colours.[17] In his unreconstructed mind such people had a particular connection to nature, along the lines of Edmund Rousseau's 'noble savage'.[18] They knew 'how to live'. This belief seems to have been encouraged by his relationship with Josephine Baker.

Le Corbusier expressed similar sentiments when in Asia, commenting on the women whom he saw when working in Chandigarh and Ahmedabad whom he admired for wearing bright colours and traditional dress. Drew, for example, spoke of his observations on the way in which saris made the women of the Punjab look more attractive than French fashions.[19] For Le Corbusier 'The men in white' provided the background for 'silk in motion. The women give colour to life in both senses of the word. vibrant or delicate colours – on the surface of the streets.'[20] This 'race of strong women' gave colour to life in both senses of the word.

Le Corbusier was evidently impressed by the women who worked on his building sites in Ahmedabad. He devoted half a page of the *Oeuvre Complète* to an image of one of the woman workers on the site for the Palais de Justice (Fig. 2.2).[21] 'I have eyes and heart still full of the power of the cows and buffalo, of the birds, of the peasants, of the women on my High Court site. It's a civilisation!'[22] He wanted to make a film of the 'mules, women, kids etc. on site of the Assembly Building'.[23] Here were women and men working together to bring about the new civilisation after which he so yearned.

Women at work

Le Corbusier was very familiar with the idea of working women. His mother worked as a piano teacher to bring additional income to the family (Fig. 2.3)[24] and women workers seem to have been present in the watch-making workshops of La Chaux de Fonds.[25] It is unsurprising, therefore, that he seems to have felt comfortable with the idea of women working within the realm of architecture, in spite of the fact that, as Claire Laubier observes, 'only work reflecting traditional feminine [soft, caring] qualities

Figure 2.2 Women workers on the site of the Palais de Justice from Le Corbusier's *Oeuvre Complète Volume 6*.

Figure 2.3 C.E. Jeanneret sketch of Madame Jeanneret giving a piano lesson, 18 December 1915.

was envisaged' for women of the middle classes during that time.[26] Griselda Pollock observes that during the late nineteenth century there was still a feeling that the public realm was a risky place for women, one where 'one might risk losing one's virtue, dirtying oneself', while for a man it represented a place to be lost in the crowd away from the demands of respectability.[27] Such sentiments remain implicit in the work of Le Corbusier. He was fully aware that the city remained a hostile territory for women.

'Little Paris birds'

As well as being interested in women of other cultures, Le Corbusier took an interest in the predicament of those he saw closer to home, whom he called 'the little Paris birds'. Although young, single and chic he perceived that the lives of these women were hard. The poor 'shop girl' spent long hours in uncom-

fortable proximity to lustful men in buses and trains as she travelled to and from work. Brought up on a diet of Hollywood films, 'Cinderella's happy ending' was not for her.[28] Le Corbusier remained unconvinced that in reality 'all those Prince Charmings as rich as Croesus' would have 'but one desire; to marry poor little typists'.[29]

In *The Radiant City* Le Corbusier described a dialogue that took place between him and his secretary. I quote it in full as it reveals a great deal about the architect in his dealings with women:

'Can't you manage to arrive on time, at 8:30?'
She is very sorry. 'I live in the suburbs, the stations are crowded, and if I miss my train I'm late.'

'Oh, I didn't know you lived in the suburbs.'
She began again, more boldly. 'Look, you can't possibly imagine what it's like, all the trains are packed solid, morning, noon and night. And sometimes the men aren't too pleasant, we're all

squashed together like in the subway and you have to look out!

'I catch the 7.45 and I have to walk nearly half an hour along muddy roads to get it. When it rains it's terrible and when it's windy it's worse, and in the winter it's dark.

'I get up at 5. I wash my stockings and blouse, I press my dress and make my breakfast . . .'

'Why don't you do all that in the evening, after 6:30?'

She:

'6:30! I want you to know that at 5.50 the letters are ready for you to sign, but when I open the door you're talking with someone. At six you're still talking. At 6.25 you call me in and it takes you ten or fifteen minutes to sign them. You say to yourself: "she can go home now." But the letters have to be mailed. So I run to the post office. I can't possibly make the 7 o'clock train, the 7.30 or the 7.45.

'When I get home it's 8:30 or 9. I have dinner. "Then do something?" I'm tired and nervous. I've been up since 5, and I just don't have the courage to start on something else . . .'

I am beginning to be deeply interested in this daily round that reveals such a series of anxieties:

'Anyway, Sunday must be pretty nice in the suburbs, isn't it?'

She:

'Sunday! It's dreadful. I'm bored to death. You see, I never see anyone, I don't know anyone . . .'

'But that's ridiculous: nobody's alone like that in the world, especially a pretty girl like you.'

She:

'I've been coming to Paris every day for ten years. My mother's pretty old, she often feels sad and depressed, and we have to be terribly careful about money. My mother knows a few people here and there that she meets when she does the shopping. We have a few relatives who live in other suburbs. What's the point of getting into a crowded train again, on a Sunday, to go and see them? We're too tired. And if we did, we'd find the same kind of people, stuck in the same kind of lives. Go for a walk? Of course we can't [,] the suburbs aren't much fun to walk in. It's not like the real country.

'I'd like to know some people of my own age. Men? Where would I meet any? Look, how can I make contact with anyone of my own age? In the train? If you knew what that kind of thing leads to . . . I've spent the best years of my life in the train. Ten years! Since I was seventeen. My youth and all of life's dangers have passed me by in the train. I often feel pretty low, and that can lead to the kind of adventure that only brings danger and bitterness and the rest. I haven't given up hope, don't worry!

'But life isn't much fun. *If you only knew how bored I get!*'

All this brought me up short. I had thought that life was cheerful, bright and amusing for these little Paris birds, so trim, with their heads in the air and their chic, miraculously made out of nothing.[30]

Whilst Le Corbusier includes this exchange as a piece of propaganda for his urbanistic ideals, it also indicates an unusual degree of empathy with his beleaguered secretary. It should be noted that Jeanne Heilbuth, Le Corbusier's secretary (though not necessarily the one referred to in the extract), worked devotedly for him for decades, right up to the end of his life. Her letters to her employer are very affectionate, full of gratitude for his kindly acts.[31] Evidently a spirited and intelligent woman, a central figure in his office (Fig.2.4), she wrote him friendly postcards, with apposite illustrations, from such adventurous holiday destinations as Lima in Peru.[32] It seems that Le Corbusier genuinely did take the interest in her wellbeing that is suggested by the extract.

Evidently Le Corbusier made a point of giving attention and thanks to those in more servile positions including, in many cases, women. When it came to advising his mother on employing a maid he was emphatic that she should be paid well above the going rate: 'one must not assassinate existence with domestic issues'.[33] Jardot writes of 'a letter, which he illustrated, full of fun and charming perception, addressed by way of apology to a friend's cook whom Le Corbusier had not been able to congratulate when taking leave of his host'.[34] Le Corbusier noted that he was invited to visit a brothel, the first building erected in the middle of the site for his scheme in

Figure 2.4   Le Corbusier and Jeanne Heilbuth, 1959.

Nemours, Africa, in 1934. 'It was a Saturday; the ladies, in their petticoats and with handkerchiefs knotted about their perms, were scrubbing the cement floor of this paradise due to open its doors that evening.'[35] In short he was highly observant. His interest in women did not focus solely on those at the top of the social scale.

Married women

After the Second World War there was great pressure upon the women of France from both government and Church to stay at home and procreate. Certainly Le Corbusier seems to have been prey to the propaganda surrounding him as he was of the opinion that the best place for a mother was in the home. This does not necessarily mean that he was 'sexist', as the issue of the best place for mothers is one that wages war in the consciences of working mothers to this day. Whilst advocating that the mother of the family should stay at home, Le Corbusier made the point that women should work the same hours as men, his suggestion being that their work should be perceived in the same way. Writing at the time when journal-

ists were only just beginning to acknowledge the economic value of woman's work in the home, Le Corbusier was radical in thus emphasising its importance.[36] He observed that

> . . . the economic and social boom that followed the Great war, that began during the war itself, has made woman a worker too and uprooted her from her former position at the center of home and family life. This tendency (especially strong in Russia: female emancipation and freedom = ideal = illusion) is perhaps leading us into error. If the wife goes back to her home, to her children, then there will be less labour on the market. The result would be less industrial unemployment. But take care! If the husband's working day is reduced to a mere 5 hours, then we must be careful not to force the wife back into the 12 to 16 hours of household tasks from which she has recently so energetically escaped. What is sauce for the goose is sauce for the gander: only 5 hours of house-work per day as well . . . The problem is to design a city for husbands, for wives, and for children, *in which the average working day is only 5 hours.*[37]

The suggestion hidden within this statement is that, in Le Corbusier's utopian vision, men would come to play a greater role within the household. In consigning mothers to the home, he anticipated a rather different role for them than that often conveyed by the term housewife, in other words exhausted drudge and lonely domestic slave. Sharing in the minimum of household tasks, they would live in close relationship with their families, within a supportive community with free access to recreational and cultural facilities, sun, space and greenery with time to develop themselves both physically and intellectually.

Women writers

When he moved to Paris in 1917, Le Corbusier lived on the fringes of a social circle that included a number of important and well-known intellectual women. He was acquaintances if not friends with many of those who frequented the salon of the American writer Nathalie Barney (with whom he shared the same address, in Rue Jacob).[38] Evidently she complained at the noise of some building work going on in Le Corbusier's apartment as the files in the Fondation Le Corbusier contain a placatory letter which emphasised what a 'discreet' neighbour he was (Barney was well known for her scandalous parties involving numbers of naked women in her garden).[39] During the twenties her salon attracted most of the rich and titled intellectuals who provided the backing for many of the artistic breakthroughs that were being achieved at that time.

In one letter of 1926, Le Corbusier wrote to his mother of the fact that he had met Colette the previous evening. The renowned author Colette Sidonie Gabrielle (1873–1954) was famously homosexual, part of a circle of powerful and intelligent women that included Barney, Romaine Brooks and Gertrude Stein. Shari Benstock observes that male homosexuality was at that time generally seen as a threat to the roots of society while female homosexuality received more indulgent treatment as it was a subject of erotic interest to men.[40] It was certainly a subject of interest to Le Corbusier as can be seen from a number of drawings that he made of women pleasuring one another (Fig. 2.5). Whilst he may have experienced a voyeuristic pleasure in creating such images, he was simultaneously acknowledging womens' need for

sexual fulfilment. Benstock notes that 'the dominant heterosexual culture in general would not have acknowledged woman's choice for a homosexual rather than a heterosexual life because this culture did not recognise woman's desire in any form'.[41] For this reason the openness with which Colette acknowledged the extent of women's sexual experience and desires made her, as Perry puts it, 'a controversial figure within the literary establishment and something of a heroine within some feminist circles'.[42] In the opinion of Benstock, Colette expressed through her work a lack of ease with the then current 'polarities of male and female sexuality'.[43] Early in the twentieth century Colette had cropped her hair and had begun to wear less restrictive clothing than the norm. Benstock writes that she and her follower, the fashion designer Coco Chanel, 'symbolised for many French the deterioration of feminine virtue'.[44] Evidently she got on well with Le Corbusier as he wrote to his mother of the fact that Colette wanted to sell her home in order to live in a 'Corbusièrie', the main issue being to get rid of her servants, whom he described as 'vampires'. Le Corbusier, evidently undeterred by her fearsome reputation, described her admiringly as a captivating woman.[45]

Le Corbusier also wrote to his mother in 1928 of an agreeable dinner that he had attended with the Princesse de Polignac and the poetess the Comtesse de Noailles. He was to recall this event in the pages

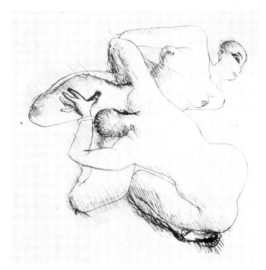

Figure 2.5 Le Corbusier, sketch of lesbians.

of his *Oeuvre Complète*.[46] Anna de Noailles, a close friend of Proust and the famously homosexual artist and writer Jean Cocteau, had been honoured by the French Academy for her poetry and was a renowned novelist who favoured the theme of women in love as a subject.[47] She was known for the way in which she rebelled against established norms of behaviour for women.[48] Benstock writes that, although she counted Cocteau amongst her friends, the Comtesse had a repugnance for lesbians such as Barney.[49]

The Princesse de Polignac (a friend of Barney), née Winaretta Singer, was a wealthy American heiress to the sewing machine fortune. She had entered into a marriage of convenience with the impoverished Prince Edmond de Polignac in which both husband and wife led fairly separate lives while sharing a great love of music, founding together a highly influential music salon. Apparently the Princesse 'collected' attractive women as well as composers.[50] Le Corbusier was to work on a scheme for a villa for her in 1926. Although it was never realised, she assisted him in securing the commission for his Cité de Refuge scheme in Paris (1933). Le Corbusier unsuccessfully asked her to become a financial backer for *L'Esprit Nouveau*.[51] Evidently he had no difficulty in accepting patronage from a wealthy intellectual woman of dubious sexuality.

Women clients

Le Corbusier was fully aware of the growing economic strength of women. Indeed he seems to have sought their attention, understanding them to be more receptive to his ideas and possibly his charms. Certainly women – rich women – played an important role in promoting his work across the world. Through their salons he was able to gain introductions to possible clients and extend the notoriety of his ideas.

A number of Le Corbusier's clients were women. They were to play a decisive role in seven of his projects. One of his first clients was Camille Schwob (1882–1944), the older sister of his friend Marcel Levaillant. He remodelled her apartment at 73 Rue Léopold-Robert in La Chaux de Fonds in 1913. According to Arthur Rüegg, she took Le Corbusier's side in a disagreement with her husband when he designed and built the Villa Schwob (1917) for

them.[52] One can only assume she played an active role in securing his commission. Of the fifteen projects covered in Tim Benton's book *The Villas of Le Corbusier 1920–1930*, eight involved female clients. This gives some idea of the extent to which Le Corbusier would have been used to working with women of financial power and influence. In this section I shall attempt to show something of what Le Corbusier was like in his dealings with such women by briefly describing four commissions in which they played a central role.

Villa Meyer, 1925

Although never built, the Villa Meyer project provides good evidence of one approach Le Corbusier took to his women clients: that of an aggrieved lover. Benton writes of 'the illustrated letter' written to Mme Meyer, wife of Pierre Meyer (clients for the Villa Meyer project 1925) written 'in the flirtatious banter of an experienced raconteur'.[53]

> Behind the swimming pool and the service rooms, you would take breakfast . . . From the boudoir, you have gone up onto a roof with neither slates nor tiles, but a solarium and swimming pool with grass growing between the paving slabs. Above you is the sky. With the surrounding walls, no one could see you. In the evening you would see the stars and the sombre mass of the trees in the Folie St James . . . you could imagine yourself far from Paris.[54]

Benton notes that 'Le Corbusier had a very interesting notion of the private, and in letters like this it is clear that this idea of the private life of his (female) clients interested him'.[55] When apparently Mme Meyer did not reply, Le Corbusier wrote back in what Benton calls 'the tone of an offended troubadour':

> My paternity is suffering! You are cruel, Madam to make us wait so long! I have told you the infinite trouble we have taken with your project and we were celebrating to see it emerge into the light of day. A house which remains on paper is still-birth. Let me tell you that my suffering is truly that of an expectant father.[56]

The Meyers were expecting a child at this time, so he was evidently attempting to play upon her maternal feelings.[57] Le Corbusier also entered into correspondence with Mme Hirtz, the mother of Mme Meyer, who was apparently going to pay for the new house.[58] However, the project was shelved because of financial difficulties, a familiar story in any architect's life.

Villa Stein de Monzie, 1928

Benton notes that 'although the best known clients for the Villa [Stein de Monzie] are Michael and Sarah Stein, the house was built on the land of Gabrielle de Monzie, and it is to her that most of the formal documents are addressed'.[59] Le Corbusier wrote of Michael Stein that he was 'Gertrude Stein's brother' and 'a wonderful man, a splendid client'. Significantly, he put his client into context by mentioning his relationship with his sister, a 'woman modernist' who chose to flout accepted standards of behaviour.[60] Le Corbusier also noted that Sarah Stein had been 'the first to buy a picture by Matisse'.[61] This was high praise in Le Corbusier's terms and evidence of extreme discernment and good taste.

The Steins, both Christian Scientists, obsessed by health as well as being patrons of the arts,[62] lived with their friend Madame de Monzie and her daughter, sharing much while retaining separate private lives.[63] In order to accommodate this arrangement Le Corbusier would have to provide two suites of rooms of equal size and status rather than the more conventional arrangement of one master bedroom surrounded by rooms of lesser status (Figs 2.6 & 2.7). Alice Friedman notes that Le Corbusier took this very literally in his initial sketches for the project, which

Figure 2.6   Villa Stein de Monzie, 1928.

show rooms of equal size and similar shape positioned symmetrically.[64] She concludes that the house was 'viewed by the clients and their architect as an image of a way of life shaped by a nexus of ideas and values, a life deliberately and self consciously constructed in response to the challenges of the modern world and the new ways in which women and men could relate to one another'.[65]

Villa de Mandrot, Le Pradet, 1929–31

Being a woman did not protect a client from Le Corbusier's ire, as can be seen from his relationship with Mme de Mandrot. This adventurous woman, an active promoter of Modernism, had lent her chateau at La Sarraz in Switzerland for the use of the first CIAM congress.[66] Le Corbusier prepared some designs for the interior of her villa at Le Pradet, built in 1930 (Fig. 2.8). Jencks refers to this low cost rubble building as 'an ironic house for a rich hostess'. According to Jencks she left the house because it had so many building defects. Le Corbusier wrote of the building: 'Your house is not one of our best . . . It seemed that Madame de Mandrot, after the act of La Sarraz, which made her enter by the gate of honour into the world of modern architecture, would have been ready to live in a modern house. You have told us you cannot. What the hell, then!'[67]

Heidi Weber House, 1964/65

A far more successful collaboration was that between Le Corbusier and Heidi Weber who played a very active role in the design of the Heidi Weber House (1964/5), an experimental steel house on the shore of the lake at Zurich (Fig. 2.9), perhaps because he may, by that time, have mellowed with age. This building was to have a double function – those of 'a private museum and a place where Le Corbusier's painting sculpture, graphic works and books' were to be made available to the public.[68]

Weber had been very impressed by Le Corbusier's paintings upon visiting an exhibition of his work in 1958 (Fig. 2.10). She became interested in selling his furniture in her interior design shop in Zurich and met him the same year. She records:

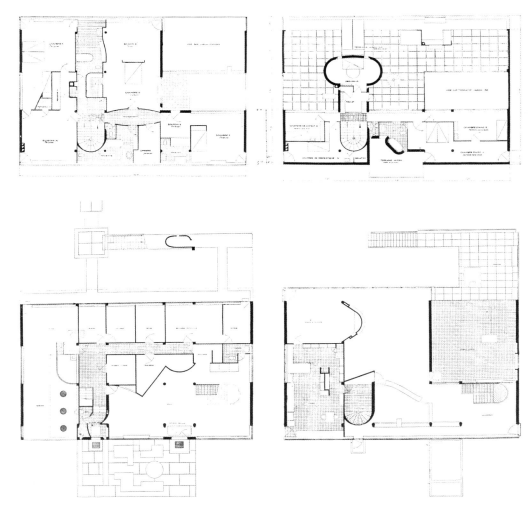

Figure 2.7 Plans of Villa Stein de Monzie.

Figure 2.8 Villa de Mandrot, Le Pradet, 1929–31.

Figure 2.9 Heidi Weber House, 1964.

Figure 2.10 Le Corbusier and Heidi Weber, 1960.

My first personal encounter with Le Corbusier turned out quite opposite from my expectations. Acquaintances had described him to me as closed and distant almost to arrogance; the man and artist whom I met in the middle of August 1958 in his small cabin on Cap Martin was friendly, attentive, open and amiable. From the very first instant I had a feeling of trust.[69]

This point marked the beginning of an intensive and fruitful collaboration that lasted till his death in 1965 (she visited him every other week). It was she who came up with the idea of building the house and exhibition pavilion beside the lake at Zurich. Le Corbusier sent her a couple of colourful sketches that Weber then sent to the planning office for approval. What followed was a succession of design changes and new applications for approvals. Work started on the basement in spring 1964. In Weber's opinion Le Corbusier treated her very much as he would a male client.[70] Theirs was a real partnership. It was in 1965 that Le Corbusier asked Weber whether she would mind if the structure was built in steel. This suggestion 'thrilled' his client who proudly proclaims that 22,000 screws were used in the production of her house.[71] Here we have a clear case of a woman client sanctioning his risky and innovative proposals.

Summary

These are not the sole cases where women played an important role in the design for a house. There are a number of other conspicuous examples. Barbara Church had a significant input into the design for the Villa Church of 1929,[72] while Madame Savoye, not her husband, wrote the initial brief for the Villa Savoye.[73] Lotti Raaf, fiancée of Le Corbusier's brother Albert, seems to have been the client for their house the Maison Jeanneret (1925). She took a great deal of interest in the design of her house, suggesting the inclusion of push button light switches and a spray system bidet.[74] Le Corbusier's own mother presumably would have had a say in the design for her house by the lake at Vevey, and Mona Sarabhai was to commission Le Corbusier to construct a villa in 1955 'on her paternal estate, in the shade of the beautiful trees which covered it'.[75] Moreover, correspondence such as that with Madame Delgado, whom Le Corbusier never actually met, regarding the design of the Delgado chapel suggests that he was, in the main, co-operative, respectful and professional in his dealings with his women clients. After an inspiring chat with Madame Jaoul, client for the Jaoul Houses 'who was very kind', Minette De Silva planned to write a 'very sympathetic' book on Le Corbusier's 'client-architect relationship' as 'few people know of this facet of his life and work'.[76] Evidently it was one of which she felt he should be proud.

Women collaborators

Not only did Le Corbusier work for women clients, he also worked on a day-to-day basis, with a number of women who promoted his work and provided support in various ways. The extent of his collaboration with the female sex would appear to be unusual for a man of his times. My suggestion is that he may have actively sought their assistance in this way believing them to be his 'best propagandists'.

Le Corbusier's 'best propagandists'

Le Corbusier worked with many women, particularly as promoters of his ideas, as was the case of Héléna Strassova who became his exclusive literary agent in 1951 with 'all powers over his translations, works and editions in all countries' – a very significant role.[77] Evidently he had every confidence in her ability as a professional. Le Corbusier wrote to her in 1960 in appreciation of their ten-year collaboration and their correspondence is one of the largest in the archives of the Fondation Le Corbusier. Whilst their relationship was clearly professional, this did not stop them from becoming good friends.

When Le Corbusier went on tour, women were often to play a large part in promulgating his work. Mme Kamenef (the sister of Trotsky and director of *Vox*, an intellectual journal) organised Le Corbusier's second conference on urbanism in Moscow.[78] On his tour of South America Le Corbusier received the assistance of Madame Ocampo, the editor of an Argentinian poetry journal, a 'glamorous and very wealthy lady'.[79] She was to become a friend of Le Corbusier's, helping him with the organisation of his lecture tour in Argentina in 1929.[80] Le Corbusier wrote of Madame Ocampo as being 'alone in making a decisive gesture in architecture by building a house considered scandalous'. He wrote of 'two million inhabitants' of Buenos Aires, 'emigrants with the worst tenderness for junk, colliding with the *willpower* of one woman'.[81]

Similarly, on his tour of America, women were a primary source of practical support. In October 1936 Le Corbusier engaged photographer Thérèse Bonney to be his agent there. He also enlisted the help of Alma Clayburgh, a society hostess, to represent his interests amongst the rich upper classes.[82] A further powerful woman with whom Le Corbusier was in contact was Hilla Rebay (1890–1967) the first director of the Guggenheim Museum in New York.[83]

Jane Drew would promote his work through books and exhibitions in Britain.[84] Again and again Le Corbusier enlisted women to his aid believing them to be tireless promoters of his message.

Intellectual support

Le Corbusier was not afraid to use the opinions of women to reinforce his arguments. Of particular importance for this proposition is the work of Mlle Elisa Maillard, apparently attached to the Musée de Cluny and the author of what Le Corbusier called 'an excellent book on regulating lines, *Du nombre d'or*,

published by André Tournon et Cie'.[85] Late in October 1948 Le Corbusier wrote to Mlle Maillard asking her to consult with 'her colleagues at the Sorbonne' on a number of issues pertaining to the Modulor.[86] With her help, exemplified by a drawing 'the answer of the compass', included in the Modulor, he was able to arrive at the final version of this system of proportion.[87] She thus played an essential role in its development.

In *Modulor 2* Le Corbusier wrote of a letter that he received from Jacqueline Tyrwhitt, to whom he referred as 'the organizer of the Eighth CIAM Congress held at Hoddesdon, near London, in 1951, and of the Regional symposium on "Principles of Scientific Buildings, Design and Construction and Their application in Tropical Countries" held in New Delhi in December 1952"'. Tyrwhitt wrote that she was using the Modulor in her teaching activities. For Le Corbusier her endorsement of the Modulor was worthy of mention in his book. Even the view of 'a woman who is professor of art history at Vassar' that 'The Beaux-Arts School in Paris has done us harm here in the United States' was seen to be of value.[88] A further example is that of Marie Dornoy whose book on French architecture received his particular approval.[89] Whilst he obviously did not make as many references to the work of women as to that of men, it is the fact that he made any references at all to them that is significant.

Women designers

Unlike many of his contemporaries Le Corbusier seems to have experienced little difficulty with the idea of women working within the domain of architecture.[90] He believed that:

> The architect's vocation is open to women in all matters connected with housing. Architecture is no longer the right term for the activity that is expected. The vocation must be broadened. Those who devote themselves to it must always be faced with realities: the workshop, the factory, the building site. Those who have acquired sufficient knowledge in this field might be awarded a 'diploma of housing' and authorized to build and equip homes.

The diploma given today is a barrier to much of this potential energy. The type of mind necessary to win the official diploma is not necessarily the same as that which will devote a lifetime to the service of men in their homes.[91]

Whilst the last statement, suggesting that women are only suitable to work on domestic architecture, might make female architects sigh with exasperation, it should be remembered that Le Corbusier believed housing to be the single most fundamentally important form of building. As such it would be safe in women's hands. It should also be remembered that for any architect to suggest that women should have any role in the construction process was at that time radical in the extreme.

I will now examine his relationship with three well-known women designers, Charlotte Perriand, Eileen Gray and Jane Drew, in order to gain a better insight into his view of women designers.

Charlotte Perriand

One afternoon, a portfolio of drawings under my arm, somewhat intimidated by the austerity of the premises, I found myself face to face with Le Corbusier's large eye-glasses, which concealed his gaze. His greeting was rather cold and distant. 'What do you want?' 'To work with you.' He glanced quickly through my drawings. 'We don't embroider cushions here,' was his response. He led me to the door. In a final attempt I left my address and told him about my installation at the Salon d'Automne – without any hope that he would see it. I went away feeling almost relieved. No one could say that my charm had worked on him.[92]

Perriand's exhibit, a design for a 'Bar in the attic' at the Salon d'Automne exhibition of 1927, evidently impressed Le Corbusier as she began work in the Rue de Sèvres in October of that year, remaining there for a decade. Together they formed a successful collaboration in which, as Mary McLeod notes, it is difficult to assign authorship.[93] For Le Corbusier she was his 'associate for the interior equipment of dwellings'

(Fig. 2.11), giving her credit as a designer and an equal.[94] McLeod recalls that

Perriand was not shy about criticising Le Corbusier's political views or social relations, but she also said to me on many occasions that he always treated her as the equal of any male employee. She had a certificate from him saying that she had the full responsibility for the firms 'domestic equipment', and he regularly acknowledged her contribution in his publications.[95]

According to McLeod it was generally Le Corbusier who would set a design problem which Perriand would then develop in detail, sometimes with the help of Pierre Jeanneret, Le Corbusier's partner.[96] She collaborated with Le Corbusier and Jeanneret in the design of the *siège à dosier basculant* (chair with tilting back), the *grand-confort* and the *chaise longue* of 1928–9.[97] She also prepared a number of other furniture designs in her own right.

Le Corbusier and Perriand remained friends after her departure from his atelier. In a letter of 1946 Le Corbusier wrote to her in admiration of her 'album on Japan'. It is evident from the tone of his letter that he believed her to be an esteemed colleague and friend.[98] They were to continue collaborating over a number of projects, for example the Brazilian Pavilion in Paris in 1958.[99]

Eileen Gray

Eileen Gray (1878–1976) was an Irish born designer who settled in Paris and, during the 1910s and early

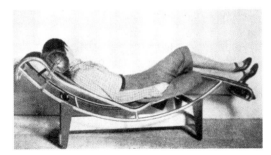

Figure 2.11   Photograph of Charlotte Perriand lying on Le Corbusier and Perriand's chaise longue.

1920s, became known for her lacquered furniture and interiors. She started to experiment with architecture when she began a six-year collaboration with Jean Badovici the editor of L'*Architecture Vivante*. Between 1927 and 1929 she built a modernist villa, E.1027, in Roquebrune on the Mediterranean, for both their use. In the opinion of Caroline Constant, the building 'represents a sophisticated critique of Le Corbusier's spatial principles'.[100] Gray also collaborated with Badovici on the renovation of an old stone structure in Vézelay to which Le Corbusier was a frequent visitor.[101]

Colomina has written extensively on Le Corbusier's offensive role in despoiling E.1027 through his painting of a number of murals there.[102] Constant presents the events that took place there in a rather more measured tone as does Christopher Pearson, who observes that in certain critiques 'Le Corbusier is portrayed as almost comically depraved, coming off no less than a lesbian bashing colonialist with Nazi sympathies'.[103]

Constant writes that Le Corbusier was an admirer of Gray's architecture, displaying a proposal that she made for a vacation and leisure centre (1936–37) amongst the work of other CIAM members in his Pavillon des Temps Nouveaux. According to Pearson they were on 'good' but fairly 'formal' terms with one another.[104] Significantly, Le Corbusier had written to Gray in 1938 registering his appreciation of E.1027:

> I genuinely regret having arrived here too late to have been able to spend some time with you . . . I hope that you will give us the pleasure of paying us a visit in Paris. I would be delighted to relate how much those few days spent in your house have made me appreciate that rare spirit that dictates all of its organisation, both inside and outside, and has given the modern furniture and equipment a form that is so dignified charming and full of wit.[105]

Evidently he was able to appreciate her talents as an architect. Not only was her architecture charming, a word that one might imagine him using, possibly in a patronizing way, to a woman but it was also dignified, suggesting the depth of his respect for her work.

Gray apparently moved out of the house in 1932. It was a number of years after her departure that Badovici made what Pearson calls the rather 'insensitive decision' to allow Le Corbusier to take a paint-

brush to the building.[106] In the summer of 1938 he began work on a mural depicting three reclining women outlined in black. As its name suggests *Sous les pilotis* took a position at the base of the building. To its left, on a low wall, Le Corbusier made a depiction of a striped beach pebble, like those to be found on the beach at Cap Martin below. This, according to some commentators, represented a form of self-portrait.[107]

Constant notes that the subject of *Sous les pilotis*, three women, was a recurrent theme in his work at that time, and should not 'necessarily be interpreted as a commentary on Gray's bisexuality'.[108] However, in Pearson's opinion the murals present 'a jumble of interrelated associations' which emerged 'from Le Corbusier's conceptions of Mediterraneanism, Orientalism, antiquity and the "primitive," all held together by an overarching emphasis on sexuality.'[109] This makes it rather more likely that the mural was a statement about Gray's sexual proclivities.

A second mural was painted that same year at the end of the living room on a partition that screened off a washroom from the main space. In bright colours it depicted a large female figure with bare teeth. It was particularly inappropriate to the space which, as Pearson observes, was specifically designed for relaxation.[110]

Figure 2.12   Le Corbusier painting murals at E.1027.

Over the following year Le Corbusier painted five further murals – he can be seen at work in the photograph (Fig. 2.12). Firstly he attempted to 'demolish' the wall of the porch by painting on it a large, brightly coloured woman – what Pearson calls a 'guardian deity figure'.[111] Le Corbusier believed that, through the judicious use of painting, it was possible to make an undesirable wall disappear. Pearson notes that here again Le Corbusier was directly flouting Gray's architectural intentions as she had intended this as a pure meditative space.[112] Whilst it was obviously reprehensible to alter the house in this way, Le Corbusier evidently had a strongly held belief that the monumental women with whom he adorned the cool pale walls of E.1027 provided an important foil to the space. As Pearson observes, they represent 'another manifestation of Le Corbusier's urge to bring violent and chaotic elements into value by juxtaposing them against a pristine measured field'.[113] It will be seen in Chapter 5 that by promulgating such feminine deity figures Le Corbusier was attempting to create a sense of sexual balance within religion. I suspect that he did find the architecture of E.1027 imbalanced in gender terms, believing that his murals could in some way rectify the situation. It seems likely that he did not specifically intend to upset Gray and Badovici: his main concern was the pursuit of his own particular thesis, in this case rather insensitively it seems. Pearson describes his behaviour as 'remarkably cavalier', believing that the 'assertive imagery of the murals cannot be ignored'.[114]

Le Corbusier wrote in his *Oeuvre Complète* that the murals were 'not painted on the best walls of the villa'. On the contrary, they burst out from dull, sad walls 'where nothing is happening'.[115] Whilst this could be seen as a slight on Gray's architecture it also reads as guilty self-justification on Le Corbusier's part. According to Constant, Gray urged Badovici to write a letter to him registering his annoyance at Le Corbusier's published criticisms of the house.[116] Le Corbusier's response was hostile: he wrote that he had perhaps misunderstood 'the underlying sense' of Badovici's thoughts. Indeed he pointed to Gray's use of Corbusian signage around the house as some kind of precedent.[117] The exchange led to a long-term falling out between the two men.[118]

The despoiling of E.1027 does not seem to have angered Gray so much that she lost her respect for Le Corbusier altogether. She was, for example, to comment favourably upon his exhibition at the Musée d'Art Moderne in Paris in 1953.[119] Whilst it is impossible to know what really occurred in the complicated web of misunderstandings that took place at Cap Martin, it is my belief that Le Corbusier did not intend the painting of the murals to be seen as the out-and-out attack depicted by Colomina, and there is no proof to indicate that Gray's gender acted as a provocation to him in this case. Mary McLeod makes the important point that 'Colomina's reading' of Le Corbusier's work 'played an important polemical role during a particular time period in architectural history'.[120] It should be noted that he had a habit of painting murals in the houses of his friends – indeed he and his friend the artist Fernand Léger had already completed murals at Badovici's house in Vézelay in 1940, suggesting that he may have thought that it was an acceptable thing to do.

Jane Drew

Late in life Le Corbusier was to work closely with another female designer, the architect Jane Drew. 'Le Corbusier was an extraordinarily good friend to me' reminisced Drew (Fig. 2.13).[121] She wrote movingly of her close relationship with him, a man to whom she was 'very attached', in an essay in Russell Walden's book *The Open Hand*. Drew made friends with Le Corbusier at successive CIAM meetings, the first being that at Bridgewater in Somerset in 1947. After that he

Figure 2.13 Le Corbusier and Jane Drew.

regarded her as a 'special friend', sending her numerous letters and postcards along with 'a constant stream of paintings and drawings' until his death 'showing how seriously he treated friendship'. Guardedly she admitted the extent of her affection for him.[122] Together with her husband Maxwell Fry, they worked together on the scheme for Chandigarh.[123] According to Drew, Le Corbusier had initially refused the project as he was busy with Ronchamp, but had eventually agreed to come on board when he knew that she and Fry had been appointed.[124] Le Corbusier and Drew seem to have had a workmanlike collaboration as can be seen from notes in his sketchbook reminding himself to ask Drew about this or that technicality.[125] She herself was treated 'like a man' by the Indian team, who referred to her as 'respected Sir'.[126]

Drew wrote of the way in which Le Corbusier incorporated images of the design team into the

Figure 2.14 Le Corbusier sketch, dated 1952, of himself and his collaborators on Chandigarh: Jane Drew, Maxwell Fry and Pierre Jeanneret as animals and birds.

enamel of the doors for the Palace of the Assembly at Chandigarh in 1962. Here she is represented as a large goat towering over the rest of the group with her husband below suckling from her teats (Fig. 2.14). In front, oblivious, Pierre Jeanneret, whom Drew referred to as a 'strutting little man', can be seen as a cockerel pecking at the ground.[127] Le Corbusier himself, the crow, appears with his back to the whole scene. Evidently the suggestion is that Drew herself in some way dominated the three men, particularly Fry who is infantilised by Le Corbusier's representation.

Le Corbusier did not denigrate her for being a female; on the contrary, Drew observed that 'his kindness and unselfishness to me may well have been partly or largely due to my being a woman, but he continued it when our work association was over'.[128]

Conclusion

Le Corbusier recognised the changing role of women and their need to work outside the home. Operating at a time when there was great confusion about gender roles, he was pioneering in his ability to collaborate with and acknowledge the design ability of women. Both Perriand and Drew have testified to his impartial treatment of them. Women were for Le Corbusier important agents in the march for progress; he would for this reason make a special effort to utilise their energies.

Notes

1 Le Corbusier, *Journey to the East* (Cambridge, MA: MIT Press, 1987), p.206.
2 J. Drew, 'Le Corbusier as I knew him' in R. Walden, (ed.), *The Open Hand* (Cambridge, MA: MIT Press, 1982), p.367.
3 J. Drew interview with M. Garlake, 20–21 May 1995, National Life Story Collection, British Library, F823.
4 M. Bacon, *Le Corbusier in America* (Cambridge, MA: MIT Press, 2001), p.227.
5 Le Corbusier, *When the Cathedrals were White: A Journey to the Country of the Timid People* (New York: Reynal and Hitchcock, 1947), p.149.
6 Bacon, *Le Corbusier in America*, p.211.
7 Le Corbusier, *When the Cathedrals were White*, p.135.
8 Ibid., p.138.
9 Ibid., p.137.
10 Le Corbusier, *Sketchbooks Volume 1* (London: Thames and Hudson, 1981), sketch 97.

11 Le Corbusier, *The Decorative Art of Today* (London: Architectural Press, 1987), p.43.

12 Le Corbusier, *When the Cathedrals were White*, p.137.

13 Ibid., p.138.

14 Le Corbusier, *When the Cathedrals were White*, p.149.

15 Ibid., p.147.

16 Ibid.

17 Le Corbusier, *Sketchbooks Volume 2* (London: Thames and Hudson, 1981), sketch 444.

18 Le Corbusier's interest in Rousseau is discussed extensively in A.M. Vogt, *Le Corbusier, The Noble Savage: Towards an Archaeology of Modernism* (Cambridge, MA: MIT Press, 1998).

19 Le Corbusier, *Sketchbooks Volume 2*, sketch 646.

20 Ibid., sketch 622.

21 Le Corbusier, *Oeuvre Complète Volume 6, 1952–1957* (Zurich: Les Editions d'Architecture, 1995), p.87.

22 Le Corbusier, *Sketchbooks Volume 2*, sketch 921.

23 Le Corbusier, *Sketchbooks Volume 4, 1957–1964* (Cambridge, MA: MIT Press, 1982), sketch 798.

24 Lowman observes that she must have contributed to the household budget. J. Lowman, 'Le Corbusier 1900–1925: The Years of Transition.' Unpublished doctoral dissertation, University of London (1979), p.20.

25 See photographic evidence in J. Gubler (ed.), *Le Corbusier: Early works by Charles-Edouard Jeanneret-Gris* (London: Academy, 1987), p.120.

26 C. Laubier, *The Condition of Women in France: 1945 to the Present* (London: Routledge, 1990), p.2.

27 G. Pollock, 'Modernity and the Spaces of Feminism' in F. Frasina (ed.), *Art in Modern Culture* (London: Phaidon, 1992), p.131.

28 Le Corbusier, *The Radiant City* (London: Faber, 1967), p.92.

29 Ibid., p.15.

30 Ibid., pp.12–13.

31 Letter Heilbuth to Le Corbusier, 10.11.58, Fondation Le Corbusier (hereafter referred to as FLC) E2.4.202.

32 Postcard Heilbuth to Le Corbusier, FLC E3.4.563.

33 Letter Le Corbusier to his mother, 11.08.1948, FLC R2.4.135.

34 Le Corbusier, *My Work* (London: Architectural Press, 1960), pp.12–13.

35 Ibid., p.115.

36 Ibid., p.85.

37 Le Corbusier, *The Radiant City*, p.112.

38 S. Von Moos, & A. Rüegg (eds), *Le Corbusier Before Le Corbusier* (New Haven, CT: Yale University Press, 2002), p.267.

39 Letter Le Corbusier to Mademoiselle Clifford Barney, FLC E1.6.32.

40 S. Benstock, *Women of the Left Bank* (London: Virago, 1994), p.54.

41 Benstock, *Women of the Left Bank*, p.54.

42 G. Perry, *Women Artists and the Parisian Avant-Garde* (Manchester: Manchester University Press, 1995), p.132.

43 Benstock, *Women of the Left Bank*, p.58.

44 Ibid., p.74.

45 Letter Le Corbusier to his mother, 1926 in Jenger, J. *Le Corbusier Choix de Lettres* (Basel: Birkhauser, 2002), p.172.

46 Le Corbusier, *Oeuvre Complète Volume 6, 1952–1957* (Zurich: Les Editions d'Architecture, 1995), p.158.

47 Benstock, *Women of the Left Bank*, p.69.

48 Ibid., p.75.

49 Ibid., p.61.

50 G. Wickes, *The Amazon of Letters* (New York: Putnam & Sons, 1976), p.107.

51 Letter Le Corbusier to the Princesse de Polignac, 16.03.32, FLC A1.19.273.

52 A. Rüegg, 'Marcel Levaillant and "La Question du Mobilier"', in von Moos & Rüegg, *Le Corbusier before Le Corbusier*, p.113.

53 Letter Le Corbusier to Madame Meyer, FLC 31525, October 1925 cited in T. Benton, *The Villas of Le Corbusier* (London: Yale University Press, 1987), p.143.

54 Ibid, p144.

55 Ibid.

56 Letter Le Corbusier to Madame Meyer, 24.02.26, FLC H3.1.16.

57 Benton, *The Villas of Le Corbusier*, p.145.

58 Ibid., p.147.

59 Ibid., p.166.

60 Perry, *Women Artists and the Parisian Avant-Garde*, p.91.

61 Le Corbusier, *My Work*, p.76.

62 In the late nineteenth century the collection of art was seen as the remit of men. See for example Edmond de Goncourt, *La Maison d'un artiste* (Paris: Charpentier, 1881), pp.2–3. Quoted in Leora Auslander, 'The Gendering of Consumer Practices in Nineteenth Century France', in Victoria de Grazia (ed.), *The Sex of Things* (Berkeley: University of California Press, 1960), p.90.

63 A.T. Friedman, *Women and the Making of the Modern House* (New York: Harry N. Abrams, 1998), p.96.

64 Ibid., p.113.

65 Ibid., p.98.

66 Le Corbusier, *The Radiant City*, p.19.

67 Quoted in C. Jencks, *Le Corbusier and the Continual Revolution in Architecture* (New York: Monacelli Press, 2000), p.208.

68 Le Corbusier, *Oeuvre Complète Volume 7, 1957–1965* (Zurich: Les Editions d'Architecture, 1995), p.24.

69 H. Weber, Le Corbusier, *Das Grafische Werk* (Zurich: Editions Heidi Weber, 1988).

70 Meeting Heidi Weber with Gisela Loehlein, Zurich, 13 July 2002.

71 Apparently, after Le Corbusier's death, the architects in Le Corbusier's office (of whom she seems to have had rather a low opinion) tried to persuade her to have the

joints welded – a change that she adamantly resisted. Ibid.

72 Benton, *The Villas of Le Corbusier*, p.129.

73 Ibid., p.202.

74 Interview Lowman and Albert Jeanneret, Vevey, June 1972. J. Lowman, 'Le Corbusier 1900–1925: The Years of Transition', p.229.

75 Le Corbusier, *Oeuvre Complète Volume 5, 1946–1952* (Zurich: Les Editions d'Architecture, 1995), p.160.

76 Letter Minette De Silva to André Wogensky, 01.06.79, FLC R3.4.512.

77 Contract between Le Corbusier and Strassova, 12.04.60, FLC U3.23.

78 Letter Le Corbusier to Yvonne, 24.10.1928, FLC R1.12.315.

79 Benton, *The Villas of Le Corbusier*, p.150.

80 Ibid., p152.

81 Le Corbusier, *Precisions* (Cambridge, MA: MIT Press, 1990), p.15.

82 Bacon, *Le Corbusier in America*, p.197.

83 Jenger, *Le Corbusier Choix de Lettres*, p.254.

84 Letter Jane Drew to Le Corbusier, 11.2.59, FLC E1.19.79.

85 Le Corbusier, *Modulor* (London: Faber, 1954), p.38.

86 Ibid., p.229.

87 Ibid., pp.235–37.

88 Le Corbusier, *When the Cathedrals were White*, p.114.

89 Le Corbusier, *Le Corbusier Talks with Students* (New York: Princeton University Press, 1999), p.29. See letter Le Corbusier to Marie Dornoy, 15.3.1938, FLC E1.19.15 that he wrote in appreciation of her book.

90 He wrote for example of a Madame Chowdhury being a totally capable architect. Letter Le Corbusier to Paule Gabriel, 30.5.1963 in Jenger, *Le Corbusier Choix de Lettres*, p.491.

91 From an article originally published in Le Point in 1948 and cited in Le Corbusier, *Modulor* 2 (London: Faber, 1958), p.162.

92 C. Perriand, *Une Vie de crèation* (Paris: Editions Odile Jacob), p.25 cited in G.H. Marcus, *Le Corbusier: Inside the Machine for Living* (New York: Monacelli, 2000), p.85.

93 McLeod, who had unique access to Perriand, is currently compiling a book on her work.

94 Le Corbusier, *Precisions*, p.113.

95 K. Ven Herck (ed.), 'First Interlude: on the nuances of historical emancipation', *The Journal of Architecture*, 7, Autumn 2002, p.245.

96 Pierre Jeanneret and Perriand began a relationship which lasted up to the Second World War. Apparently Pierre was very fond of her, but they never formalised their relationship. Separated by force during the War, Perriand was to marry elsewhere. Interview Lowman with Mme J. Vauthier, Pierre Jeanneret's niece, June 1972. Lowman, 'Le Corbusier 1900–1925: The Years of Transition', p.233.

97 M. McLeod, 'Charlotte Perriand: Her First Decade as a Designer', *AA files*, 13, 1987, pp.3–13.

98 Letter Le Corbusier to Charlotte Perriand, 02.05.46 in Jenger, *Le Corbusier Choix de Lettres*, p.286.

99 Letter Le Corbusier to Perriand, FLC K1.15.129.

100 C. Constant, *Eileen Gray* (London, Phaidon, 2000), p.67.

101 Ibid., p.85.

102 B. Colomina, 'War on Architecture', *Assemblage* 20 (1993), pp.28–29. B. Colomina, 'Battle lines: E.1027', in D. Agrest (ed.), *The Sex of Architecture* (New York: Harry N. Abrams, 1996), pp.167–190. See also B. Colomina, *Privacy and Publicity* (Cambridge, MA: MIT Press, 1994), p.84–88. The murals can be seen in Le Corbusier, *Oeuvre Complète Volume 4, 1938–1946* (Zurich: Les Editions d'Architecture, 1995), pp.158–159.

103 C. Pearson, 'Integrations of Art and Architecture in the Work of Le Corbusier. Theory and Practice from Ornamentalism to the "Synthesis of the Major Arts"', unpublished PhD thesis, Stanford University (1995), p.301.

104 Ibid., p.288.

105 Letter Le Corbusier to Eileen Gray, Cap Martin, 28 April 1938 (private collection, London). Cited in Constant, *Eileen Gray*, p.125.

106 Pearson, 'Integrations of Art and Architecture in the work of Le Corbusier', p.289.

107 Ibid., p.290.

108 Constant, *Eileen Gray*, p.203, note 48.

109 Pearson, 'Integrations of Art and Architecture in the Work of Le Corbusier', p.298. In his belief that Le Corbusier began to associate 'muralism with sexuality' having seen the ancient murals with 'priapic and orgiastic' themes while on his journey to the East. See his description of the fresco in the House of the Vetii. *Le Corbusier, Voyage d'Orient. Carnets Volume 4* (Milan: Electa and Paris: Fondation Le Corbusier, 1987), p.46.

110 Pearson, 'Integrations of Art and Architecture in the Work of Le Corbusier', p.293.

111 Ibid., p.295.

112 Ibid.

113 Ibid., p.301.

114 Ibid., p.297.

115 Le Corbusier, *Oeuvre Complète Volume 4*, p.158.

116 Letter Jean Badovici to Le Corbusier, 30.12.1949, originally FLC E1–592, but no longer catalogued with Badovici correspondence. Cited by Constant, *Eileen Gray*, p.123.

117 Le Corbusier to Jean Badovici, 01.01.1950, FLC E1.5.99. Cited in Constant, *Eileen Gray*, p.123.

118 Ibid.

119 Ibid., p.125.

120 Quoted in Ven Herck (ed.), 'First Interlude', p.245.

121 J. Drew interview with M. Garlake, 20–21 May 1995, National Life Story Collection, British Library, F823.

122 Drew wrote of the fact that she was 'not yet at peace with myself, after Le Corbusier's departure. 'The only

reason I make faces when you go is that I cannot like you going'. Letter Jane Drew to Le Corbusier, 07.05.54, FLC E1.19.56.

123 Walden (ed.), *The Open Hand*, p.366.

124 J. Drew interview with M. Garlake, 20–21 May 1995, National Life Story Collection, British Library, F823.

125 Le Corbusier, *Sketchbooks Volume 2*, sketch 1026.

126 J. Drew interview with M. Garlake, 20–21 May 1995, National Life Story Collection, British Library, F823.

127 Ibid. Apparently Le Corbusier was not very 'nice' to Jeanneret, preferring to send messages to Nehru through Drew.

128 Walden (ed.), *The Open Hand*, p.372.

3 Feminism, Fashion and Physical Culture

What again shall we say of the actual acquirement of knowledge? – is the body, if invited to share in the enquiry, a hinderer or a helper?'[1]

Feminism, it will be seen, was very much part of the cultural agenda in the period during which Le Corbusier was most active; it formed part of a general questioning of sexual roles that was taking place in avant-garde circles at that time. The 'woman question', as it came to be known, attracted wide public interest between the wars.[2] Le Corbusier's treatment of women, examined in the last two chapters, should be seen in this context.

Evidently Le Corbusier took an interest in the subject of feminism as he owned a small pamphlet on the subject, written by Antoine Mesclon and entitled *Le Feminisme et l'Homme*.[3] For Mesclon 'the equality of the sexes is inscribed in natural law'.[4] He asked the question whether mothers deserve the same respect as other people. Patently the answer, for Mesclon, was yes. This was a statement that must have struck a chord with Le Corbusier who held his mother in high esteem.

The cause of woman's suffrage was one that was unpopular in Catholic right wing circles in France, suggesting that it might, for this very reason, have held some subversive appeal for the architect who always saw himself as an outsider. Le Corbusier made angry annotations to his friend René Allendy's reference to the 'sufficient liberation' of women in his book *Capitalisme et Sexualité*. For Le Corbusier there was no such thing – liberation should be total.[5] In *Le Corbusier Lui-même*, written by his friend Jean Petit, the significant events of each year are given next to a list of the events in Le Corbusier's life. Those for 1908 are given as: 'The suffragettes in England. Braque and Picasso' in that order, suggesting that this first phenomenon was at least of comparative importance, or perhaps greater importance, for Le Corbusier than

the rise of Braque and Picasso, whose work we know had a tremendous impact on him.[6] Gill Perry writes of the paucity of evidence to prove that bohemian artistic circles were a 'breeding ground for clearly feminist ideas'.[7] This is what makes Le Corbusier's interest in feminism all the more significant.

In his book *Passion and Society*, a history of romantic love through the ages, Denis de Rougemont (briefly involved in Le Corbusier's unbuilt scheme for La Sainte Baume[8]) identified a general movement in French society after the Second World War to elevate the role of the feminine. In his opinion there was

> A strong revival of mariology[9] in the Roman Catholic Church with its popular millions; the most recent work of C. G. Jung and his school, on the eternal Sophia, wisdom, and mother-Virgin; and also (and really otherwise) the revival of interest in Catharism shown by the avant-garde of European literature and in the elevation of the 'Child-Woman', saviour of rational man, or the repeated announcement that the feminine principle is about to get even with patriarchal pretensions.[10]

He cited books such as *Arcane 17* by Breton, the novels of Julien Gracq[11] and the studies of the great goddess by Robert Graves[12] as being important manifestations of this change.

In this chapter I will set out a number of themes that were prevalent in French feminist thought during the early twentieth century and will illustrate the ways in which they connect to the ideas of Le Corbusier. Of central importance to the feminist cause, to that of their literal liberation, was fashion and its connection to physical culture.

Feminism in France at the beginning of the twentieth century

France has a very rich tradition of feminist thought in which Hubertine Auclert (1848–1914), one of the first leading French feminist thinkers of the nineteenth century, would play a pivotal role. Auclert argued that the principles of equality and justice embedded in *Le Déclaration des Droits de l'Homme* should be applied to women as well as men.[13] For Auclert women's 'struggle focused on the four interrelated issues of education, access to the professions, women's parity in the law, and political rights'.[14] The first issue whch she tackled in 1876 was that of equal pay for equal work, a right that would not be enshrined in French law until as late as 1972.[15]

From this point on, the French suffragette movement began to gather momentum until, at the outbreak of the First World War, they stopped their fight for women's rights to concentrate on the war effort. During this period vast numbers of women began work outside the home, replacing the rapidly dwindling population of men. Following an initial decline immediately after the war, the proportion of employed married women working in factories continued to grow in spite of pro-natal policies.[16] Woman's suffrage found a place on the agenda of the the Chambre des Députés, the French lower house, but there was a three year lapse before the issue was due to be debated, a gap that resulted in a change of heart in political circles. Mitchell writes that 'during this period all the old conservative arguments concerning woman's special relation to family, employment and the Church were voiced again'.[17] Feminists were represented as revolutionaries, Bolshevism being seen as a primary cause of the breakdown of the family. The result was a ruling in the upper house of parliament, the 'Sénat', against granting French women their political rights.[18]

The experience of Occupation and Resistance during the Second World War was, according to Claire Laubier, 'a major turning point for France generally and a milestone in the history of women's emancipation'.[19] Having played such a vital role in the Resistance, it proved impossible to deny women their right to vote any longer: it was therefore granted to them on 24 August 1944. Then began an 'intense public debate about the sexual division of labour in post-armistice' France.[20] Far more women were entering the workforce and, as a result of the increase and prolongation of schooling, many were receiving a far better education than ever before. Laubier writes that 'women's participation in the electoral process forced the public at large, and women in particular, to examine their role in the social sphere and to reassess their capabilities'.[21] The subject would thus have been very much alive in the mind of Le Corbusier.

Laubier makes the point that the liberal relationships characterised by those moving in Parisian artistic and philosophical circles were limited to 'the intellectual middle class' such as Le Corbusier.[22] This was not the reality for the majority of women in the working classes for whom work became an economic necessity. The situation in France was desperate with rapidly escalating food and energy prices and cuts in the rationing of basic household goods, while the basic wage remained relatively low. It became increasingly necessary for women to work to supplement the household income. 'They worked for long hours, sometimes in appalling factory conditions, on average for two-thirds or less of the salary of male workers' writes Laubier,[23] who makes the further observation that woman's prime role was still seen as being that of wife and mother and that very little consideration was given to the fact of 'her double role as worker both inside and outside the home'[24] and her simultaneous duty to assist in the task of repopulating the country.[25]

Whilst abortion was strictly prohibited, the use of efficient contraceptives was frowned upon. For this reason they were difficult to obtain.[26] Le Corbusier's annotations to Allendy's *Capitalisme et Sexualité* suggest that he believed free knowledge of contraception to be an important step in the emancipation of women.[27] It was a subject about which he felt very strongly. In his opinion:

> The biblical dogma that begins by defining as sin the fundamental law of nature, the act of making love, has rotted our hearts, has finished by ending in this twentieth century in notions of honour and honesty that are facades sometimes hiding lies and

crimes . . . Is it not an anguishing sight to see the daily papers describing this scandalous drama – an offence to human dignity – of a poor girl who has had an abortion? Do you want to know why she had an abortion? Search: architecture and planning for it expresses the way of thinking of a period and today we are suffocating under constraint.[28]

For Le Corbusier, architecture and planning would also provide the solution to problems such as these, so wide was their remit. This is an issue that will be explored further in Chapter 7.

Laubier writes that 'Matrimonial laws of paternal authority upheld the husband's supremacy as the head of the family'.[29] Multiple annotations by Le Corbusier on his copy of Allendy's *Capitalisme et Sexualité* indicate that he was fully aware of the problem of women's role as 'slave' within the family.[30] The tradition that allowed parents to choose a suitable husband for their daughter was to continue beyond the close of the Second World War but, as women became more active in the public realm, they had greater opportunities to meet men outside the home. Increasingly love, rather than the more practical issues of connection or material gain, became the primary reason for marriage.[31] The idea that each person could and should find their ideal opposite half would be entrenched in Le Corbusier's own philosophy of life.

As women began to work outside the home, they started, for the first time, to realise their own economic power. Manufacturers began to understand the importance of appealing to a feminine market. Mo Price notes that there was, for this reason, 'a perception of the dangerous feminisation of culture operating alongside a debilitating feminisation of industry'.[32] She writes:

On both fronts, cultural and economic, critics adopted a similar strategy to simultaneously scapegoat women for undesirable, dissident tendencies within the national character and symbolically disarm femininity of its political potential. Feminine agency, whether imagined cultural intervention or actual industrial action, was rhetorically disengaged from its material base (thus overlooking the socio-economic and ideological apparatuses of

sexual power) and recast in a realm of essentialist psycho-sexual behaviour: women's activism was taken to be a manifestation of (pathological) feminine subjectivity. Thus by exerting control over the notion of woman as a desiring subject, femininity could be restored to its traditional position in the objectification of masculine desire.[33]

In taking the needs and desires of women seriously Le Corbusier would be working against the grain of society, a role that he seemed to relish.

Feminism and physical culture

During the early decades of the twentieth century new emphasis began to be placed upon the importance of exercise, sunlight and fresh air. It was for this reason that the seaside resorts of the South of France suddenly came very much into vogue. Le Corbusier himself would begin to holiday regularly on the coast of Provence, sea bathing being a favourite occupation for him. The importance of exercise was also of central importance to the cause of French feminism at that time.

The Anti-Corset League

Of major importance to the work of Auclert was an idea that may seem astonishing to us now, one that gave momentum to a campaign against the corset that began to emerge in about 1910; it was her belief that women should have the right to control the mobility of their own bodies.[34] The possibility that over the years women had been weakened by wearing corsets came to be widely discussed in the early part of the twentieth century. There was, at that time, a commonly held belief that women were inherently weak, both mentally and physically, but the idea that this weakness could have been caused by a factor outside woman herself was one that was entirely radical and new.

Increasingly women were encouraged to exercise and look after themselves in order to recover the full use of their bodies and indeed their minds. Claudine Mitchell, who has done much to bring the Anti-Corset League to our attention, records that it was promoted by a number of agencies of differing political persuasions and divers socio-cultural identities. The most active was the so-called 'league against the mutilation of the body by the corset', which succeeded in transforming the issue in a nationwide campaign. The arguments deployed by the League fell into two main categories: one that dealt with the issue of women's health, the other with that of female beauty. Both sets of arguments involved notions of female psychology. In these discussions there emerged a new concern for the relations between the physiological, the mental and the affective. It was argued that the physiological effects resulting from wearing a corset affected women in many other ways.[35]

The Anti-Corset League understood that if their campaign was to be at all successful they would need to promote and make fashionable a new vision of female beauty. It was therefore necessary to prove that a woman's natural body shape was more beautiful than that of her corseted sisters. Classical sculptures of women would provide excellent proof of the validity of their cause. In one of their propaganda leaflets the *Venus de Milo*, timeless paragon of beauty, appears with her torso squashed as if by corsets. Mitchell makes the important point that there was at this time 'a slippage of meaning' between the words 'normal' and 'natural' and 'the League advertised their campaign under the general motto of: 'For the natural beauty of women'.[36]

Figure 3.1
Le Corbusier, *Le Corset*, 1947.

Le Corbusier may well have been party to such an argument. His friend Matila Ghyka wrote extensively on the subject of feminine beauty and its relationship to proportion in his book *Nombre d'or*, a text that had great influence on the architect.[37] Indeed, Le Corbusier seems to have been alluding to this subject when he wrote in *Towards a New Architecture*,

> We say a face is handsome when precision of the modelling and the disposition of the features reveal proportions within us and beyond our senses, a resonance, a sort of sounding board which begins to vibrate. An indefinable trace of the absolute which lies in the depth of our being.[38]

Given that this was the case it seems highly unlikely that the contorted form of the corseted body would be one that held any appeal for Le Corbusier, as he does not seem to have appreciated cosmetic artifice in general. Jane Drew remembered that he discovered that underarm hair was 'beautiful and to him added to a woman's attractiveness'.[39] Apparently he was particularly disgusted by the idea of deodorant.[40] He seems to have favoured women whom he saw as 'natural'; women at ease with their bodies and with themselves. Jencks observes that the women in Le Corbusier's paintings are 'not pudgy or voluptuous like a Rubens, nor quite as calm and statuesque as Picasso's neoclassical nudes of the 1920s. Rather, they are gargantuan, muscular and peasantlike'.[41] They are, in other words, active and strong, unfettered by corsets. In his enthusiasm for natural beauty and physical culture Le Corbusier espoused a tenet of the French feminist cause (albeit of some twenty years before).

For the early French feminists the rejection of the corset stood for a new, free and physical way of being like that described by Le Corbusier on his visit to Vassar where he saw the students designing and building stage sets in 'overalls or bathing suits'.[42] While he evidently found 'these beautiful bodies, made healthy and trim by physical training'[43] erotic, he also approved of the ability these girls displayed in executing tasks more usually ascribed to men. Le Corbusier approved of the fact that their bodies were free, active and lithe. These women were enjoying their freedom to move and to act, unencumbered by corsets or social conventions. As later comments made by Le Corbusier show, they also enjoyed their freedom to flirt.

Le Corbusier wrote: 'Modern women has cut her hair. Our eyes have learned the form of her legs. The corset is out. "Etiquette" is out.'[44] Significantly, Le Corbusier was to begin a series of paintings entitled *Le Corset* in 1934. These paintings typically contain two women, one tightly laced, with coiffed hair and an enigmatic expression, the other opposite, somehow loose, flowing, natural and all-encompassing. In a further version of the painting, dated 1947, the corseted woman appears artificially benign, her unbridled sister less so (Fig. 3.1). It is as though Le Corbusier is portraying two sides of womanhood, the latter, according to Drew and others, being the sort which he favoured. Le Corbusier's binary view of women will be explored further in Chapter 5.

Dance

Mitchell observes that the debate about the desirability of the natural body was fuelled as much by the work of the American dancer Isadora Duncan as it was by those who were campaigning for women's freedom of movement.[45] Duncan had become famous by pioneering a 'natural' dance movement in Paris during the postwar period and setting up a successful teaching studio in Paris. She used as a basis for her teaching ideas developed out of 'the forms in art'. Mitchell defines these as the 'rhythmic patterns and movements' that Duncan had 'evolved' when studying Greek art in the British Museum and the Louvre as well as 'movements in nature'.[46]

Le Corbusier had direct links to the world of classically inspired dance through the person of his brother Albert with whom he was very close.[47] In 1909 Albert attended a series of lectures given by Emile Jacques Dalcroze on the new eurythmical approach to the study and appreciation of music through a system of musical education that was based upon rhythm as expressed by the body through gymnastic-type movement. Christopher Green refers to the eurythmics of Dalcroze as one of the popular manifestations of the 'new classicism'.[48] It was then that Albert decided to join Dalcroze's academy at Hellerau to study eurythmics. The young Le Corbusier went to visit his brother at this 'spiritual centre, or one that wished to be so'.[49] Albert was to become a junior assistant there in 1911.[50]

Upon publication, Le Corbusier sent a copy of *Towards a New Architect* to Dalcroze. In the accompanying letter he described him as one of those personalities that through his labour would help the development of a 'veritable new spirit', adding that he knew that he would be sympathetic to their cause.[51] Evidently he felt that there were parallels between his evolving Orphic ideas and those of Dalcroze.

Albert arrived in Paris in 1919 to teach eurythmics at the Conservatoire Rameau. It was at this point that he moved in with Le Corbusier at his apartment in Rue Jacob. Albert's plan was to start a school of eurythmics – dance and gymnastics based on Dalcroze's principles. Financial backing came from a group of South American students who, in the opinion of Joyce Lowman, may have followed Isadora Duncan to Paris after her South American trip. Albert was to hold eurythmics classes for all ages during the day and gymnastic and basketball sessions in the evening which were popular with his brother.[52] At about this time Le Corbusier started living with Yvonne.[53] Apparently he began to put pressure on his brother to marry Lotti Raaf, a dancer from a Swedish ballet company with her own income, possibly because he wanted his apartment to himself once more.[54]

Advertisements for the school appeared in Le Corbusier's and Ozenfant's journal *L'Esprit Nouveau*[55] in which Albert wrote of an education based on musical rhythm creating harmony between the body and the spirit. He tried to unite the organic movements of the body with abstract musical compositions.[56] He also contributed to the second edition of the journal in the form of a two-part article entitled 'La Rythmique'.

Through the person of Albert, Le Corbusier would have been fully aware of the idea that movement too could be used to bring about the state of harmony that he so desired. Like certain feminists, the two brothers would emphasise the importance of allowing the unfettered body free range to move organically in harmony with nature.

Sport

Like dance, sport would play an important role in the liberation of women. Throughout the 1920s the suffragist journal *La Française* was to argue fiercely for its promotion. Jane Misme its founder and editor wrote thus: 'We used to believe and we still believe that women's right to physical exercise and its pleasures is the basis of all other women's rights. Women have been enslaved'.[57] Sport would play a vital role in 'reconstructing the relation between the intellectual and the corporeal' by helping women to regain control of their own bodies.[58]

Figure 3.2   Le Corbusier mural illustrating the principles of the Radiant City at the Pavillon des Temps Nouveaux, World Fair, Paris 1937.

The reconstruction of the link between the intellectual and the corporeal was one of Le Corbusier's main concerns: 'cultivate the body and the mind' he stated with emphasis in one of his sketchbooks.[59] Le Corbusier wrote of his Radiant City plan, developed during the early 1930s, that it would be a place where 'the basic pleasures: satisfaction of psycho-physiological needs, collective participation and the freedom of the individual' would be of central importance and, he added intriguingly, it was a place for the 'rebirth of the body'.[60] He illustrated this in a mural depicting the principles of the 'radiant city' at the Pavillon des Temps Nouveaux for the World Fair in Paris in 1937 (Fig. 3.2). Communal sports facilities would be provided as part of his mass housing schemes, an example being the 'room of physical culture' on the roof of the Unité in Marseilles.[61] Such facilities would not be for the sole use of men.

> Everyone – men, women, children – at any age and on every day of the year, can 'take off his jacket' when he gets home, go down in front of the building where he lives and play a game of basketball, of tennis, of soccer . . .[62]

Le Corbusier made frequent approving comments about athletic women – not just, it seems, because he found them visually pleasing, but also because they were conforming to his vision of a world where the physical and the spiritual were intimately linked.[63]

Fashion

Margalit Shinar suggests that Le Corbusier only wrote admiringly of products of masculine culture, citing his statement in his first and most influential book *Towards a New Architecture* that 'modern aesthetics' have 'been created by engineers, designers of machines, motorcars, factories, bridges and grain elevators, men who are "healthy and virile"'.[64] However, it needs to be said that Le Corbusier also exhibited a continuing interest in women's fashion, understanding its importance in the making of a modern society and in the liberation of women.[65] I sense that he played down such interests in his early work fearing that they would do little for his credibility as an architect.

Fashionable society

Le Corbusier first became immersed in the Parisian fashion scene while working with Ozenfant in the early 1920s who was, for a period, manager of a smart fashion house. Their first Purist exhibition was put on display in the fashion house Maison Jovet, owned by Germaine Bongard. She often held soirées for painters and poets at which Ozenfant was a regular guest.[66] An advertisement for Maison Jovet appeared in Ozenfant and Le Corbusier's *L'Esprit Nouveau*.[67]

Paul Poiret and the development of a new feminine aesthetic

When, in 1920, Le Corbusier first exhibited his idea for the Citrohan houses, cellular units suitable for mass production, they attracted a variety of enquiries from possible clients including one from Bongard's brother, the fashion designer Paul Poiret, this last resulting in a sketch scheme.[68] He had met Poiret at Auguste Perret's Society for the Protection of the Arts.[69] Le Corbusier's connection to the man suggests that he would have been fully *au fait* with Poiret's life and work.

Poiret has an important role in the events described here as he is generally credited with ridding the lives of women of corsets.[70] Indeed, he transformed the way in which women dressed, producing a completely new physical aesthetic.[71] Although he did much to free up women's bodies, his women were not exactly exemplars of feminist rectitude. Inspired by the East (at that time very much in fashion) Poiret's work was associated with a new, and possibly subversive eroticism. His feminine ideal was a decorative and beguiling odalisque, her non-conformism signified by her identification with sensuousness and pleasure. As Caroline Evans and Minna Thornton write, the Poiret women moved in an interior world, a seductive 'elsewhere'.[72]

In the opinion of these writers, Poiret held a view of women as 'purveyors of domestic charm and decorativeness'.[73] He bemoaned the crisp unexpansive manly styles of Coco Chanel then coming into vogue: 'Formerly women were architectural, like the prows of ships, and very beautiful. Now they resemble little undernourished telephone clerks'.[74] While Le Corbusier himself was to advocate simplicity and practicality in modern dress, it will be seen that the women in his paintings share that 'architectural' quality of women described by Poiret.

Not only were women changing their style of dress, they were also changing their hair. Both played an important role in defining new sexual roles, as Le Corbusier was fully aware. Between 1918 and 1925 short bobbed styles came into vogue. The year 1922 saw the publication of an overnight bestseller, Victor Margueritte's novel *La Garçonne*, about a 'modern' young woman who shrugged off her bourgeois family life by cutting her hair, dressing as a man and adopting a bohemian lifestyle in Paris.[75] For Le Corbusier women's fashion was significant because it provided an illustration of the way in which they were prepared to shed conventions in favour of convenience and a new more modern way of life. Le Corbusier wrote:

> Women have preceded us. They have carried out the reform of their clothing. They found themselves at a dead end: to follow fashion was to give up the advantages of modern techniques, of modern life. Renounce sports, and, an even more material problem, be unable to take on the jobs that have made women a fertile part of contemporary production and allowed them to *earn their living*. To follow fashion: they couldn't have anything to do with cars, they couldn't take the metro or a bus, nor move lively in an office or a store. To carry out the daily *construction* of a 'toilette', hairdo, boots, buttoning a dress, they would not have had time to sleep . . .

> So women cut their hair and their skirts and their sleeves. They went off bareheaded, arms naked, legs free. And were dressed in five minutes. And they are beautiful; they lure us with the charm of their graces of which the designers have accepted taking advantage . . .

> The courage, the liveliness, the spirit of invention with which women have operated the revolution in clothing are a miracle of modern times. Thank you!

> We men, a sad question! In dress clothes, we wear starched collars and resemble the generals of the Grande Armée. In street clothes we are not at ease. We need to carry an arsenal of papers and small tools on us. The pocket, pockets, should be the keystone of modern clothing. Try to carry everything you need: you've destroyed the line of your costume; you are not longer 'correct'. One must chose between working and being elegant . . .

> The English suit we wear had nevertheless succeeded in something important. It had neutralised us. In town it is useful to have a neutral appearance. The important sign is no longer the ostrich feathers of the hat, it is in the eyes. That's enough.
> . . . We office workers are beaten by a serious length by women.

> Thus, the spirit of reform has only just appeared. It remains for it to influence all the acts of life.[76]

This last statement is of great significance. Le Corbusier discovered that the spirit of reform found its first expression in that most unlikely and changeable manifestation of culture, women's fashion.

Such sentiments must have been his guide when he decided to write an article for *Harper's Bazaar* on 'costume for the woman of today', which he described thus:

> This is a dress for contemporary woman, not an *haute couture* creation. It is meant to be more classic than ephemeral. This distinction is not absolute, it simply delineates two different ways that women can dress, both of which are acceptable.
> On this drawing four young women and a leg can be seen [sic].
> The first woman is wearing a piece of fabric, split in the middle for the head with no special cut. It is the 'poncho' of the Andes adapted to city life and of proportional dimension.
> The second figure shows the dress with the 'poncho' off. It is then as much an indoor outfit as an outdoor one. The dress is all in one piece; it is gathered at the waist and hangs in many pleats down to the floor.
> For the third figure the pleated dress has been pulled up with two hands, lifted to the knees or thereabouts, and held just under the waist by a

separate elasticated band, which allows the excess fabric to give a padded effect (once more it all depends upon the quality of the fabric). This is a comfortable dress in which to walk, work, do things, step into a car, on board a bus, and to go about one's business.

The fourth figure represents a person sitting down on the floor – why not? You could also sit down on a low couch or a mattress. The living room of a modern house is no longer limited to chairs and armchairs, which do not represent the totality of natural possibilities for groups of eminently mobile furniture. The heavily pleated dress allows for multiple seating positions.

For all four figures, the legs are bare, as are the feet in stylishly concocted sandals, yet they are good for walks with their practical heels . . .[77]

Figure 3.3 'Clothes for the women of today', a drawing by Le Corbusier for publication in *Harper's Bazaar*, February 1952.

This curious description combines freedom and practicality with sensuality, the poncho, a very traditional and simple form of clothing, being suggestive of both colour and life (Fig. 3.3).[78] Kurt Forster has written of the way in which Le Corbusier saw the house and the articles it contained as an extension of the body.[79] Here clothing is blurred into furnishing in a highly unusual way.

Male adornment

Le Corbusier bemoaned the way in which men had been left behind by women in shrugging off their old way of dressing and their old way of life. During his early career Le Corbusier had celebrated the neutrality of the traditional European male suit. According to Adolf Loos, the subtlety and anonymity of such garb were major indicators of modernity.[80] Tag Gronberg writes that 'Le Corbusier's modern city was ostensibly based on anonymous, unostentatious components, on standardised objects and architecture as embodied by the anonymity of the suited male body.'[81] However, he seems to have undergone a change of heart on this issue after the war when he developed what Pearson calls a 'renewed sympathy for "ornament"'.[82] Le Corbusier wrote in *Talks with Students* that

Nowadays people are unaware of the power of colour as it was used in Doric or medieval times. They know nothing of the clarity or glitter of golds, or mirrors, or silks, or brocades or of Louis XIV and Louis XV felts. The strength, health and joy of aristocrats in other times strike our grocer types as lacking the necessary degree of refinement. That revolution of consciousness belatedly emerging now after having too long burdened society, will one day even affect our dress. Women have already taken the lead. Their styles and fashions are bold, sensitive, expressive. Just look at the young girls of 1942. Their hair styles reflect a healthy and optimistic outlook. They go forth crowned in gold or ebony. But in the reign of Louis XIV or during the Renaissance, you boys are the ones who would have been as radiant as archangels with hair like theirs, and strong as Mars and handsome as Apollo. But the women have stolen your thunder![83]

'Our clothing is completely unadapted to our needs. We have also abandoned the use of colour, one of the sure signs of life' wrote Le Corbusier[84], casting off his early predilection for sobriety in matters of dress. It was his belief that 'To a renaissance of vitality corresponds a direct action of colour. (We can see by the publicity on the walls, in the city, outside the cities and in the countryside, through automobile publicity, in women's fashion, in sport, on the beach, etc). Colour expresses life.'[85] Such vitality, expressed through women's fashion, would now play an important role in the pursuit of modernity.

Contrary to popular myth, even in his earliest work, Le Corbusier was fascinated by the possibilities presented through the use of colour. He wrote approvingly of the colourful clothes of women, contrasting their appearance with the drabness of Nazi soldiers. He wrote of the way in which the women of Paris had managed to maintain 'their customary elegance' throughout the war. 'They managed the trick of being desirable; without hats, they had invented ways of turning their hair into gold, bronze, or ebony helmets, a warlike coiffure which made them luminous and magnificent. Feminine centaurs on bicycles cutting through the fog of Paris in the springtime or in the dog days, legs, hair, faces, breasts whipped by the wind, indifferent but disturbing, they passed under the noses of the sinister-purposed, drearily coloured "green mustard" soldiers . . .'[86]

Le Corbusier expressed his own desire for colour when dressing for dinner on one of his transatlantic voyages:

On board I asked the purser for dinner clothes with some colour: the stewards dressed in vermilion are in keeping with the pomp of the ship; at dinner the rest of us are like people at a country funeral; the beautiful women seem like flowers in the splendours of their gowns. It is a curious end-result of civilisation that men who used to wear ostrich plumes on their heads, rose, white and royal blue, a vesture of brocades or shimmering silk, should no longer know how to do anything but thrust their hands into the pockets of their black trousers . . . The question has to be reconsidered and the transformation of masculine costume is necessary. It is as difficult as changing the ethics and institutional state of a society. Costume is the expression of a civilisation. Costume reveals the most fundamental feelings: through it we show our dignity, our distinction, our frivolity, or our basic ambitions. Though standardised, masculine dress does not escape individual decision. But is it no longer suitable. From what persists, we have proof that the machine age revolution has not reached maturity.[87]

There are a number of possibilities that may explain Le Corbusier's new-found interest in colour in male dress. Firstly, he had travelled very widely and may have come to enjoy the colourful possibilities presented by indigenous clothing. Secondly, colour played a vital part in his pursuit of harmony, hence his interest in creating colour keyboards for the wallpaper firm Salubra. Colour, for Le Corbusier, had the power to affect emotions. Colour would play a vital role in the creation of the harmonious environment that he so desired. A further possibility is that he sensed a need for men to once more enjoy that side of their lives which they once did through colourful and expressive clothes. Men as well as women could be objects of desire, recipients of the gaze. He wrote, 'When polychromy appears it means that life is breaking out.'[88]

Fashion magazines

Married to an ex-model, it seems Le Corbusier was not so intellectual that he was above reading the fashion magazines which he must have found lying around his apartment. He even included illustrations and comments from them in his work. 'Flowers, sun, joy. Who is going to wear these beautiful bathing costumes created by our big stores? And how soon?' he wrote of an advertisement for bathing costumes that he included in the pages of *The Radiant City* (Fig. 3.4).[89] During his early career Le Corbusier even tried to promote his ideas through the pages of fashion magazines.[90] In 1923 he wrote to Pierre de Trevières, editor of *Les Modes de Femme de France* who had included an article on the 'city of the future' in his magazine. In his letter he praised the journalist for his understanding of the subject, sending him a pamphlet on his design for the *Ville du Trois Millions* and asked him to inform his readers of his projects.[91] Articles on Le Corbusier would appear in a number of women's magazines, presumably at his instigation, for example: 'To ease the pain of women: the vertical city' which appeared in *Journal de la Femme*.[92] Le Corbusier would himself write for women's magazines, usually focusing on his urbanistic ideas, but also touching upon the relationships between men and women, advice ('there is no need to be a Venus or a pin-up'[93]) and indeed fashion.[94] Here we see a version of a belief that seems to run through Le Corbusier's work, that of the importance of conveying

Flowers, sun, joy. Who is going to wear these beautiful bathing
costumes created by our big stores? And how soon?

Sport? Only for the players (20 players for every
20,000 spectators). Where is the sport for the 20,000
spectators? Our aim: sport for everyone. That is the
question.

Figure 3.4   Advertisement for bathing costumes included in
Le Corbusier's *The Radiant City*, 1933.

a 'sign of mass culture', not necessarily a desirable quality.[97] The painter represented women only in terms of consumerism, reproduction and leisure. In doing so 'femininity is relegated to the margins of the modern technological order'.[98] However, Le Corbusier seems to have found women's tendency towards mass culture, mass housing, mass-produced clothes and mass community to be a positive attribute. 'We must create the mass-production spirit'[99] he wrote with some urgency in the pages of *Towards a New Architecture*.

Fashion and furniture

Fashion for Le Corbusier was a phenomenon that had a direct relationship with events in the decorative arts. Charlotte Perriand exhibited the close links between the two when she wrote of being a woman of the jazz age:

> I express my own needs: I'm aware and in tune with my own age. It is mechanical: the cars in the street strike the eye. They are polished, shiny. I wear chrome beads around my neck, a belt of metal links. My studio is chromed steel; and I wear my hair *à la* Josephine Baker.[100]

McLeod observes that 'Eighteenth-century grace and eroticism find their twentieth-century equivalent' in Le Corbusier and Perriand's famous design for a chaise longue.[101] She notes the demise in distinctions between specifically masculine and feminine furniture forms at that time, distinctions that had been prevalent for centuries. 'Because tubular steel combined such traditionally male and female attributes as strength and lightness, distinctions between a woman's chair and a man's chair no longer seem relevant.'[102] Such unisex furniture would be admirably fitting for the unisex environment that Le Corbusier aimed to create, for example in his own home in the penthouse at 24 Rue Nungesser et Coli to be discussed in Chapter 7.

Conclusion

Consciously or unconsciously Le Corbusier advanced the cause of French feminism through his pronounce-

to women the relevance of his message. It seems no coincidence that Le Corbusier would be asked to design a stand for the Exposition de la Femme Française, taking place in Versailles in 1948, such was his interest in currying favour with women.[95] He also contributed an exhibition stand on the Unité in Marseilles for an international exhibition of Women held by the Women's International Democratic Federation in 1949.[96]

Mo Price notes that for the painter Fernand Léger, Le Corbusier's friend and collaborator, woman was

ments on the subject of fashion and physical culture. McLeod makes the significant point that 'What is female for Le Corbusier' is in her opinion a 'woman's willingness to shed conventions'.[103] Seen in these terms Le Corbusier had a vested interest in advocating the cause of women's liberation as it was women who would have a primary role in bringing about the new era that he so desired.

Notes

1 Plato, *Phaedo*, in S. Buchanan (ed.), *The Portable Plato* (Harmondsworth: Penguin, 1997), p.201.

2 G. Perry, *Women Artists and the Parisian Avant-Garde* (Manchester: Manchester University Press, 1995), p.142.

3 A. Mesclon, *Le Feminisme et l'Homme* (Paris: A. Mesclon, 1931) in Fondation Le Corbusier (hereafter referred to as FLC).

4 Ibid., p.4 .

5 R. Allendy, *Capitalisme et Sexualité: le conflits des instincts et les problèmes actuels* (Paris: Denoel), 1931, p.18 in FLC.

6 J. Petit, *Le Corbusier Lui-même* (Paris: Forces Vives, 1970), p.29.

7 Perry, *Women Artists and the Parisian Avant-Garde*, p.143.

8 Letter Trouin to Le Corbusier, 17.06.55, FLC P5.02.19.

9 Interest in the cult of Mary.

10 D. de Rougemont, *Passion and Society* (London: Faber and Faber, 1958), p.294. Originally published as Denis de Rougement, *L'Amour et L'Occident* (Paris: Plon, 1940).

11 For a discussion of the French novelist's treatment of the subject of women see A. Denis, *Julien Gracq* (Paris: Seghers, 1978), p.20.

12 Robert Graves, *The White Goddess* (London: Faber, 1948).

13 C. Mitchell, 'Style/Ecriture. On the classical ethos, women's sculptural practice and pre-First-World-War feminism', *Art History*, February 2002, p.6.

14 Ibid.

15 C. Mitchell, 'Facing horror: women's work, sculptural practice and the Great War', in V. Mainz and G. Pollock (eds), *Work and the Image II* (Aldershot: Ashgate, 2000), p.34.

16 M. Price, 'The missing *méchanicienne*: gender, production and order in Léger's machine aesthetic' in Mainz and Pollock (eds), *Work and the Image II*, p.95.

17 Mitchell, 'Facing horror', p.50.

18 Ibid.

19 C. Laubier, *The Condition of Women in France: 1945 to the Present* (London: Routledge, 1990), p.1.

20 Price, 'The missing *méchanicienne*', p.95.

21 Laubier, *The Condition of Women in France*, p.1.

22 Ibid., p.2.

23 Ibid.

24 Ibid.

25 Ibid., p.3.

26 Ibid.

27 Allendy, *Capitalisme et Sexualité*, p.22 in FLC.

28 Le Corbusier, *Precisions on the Present State of Architecture and City Planning* (Cambridge, MA: MIT Press, 1991), p.29.

29 Laubier, *The Condition of Women in France*, p.2.

30 Allendy, *Capitalisme et Sexualité*, pp.175–7 in FLC.

31 Laubier, *The Condition of Women in France*, p.4.

32 Price, 'The missing *méchanicienne*', p.100.

33 Ibid.

34 Mitchell, 'Style/Ecriture', p.6.

35 Ibid., pp.6–7.

36 Ibid., p.7.

37 M. Ghyka, *Nombre d'or: rites et rhythmes Pythagoriciens dans le development de la civilisation Occidental* (Paris: Gallimard, 1931) in FLC.

38 Le Corbusier, *Towards a New Architecture* (London: Architectural Press, 1982), p.187. First published 1923.

39 R. Walden, ed., *The Open Hand* (Cambridge, MA: MIT Press, 1982), p.372.

40 Le Corbusier, *Sketchbooks Volume 3, 1954–1957* (Cambridge, MA: MIT Press, 1982), sketch 640.

41 C. Jencks, *Le Corbusier and the Continual Revolution in Architecture* (New York: Monacelli Press, 2000), p.202.

42 Ibid., p.136.

43 Ibid.

44 Le Corbusier, *Precisions* (Cambridge, MA: MIT Press, 1990), p.118.

45 Mitchell, 'Style/Ecriture', p.9.

46 Mitchell, 'Style/Ecriture', p.21. See I. Duncan, *My Life* (New York: Liveright, 1995), p.128.

47 Interview Lowman and A. Jeanneret, Vevey, June 1972. J. Lowman, 'Le Corbusier 1900–1925: The Years of Transition.' Unpublished doctoral dissertation, University of London (1979), p.225.

48 C. Green, *Léger and the Avant-Garde* (New Haven, CT: Yale University Press, 1976), p.234.

49 Le Corbusier, *When the Cathedrals were White: A Journey to the Country of the Timid People* (New York: Reynal and Hitchcock), p.144.

50 Letter Jeanneret to W. Ritter, early summer 1911, FLC quoted in Lowman, 'Le Corbusier 1900–1925', p.46.

51 Letter Le Corbusier to J. Dalcroze, 12.01.1924, FLC E1.18.2.

52 Interview Lowman and A. Jeanneret, Vevey, June 1972. Lowman, 'Le Corbusier 1900–1925', p.226.

53 Ibid.

54 Lowman, 'Le Corbusier 1900–1925', pp.40 and 174.

55 *L'Esprit Nouveau* 13 and 15 (New York: Da Capo Press, 1969), pages not numbered.

56 L. Soth, 'Le Corbusier's Clients', *Art History*, 6, 2, p.192.

57 J. Misme, 'Les sportives doivent se gouverner elles mêmes', *La Française*, 7 October 1922, p.1. cited in Mitchell, 'Style/Ecriture', p.11.

58 Ibid., p.13.

59 Le Corbusier, *Sketchbooks Volume 2* (London: Thames and Hudson, 1981), sketch 502.

60 Le Corbusier, *The Radiant City* (London: Faber, 1964), p.7.

61 Le Corbusier, *Oeuvre Complète Volume 5, 1946–1952* (Zurich: Les Editions d'Architecture, 1995), p.218.

62 Le Corbusier, *The Radiant City*, p.65.

63 See Le Corbusier, *Athlète*, oil on canvas, 1937.

64 M. Shinar, 'Feminist Criticism of Urban Theory and Design, Case Study: Le Corbusier', *Journal of Urban and Cultural Studies*, 2,2, 1992, p.33. She quotes from Le Corbusier, *Towards a New Architecture*, p.31.

65 For example, Le Corbusier was to observe how good transportation meant that the people of Buenos Aires wore the suits of London and Paris fashions: Le Corbusier, *Precisions*, p.27.

66 Lowman, 'Le Corbusier 1900–1925', p.101.

67 Ibid.

68 Ibid., p.195.

69 Ibid.,p.197.

70 C. Evans and M. Thornton, *Women and Fashion* (London: Quartet, 1989), p.118.

71 Ibid., p.128.

72 Ibid.

73 Ibid.

74 Ibid.

75 See M. L. Roberts, 'Sampson and Delilah Revisited', *American Historical Review* (1993), p.659.

76 Le Corbusier, *Precisions*, p.107.

77 Letter J. Heilbuth to H. Strassova, 23.02.52, FLC U3.3.4.

78 Le Corbusier, 25.02.52, FLC U3.3.5.

79 K.W. Forster, 'Antiquity and Modernity in the La Roche-Jeanneret Houses of 1923', *Oppositions* (1979), 15/16, p.142.

80 A. Loos, 'Men's fashion', *Adolf Loos: Spoken into the Void. Collected Essays 1897–1900* (Cambridge, MA: MIT Press, 1982), pp.10–14.

81 T. Gronberg, *Design on Modernity: Exhibiting the City in 1920s Paris* (Manchester: Manchester University Press, 1998), p.41.

82 C. Pearson, 'Integrations of Art and Architecture in the work of Le Corbusier. Theory and Practice from Ornamentalism to the "Synthesis of the Major Arts"', (1995). Unpublished PhD thesis, Stanford University, p.386.

83 Le Corbusier, *Le Corbusier Talks with Students* (New York: Princeton University Press, 1999), p.67.

84 Le Corbusier, *Precisions*, p.118.

85 From the essay 'Architectural Polychromy' by Le Corbusier, in A. Rüegg (ed.), *Polychromie Architecturale: Le Corbusier's Colour Keyboards from 1931 to 1959* (Basel: Birkhäuser, 1997), p.131.

86 Le Corbusier, *When the Cathedrals were White*, p.xii.

87 Ibid., p.108.

88 Ibid., p.165.

89 Le Corbusier, *The Radiant City*, p.106.

90 Lowman, 'Le Corbusier 1900–1925', p.174.

91 Letter Le Corbusier to P. de Trevières, 05.03.1923, FLC. Cited in Lowman, 'Le Corbusier 1900–1925', p.207.

92 Josette Lyon, 'Pour soulager le peine des femmes: la cité verticale', *Journal de la Femme*, FLC X1.15.200. See also Yvanhoé Rambosson, 'L'apport Français dans les arts appliqués modernes', *Revue de la Femme*, March 1928, FLC X1.6.33.

93 Le Corbusier, article in *La Femme et la Vie*, FLC X1.17.13.

94 See for example Le Corbusier article written for *La Femme et la Vie*, 27.2.53, FLC U3.7.360.

95 H. Allen Brookes (ed.), *The Le Corbusier Archive: Palais des Nations Unies and Other Buildings and Projects, 1946–8* (New York: Garland, 1983), pp.353–355.

96 Letter Women's International Democratic Federation to Le Corbusier, 21.06.49, FLC.

97 Price, 'The missing *méchanicienne*', p.103.

98 Ibid., p.105.

99 Le Corbusier, *Towards a New Architecture*, p.210.

100 'Charlotte Perriand: un art de vivre', exhibition catalogue (Paris 1985), p.12. Cited in M. McLeod, 'Charlotte Perriand, Her First Decade as a Designer, *AA Files*, 15, 1987, p.5.

101 McLeod, 'Charlotte Perriand, Her First Decade as a Designer', p.8.

102 Ibid.

103 Ibid., p.11.

Part Two

IDEAL

4 Orphism and the Quest for Harmonious Unity

1922, at the Salon d'Automne, Paris: town-planning and architecture. Suddenly it had all come alive: the basic cell and the whole conception. L-C had taken a mistress: HARMONY.[1]

It was Le Corbusier's desire to create a harmonious unity in which all things, including men and women, coexisted in a state of balance. This could be achieved through adherence to the doctrines of Orphism, an ancient wisdom linking back to the teachings of Pythagoras and Plato. In this chapter I will illustrate the increasing prevalence of Orphic ideas in Le Corbusier's thinking, their presence in his upbringing and education and in the artistic milieu which he entered when he eventually moved to Paris.

Origins of Le Corbusier's interest in Orphism

Le Corbusier reminisced that 'my direct family, father and mother, influenced me by creating a harmonious environment'.[2] The young Le Corbusier, then Charles Edouard Jeanneret, was well versed in the Bible. However he was quick to reject the religion within which he was raised, spending much of his life in pursuit of another spiritual ideal, Orphism. The foundations for this belief were laid in his childhood and education, key influences being his fascination with Catharism and his love of Rabelais, both of which were instilled in him by his mother.

Catharism

Whilst Le Corbusier was Swiss by birth, he persistently insisted that his origins lay in the Mediterranean, his spiritual home. Indeed he believed himself to be a descendant of the Cathars, a heretical sect based in the South of France:

> I am of French origin, here for centuries. I am from the south of France, from Languedoc. I'm

from the terrible persecutions of the thirteenth century, and they dare not say so because I've already built some pretty fair churches. The interesting thing about this is that those who were not massacred were able to escape. They climbed, and they established themselves there at all the high points. There they built Languedoc houses – farmhouses from the year thirteen hundred to the year fifteen hundred. This is why, as far as I am concerned, I have always had a great affinity for the southern regions, for the Mediterranean, and I have looked for an art which is Mediterranean amid the world corruption.[3]

The Cathars believed in the presence of two gods, one good and one evil (unlike the Catholic Church which believed that the devil *et al.* were fallen angels). Their system of belief was thus highly dualistic, which may, in part, explain its appeal for Le Corbusier whose work is characterised by his obsession with opposites.

The chivalric quest for 'Our Lady' provided a focus for the songs of troubadours, whom Le Corbusier thought to be the ideological descendants of the Cathars, following the massacres of the Albigensian crusade.[4] Annotations to Le Corbusier's copy of *Escalarmonde de Foix* suggest that he believed the Cathars to be in receipt of knowledge derived from that of Plato[5] which they then passed on to the troubadours, of fourteenth-century France.[6] Further notes to the book suggest that he may have believed the tradition of courtly love, promulgated by the troubadours, to be based on the ideas of Plato[7] and of the ancient Egyptian, Hermes Trismegistus, the so-called father of alchemy.[8] The chivalric quest would also be celebrated in the work of Le Corbusier's two favourite authors, François Rabelais and Miguel de Cervantes Saavedra whose writings he encountered at an early age.

Rabelais and Cervantes

The following paragraph sits within the text of Le Corbusier's book, *My Work*:

> Revealing details: the elder sister of L-C's father, an old lady given to religion of a sensible kind – it was the second half of the 19th century – chided her nephews with words like these (L-C's parents did much the same): 'Beau ténébreux, maritorne, rodomont, médor, matamore, artaban, malandrin, fier-à-bras, fanfaron, sacripant. Tire-larigot, gode-lureau, turlupin, fanfreluche, gringalet, cocquasse (casserolle).'
>
> Some were from Cervantes, others from Rabelais, but nobody knew it, or cared about it, for this second half of the 19th century, before the coming of the machine age had already transformed men's minds. Such words were no more than traces, and had disappeared for good in the following generation. They were lost and forgotten, together with the deep reasons which had brought these peasant-craftsmen into contact with the masterpieces of earlier centuries.[9]

The clue is in the words 'revealing details'. Le Corbusier is here suggesting that the reader focuses closely on what he is about to say as it is of great significance. It suggests the extent to which Le Corbusier was evidently brought up on Rabelais and other arcane stories of the past.[10] Both Cervantes' great work *Don Quixote* and Rabelais' *Gargantua and Pantagruel* contain versions of the chivalric quest, the former for a beautiful woman, the village prostitute, who lives in Don Quixote's village, the latter for the lady of the Holy Bottle residing in her subterranean cave.

It quickly becomes evident to anyone who takes the trouble to read through the four volumes of Le Corbusier's *Sketchbooks* that Rabelais' book, published 1534, introduced to him in his youth, occupied a very important place in his life. In his words 'good Pantagruel . . . The book . . . this book is always in my hand.'[11] It is evident that Le Corbusier perceived a very serious intent hidden within this famously vulgar text. On 3 April 1954, whilst working on the Chapel of Ronchamp, Le Corbusier started a new

sketchbook, entitled H32, into which he copied, though not word for word, several pages of Book Five of *Gargantua and Pantagruel*: those pages in which Panurge visits the Oracle of the Holy Bottle in an attempt to discover whether he should get married or not – itself a loaded question.[12] In the opinion of J.M. Cohen, who edited the 1955 Penguin edition of the book, these 'final chapters, with their mathematical and allegorical account of the Temple of the Bottle, are so dull that it would be charitable to ascribe them to another hand'.[13] Yet it is quite obvious that Le Corbusier would not have concurred with such a view, as he saw something very special at work in these pages.

Although, in Cohen's opinion, there are 'no hidden meanings in Rabelais', he does admit that there must be some other significance behind Rabelais' constant references to wine and drinking. His explanation is that, for Rabelais, 'the headiest liquor of all is the liquor of learning,'[14] the mention of drink leading us directly to Bacchus the god of wine in his Greek incarnation Dionysus, at the very centre of the cult of Orphism. According to Catherine Swietlicki, Rabelais was heavily influenced by the Kabbalah, which like Orphism has its roots in the ideas of Plato and Pythagoras.[15]

Rabelais' references to grain and to wine are also evocative of the rituals of the Christian Eucharist. It should be noted that there are historical parallels between the figure of Dionysus and Jesus, a point which Le Corbusier emphasised by taking the trouble to highlight a long section of Rabelais' text in his own edition of the book, making clear connections between Jesus and another incarnation of Dionysus, Pan.[16] Dionysus and Orpheus are also intimately connected. As a result of the knowledge gained during his venture into the Underworld, Orpheus was thought of as the god of the oracles. For this reason he would have an implied role at the oracle of the Holy Bottle, Panurge's long sought destination.

Significantly, in sketchbook H32, it is Le Corbusier's consideration of the issue of proportion and harmony, both in music and art, that leads him directly on to Rabelais' description of Panurge's arrival at the sanctuary of the Holy Bottle and a complex analysis of his route in terms of number. Le Corbusier's transcription begins:

. . . arrived in the longed for isle . . . At the end of this fatal number you will find the Temple door . . . = true psychogony of Plato so celebrated by the Academicians and so little understood, of which half is composed of unity, the first two whole numbers, of two squares and of two cubes (1=2 and 3= squared 8 and 27 Total 54=Plato they descend 108 steps . . .[17]

The presence of these numbers filled Panurge with fear, such import do they carry. Scribbled calculations suggest that Le Corbusier cogitated over the meaning of these figures for some time. Rabelais may be delivering a philosophy through mathematics, available only to those with eyes to see – a favourite alchemical aphorism of Le Corbusier. For him it is this aspect of Plato that the 'Academicians' do not understand. The relationship of numbers to the original Unity is fundamental, indeed it seems likely that the understanding of such a schema comprised the first steps of an Orphic initiation.

Like Orpheus, Panurge makes his journey underground, arriving at last at a holy fountain where, as Le Corbusier records, Bacbuc the high Priestess orders him to drink 'one, two, three times':

Forthwith, changing the imagination, so will you find this Water's bouquet and body exactly that of the wine you thought of then, never again say anything is impossible to God.[18]

Le Corbusier does not bother to transcribe how Panurge and his friends then use this statement as the perfect excuse to imagine various different vintages from a variety of vineyards. I suspect this is because he treats this description as pure obfuscation on Rabelais' part. Something more profound seems to be going on here, possibly a perversion of the Christian Communion ceremony and its participation in the body of Christ, whose links with Dionysus have already been mentioned. It certainly seemed to inspire Le Corbusier, who made a note that 'behind the wall the Gods are playing, men pass from that side to this side, and from time to time, catch some words. And discover some scraps . . . the crumbs which [are] fallen from the rich man's table'.[19]

The three sips of water that Panurge drinks symbolise a feminine trinity. 'Trinity, I love that word' wrote Le Corbusier when a young man.[20] Indeed, Dionysus himself was said to be born of the triple goddess, Mother Earth, a common theme in mythology. Given that Le Corbusier had a remarkable knowledge of classical and medieval iconography it seems highly likely that he was aware of these kinds of themes. Here the three waters transform into wine, Dionysus, the masculine saviour. In this case the feminine gives access to the divine, a repeated theme in Le Corbusier's work.[21]

Then, with heavy emphasis, Bacbuc instructs Panurge to listen to the word of the Oracle 'with one ear only', thus explaining the weighty presence of the ear in Le Corbusier's later artistic representations of Panurge (Fig. 4.1). She then disguises him in an extraordinary costume involving a 'felt funnel such as hippocras wine is filtered through' as a hat and a 'brace of old style codpieces in lieu of gloves'. Le Corbusier lovingly records all this in detail. Panurge is being drawn into the mystery, he is taking on the identity of Dionysus himself. His face is ducked into the fountain and a handful of meal is thrown into his eyes, a version of the bread and the wine of Communion.[22]

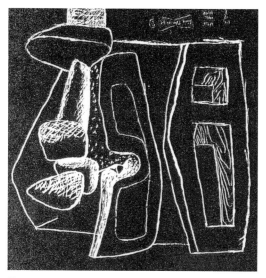

Figure 4.1   Le Corbusier, *Panurge*, 1961.

Le Corbusier then transcribes Bacbuc's instructions to Panurge to perform a ritual dance involving 'three little leaps in the air and bumping his arse on the ground seven times', during which he murmured 'who knows what conjurations in the Etruscan tongue . . . sometimes reading from a ritual book'. How serious Rabelais is in his parody we do not know. It could be that Panurge is making a connection between heaven and earth in the course of his dance. Certainly his reference to Etruria is of interest – indeed the Etruscan tombs at Cerveteri were to provide a source of inspiration for his Basilica at La Sainte Baume, the cult of love between man and woman being a central tenet of Etruscan thought.

Then Le Corbusier records the manner in which Panurge is led through a golden door into a round chapel where, in the middle of a heptagonal alabaster fountain, is the holy bottle itself, half submerged in water. Bacbuc instructs Panurge to kiss the fountain and do a ritual dance around it during which he sings

O Bottle great
with mysteries
with one ear do
I listen:
for the proffered word to sound
the Holy Bottle.

Then, in what must be one of the most startling anticlimaxes to be found within the history of literature, the bottle issues forth one word – 'TRINK'. 'You have just had the word of the Holy Bottle I say the most joyous, the most divine of words' exclaims Bacbuc translating the word of the Holy Bottle as an exhortation to drink, since 'by wine one grows divine'. Here Le Corbusier's transcription ends. Panurge is delighted with Bacbuc's interpretation. His question has been answered, though the answer is not stated. Taking with him three bottles of holy water (again the triple feminine) and the knowledge that 'great treasures and wonderful things are hidden beneath the earth' seemingly meaning that, yes, he should marry. He should engage with the body and with woman. Panurge returns home and the *Chronicles of Gargantua and Pantagruel* draw to an abrupt close.[23]

This analysis of Panurge's journey to the Oracle of the Holy Bottle reveals three points that are significant for this discussion. Firstly, it provides clear evidence of Le Corbusier's great interest in the Orphic quest and the route of initiation. Secondly, it contains a number of references to the balance between masculine and feminine elements, culminating in the hidden message that man must engage with woman, must marry. Thirdly, this important message is delivered by a woman, suggesting the importance of a female presence in the religious life of man. These ideas, encountered early in Le Corbusier's life, were to play a formative part in his development.

Education and self-education

In 1901 Le Corbusier took a course in engraving so that he might eventually follow his father into the clock making industry. He eventually transferred to the study of architecture in 1904, when he was influenced greatly by the teachings of his friend and master Charles L'Eplattenier who, building upon the work of his parents, instilled in him a quasi-religious appreciation of nature. Le Corbusier wrote of the experience:

My master said: Only nature is inspiring and true and should be the support of human endeavour. But do not make nature in the manner of landscape painters who show nothing but the exterior. Scrutinize the cause, the form, the vital development and make a synthesis in creating ornaments. He had an elevated conception of ornament – which he conceived as a microcosm.[24]

Like many of his contemporaries L'Eplattenier adhered to the Romantic idea that a close observation of nature would reveal larger truths.[25] Le Corbusier had already learnt an appreciation of the landscape from his family and from his surroundings. L'Eplattenier helped to focus this appreciation into a more cohesive theory at the same time instilling in the young man a thirst for books.

The young Le Corbusier began to see the world in terms of patterns, of lines and of geometry that would, ideally, be linked together in a cohesive whole. Strongly influenced by Rabelais, he was looking for a form of religion or belief that could link such ideas back to the profound past. It is not surprising therefore that he was very impressed by Edouard Schuré's book *Les Grands Initiés*, given to him by his teacher. Subtitled *Esquisse de l'histoire secrète des religions*, in it the lives of a number of great spiritual leaders are recorded in turn, Rama, Krishna, Hermes, Moses, Orpheus, Pythagoras, Plato and Jesus.

For a man of his time Schuré was notably pro-women. His book is dedicated to the memory of a woman and he wasted no opportunity to reinforce the importance of this sex within his 'secret history of religions'. Significantly he took a particular interest in what Richard A. Moore calls the 'primal mother'[26] and noted the inconsistency of man's treatment of woman in ancient times. On the one hand she was 'a wretched slave whom he overburdened and brutally mistreated', while on the other hand she was 'the turbulent priestess of the oak and rock, from whom he sought protection and who ruled himself in spite of himself'.[27] He emphasised the fact that women were initiated into the cults of Orpheus and Pythagoras within which they played an important role.[28] Schuré believed in

> The war of the sexes, antique war, inevitable, open or hidden, but eternal between the masculine principle and the feminine principle, between man and woman . . . where plays the secret of worlds. At the same time that the perfect fusion of masculine and feminine constitutes the same essence and the mystery of divinity itself, the equilibrium of these two principles producing the greatest civilisations.[29]

He wrote of the development of two types of cult, lunar and solar, seeing religion in terms of a union of opposites, masculine and feminine.

At the core of the book Schuré described the life of Orpheus and an initiation into the mysteries of the 'radiant spirit' Dionysus[30] to discover 'the secret of worlds, the soul of nature and the essence of God'.[31] Here the initiate encountered the 'underground Bacchus, of two sexes with the face of a bull', a figure that would appear repeatedly in Le Corbusier's painted work.[32] During the initiation Orpheus spoke of the 'pure light of Dionysos, the great sun of initiates' while he played his seven stringed lyre 'the lyre of God' to evoke 'celestial Eros, all powerful'.[33] During the

process the disciples of Orpheus chanted 'L'Evohé', a term which Schuré explains at some length:

> The cry of Evohé, pronounced in reality Hé, Van, Hé was the sacred cry of all initiates, Egyptian, Jew and Phoenician of Asia Minor and Greece. The four sacred letters pronounced: Iod-Hé, Van, Hé represented God in his eternal fusion with Nature; they embrace the totality of Being, the living Universe. Iod (Osiris) signified that divinity, the creator of intellect, the Eternal-Masculine which is in fact everywhere and beneath everything. Hé-Van-Hé represented the Eternal Feminine, Eve, Isis, Nature, within all forms visible and invisible, fecundated by him.[34]

For Schuré, belief in Orphism entailed belief in the union of opposites, masculine and feminine, as a fundamental guiding principle. It was his belief that 'Orphic word mysteriously infiltrated the veins of ancient Greece through secret routes and sanctuaries of initiation'.[35] In subsequent chapters Schuré described the ways in which such ideas influenced both Pythagoras and Plato as well as the Gnostics, the neo-Platonists and the early Church.[36]

Schuré's book finishes with a challenge to his readers to construct 'the spiritual temple',[37] the 'profound union of heroism and love, of good will and intelligence, of the Eternal Masculine with the Eternal Feminine . . . the flower of the human ideal'.[38] His words made a very strong impression upon the young Le Corbusier who, in January 1908, wrote excitedly to his parents that the book had 'opened horizons' to him which had 'filled' him with 'happiness'.[39]

At approximately the same time that he encountered Schuré, Jeanneret also read Henri Provensal's *L'Art de Demain: Vers l'Harmonie Integrale*. In the opinion of Paul Turner, whose work on Le Corbusier's early education has yet to be matched, some of the ideas to be found in Provensal can be found almost intact in his later work.[40] The book is devoted to the subject of art theory and related philosophical and spiritual questions which Provensal was to amalgamate into a theory of life. Provensal was interested in making connections between the attraction between the sexes and the attraction between atoms. All were manifestations of a larger pattern within nature. Provensal looked to the animal kingdom for irrefutable proof of this 'principle of correspondence'.[41] It is my suggestion that this idea of sexual equality as a 'natural law' would become central to Le Corbusier's work.

At around this time Le Corbusier also came into contact with the ideas of the French social philosopher Charles Fourier. Peter Serenyi has written very convincingly about the profound influence of his writings upon Le Corbusier. Central to Fourier's utopian vision of community was the ideas of sexual equality, one which may have been readily absorbed by the young man.[42]

Shari Benstock writes of the 'aesthetic of the dandy that dominated the literary and artistic culture' at the end of the nineteenth century.[43] In her opinion 'the dandy announced his opposition to cultural demands that he become a mature, adult male by exploiting (and parodying) stereotyped images of women'.[44] Le Corbusier himself seems to have absorbed something of this influence, one that extended itself into his writings about artistic pursuits such as travelling and collecting which border on the effete. His writing has something of the florid, ironic style characteristic of the period, for example in the work of Joris Karl Huysmans.

Le Corbusier met William Ritter, a painter and art critic with whom he was to develop a close relationship, in the winter of 1909.[45] Le Corbusier wrote:

> At that troubled period of finishing one's studies and beginning to know one's fellow men . . . I met a friend much older than myself in whom I could confide my doubts and incredulities because he welcomed them. William Ritter did not believe in Cézanne, and still less in Picasso, being 'all for science'. But before the phenomena of nature the struggles that rend humanity he could become strangely moved. Together we wandered across those wide regions of lakesides, uplands and Alps that are pregnant with historical significance. And little by little I gradually began to find myself, and to discover that all one can count on in life is one's own strength.[46]

The fact of Ritter's homosexuality does not seem to have troubled the young man; he was to become his mentor in all things. Jenger notes that Le Corbusier was particularly unguarded in his letters to his friend, for example writing to him of kissing a girl and feeling the next day 'the irresistible fanfares of spring'.[47] It is Jenger's belief that, at the age of 21, Le Corbusier was confused about where to channel his sexuality.[48]

Ritter was in part responsible for persuading the young Le Corbusier to embark on his 'Journey to the East' in 1911, the journey famously culminating in a memorable trip to the Parthenon, the temple of Athene Parthenos, the 'maiden'. Here all Le Corbusier's ideas about Orphism and the supremacy of ancient Greek culture received their affirmation. His travel journal was not published until 1965, shortly before his death, and when he reread the manuscript at that time he commented that 'the line of conduct of little Charles-Edouard Jeanneret at the time of Le Voyage d'Orient was the same as that of Père Corbu'.[49]

Jeanneret augmented the knowledge gained through periods of travel such as the 'Journey to the East' with hours of meticulous study in museums. Such investigations provided the raw material for much of his later work.[50] Through them he began to learn about the early religions and iconography of Europe and elsewhere, particularly through his studies of mediaeval and renaissance art; simultaneously he learnt about natural history and the patterns within nature, fundamentally linked through geometry. Such ideas were melded together with his emerging fascination for technology and the possibilities it presented. He observed that:

> the machine brings shining before us disks, spheres, the cylinders of polished steel, polished more highly than we have ever seen before: shaped with a theoretical precision and exactitude which can never be seen in nature itself. Our hand reaches out to it, and our sense of touch looks in its own way as our fingers close round it. Our senses are moved at the same time as our heart recalls from its stock of memories the disks and spheres of the gods of Egypt and the Congo. Gods! Geometry and gods sit side by side (an old human story, truth to tell, the basic and original human story).[51]

This blurring of the ancient, the natural and the machine is fundamental to Le Corbusier's thinking.

All three adhere to the laws of geometry and hence to the gods.

Synthesis

Le Corbusier wrote in *Precisions*, published in 1930, that the focus of his quest had at that point become geometry 'animated a little', as he put it, 'by the spirit of Pythagoras'.[52] He then began to direct his efforts towards devising a system of proportion that would give rise to 'a form of planning' which would 'create happiness and expel misery . . . a noble service in this age of confusion'.[53] Armed with a tape measure he would take every opportunity to take down the dimensions of places and things that were pleasing in proportion. Old buildings, Egyptian temples, paintings, cars, ships and natural phenomena such as flowers would all come under his scrutiny. The Golden Section would obviously become an important point of reference as were his readings about Pythagoras and his followers. Together they would be amalgamated into a system of proportion, the Modulor.

Le Corbusier has been criticised for basing his theory of the Modulor upon the dimensions of a European man. This was not something that he did without qualm. He was fully aware of the problems of attempting to discover a system of measure applicable to the universal community,[54] but felt in the end that it was a priority to make 'doors so that tall people should be able to go through them'.[55] Some of the tensions that he felt regarding this issue emerge in his book *Modulor 2*, in which he included a drawing prepared by his assistants Serralta and Maisonnier (Fig. 4.2). Here he commented ruefully that the drawing had started 'the square of the Modulor man' of 1.83 metres (but, since Serralta has a soft spot for the ladies, his man is a woman 1.83 metres tall: brrrh!).[56] In the opinion of Richard A. Moore, Le Corbusier saw the Modulor in terms of 'two interlocking systems, the blue, binary and red, trinary sequence'. It is his belief that for Le Corbusier the 'binary is female, infinite and dominant'.[57]

Writing in the *Modulor*, Le Corbusier was to look back at this early period of his life and describe it thus:

It was a matter of occupying a particular square on the social chessboard: a family of musicians (music heard all through my youth), a passion for drawing, a passion for the plastic arts, purity, acuity, a character which wanted to get to the heart of things, harmony. Then, suddenly, your many wanderings through the highways and byways of life serve as a detector, an intermittent contact. You stop here, there, at places where others would have gone on their way seeing nothing. And, one day, you discover . . .

I feel neither pride nor vanity or conceit in having made a discovery. I am trembling with anxiety to know and to make sure. People may tell me: 'What of it? A mere chance has brought you to the door of miracles; you have stood before it, and then you have opened it and passed through it. And so the wise men (those who know, but who, it may be, do not feel, vibrate, hold communion at every instant with life through art and the poetic emotion) will be able to explain, straighten out, pursue, expand, and make this thing useful to men.'[58]

The discovery he referred to was that of Orphism – first introduced to him through the writings of Rabelais and affirmed through his readings of Schuré and Provensal, his studies and his travels; it would be central to all his work thereafter.

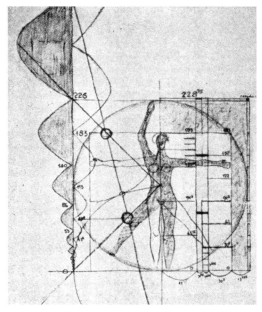

Figure 4.2   Modulor Man from Le Corbusier, *Modulor 2*.

Orphism

Orphism, an early version of Gnosticism, was described by Le Corbusier's client and friend, Edouard Trouin as 'contradictory like life . . . the only possible religion of intellectuals'.[59] For Le Corbusier it would encompass a wisdom tradition extending back to the ancient Egyptians, via alchemy, neo-Platonism, Catharism, Kabbalism, and the teachings of both Plato and Pythagoras and would be key to Le Corbusier's view of the world as a balance between male and female elements.

Orphism is traceable back to the sixth century before Christ.[60] There are frequent allusions to Orphic rites in the writings of the Graeco-Roman period, for example in the work of Plato and also in the work of the Neoplatonists.[61] The Orphic goal was to gain the necessary knowledge of the nature of God and human existence, gnosis, in order to allow the soul to leave the body at the point of death, and move up through the heavenly spheres to be reunited with God, light.[62] This would be achieved by undergoing a process of initiation.[63] According to legend, Orpheus played the lyre so sweetly that he was able to lull the gods into allowing him to visit the Underworld to find his lost love and thence to return to the land of the living. He therefore had unique knowledge of the realm of the dead. His ability to 'charm all of nature with his singing'[64] meant that he also had a special role in the propagation of musical harmony. The son of a Muse, he was identified with the god Apollo, who also played the lyre.[65]

Orpheus was said to be the prophet of a particular type of mystery-religion that the Cambridge scholar W. K. C. Guthrie, a contemporary of Le Corbusier, described as 'a modification of the mysteries of Dionysos'[66] and a 'species of the Bacchic'.[67] Dionysos, who appeared to his followers in the guise of a bull,[68] was, according to Guthrie, worshipped under many names including Pan and Apollo.[69] His cult, traditionally orgiastic in character, was eventually subsumed into that of the Orphics[70] who themselves were expected to lead an ascetic life.[71]

According to the Neoplatonist philosopher Pico della Mirandola (1463–1494), much admired by Le Corbusier,[72] the Orphics had 'a secret doctrine of number' that was understood and utilised by the ancient Egyptians, Pythagoras, Plato, Aristotle and Origen.[73] Le Corbusier underlined a section referring to this continuous thread of knowledge in Matila Ghyka's Nombre d'or and alluded to it in his book Modulor 2, extending it into the twentieth century. He wrote: 'the intuitions of Pythagoras, Plato and Pacioli[74] lead to the same result . . . Einstein's, de Broglie's[75] and Leonardo da Vinci's principles'. He described these names as 'taboo' yet, it will be argued, he felt himself to be a part of this distinguished group of artists, scientists and philosophers. Ivan Zacnic records that when Le Corbusier read over a film script based on his life by Michel Bataille, he wrote on the draft describing himself chatting on an aeroplane 'No, L.C. is always alone. Reading Orpheus, Rabelais, Cervantes'.[76] Such was the fundamental role of Orpheus in Le Corbusier's thinking.

Orphism has been given a number of different interpretations depending often upon the subjective viewpoint of the individual interpreter. For Le Corbusier, it seems to have served to draw together the many seemingly disparate areas of interest that he addressed in his work: the ideas of Plato and Pythagoras, alchemy, Pico della Mirandola, the Kaballah, geometry, harmony, courtly love, the relationship of the spirit with the body, the union of opposites and Catharism (already addressed at the beginning of this chapter) all of which were, for Le Corbusier, Orphic in essence. I will now expand on these various aspects, indicating the ways in which they impacted on his developing view of the cosmos as a balance between masculine and feminine elements.

Pythagoras

Pythagoras, a follower of Orphism, founded a religious order at Croton in the late sixth century B.C.[77] Le Corbusier appears to have gained the majority of his knowledge of this ancient philosopher through his reading of Schuré. Like the Orphics, the Pythagoreans were ascetic in their approach to life and looked upon Apollo as a figure of veneration.[78] Pythagoras took it upon himself to discover a way to express his view of the cosmos rationally, by means of numbers.[79] He set up a community in which both men and women could be initiated into his beliefs.[80]

In his own account of Pythagoras' life, Schuré emphasised the philosopher's belief in seeing the world in terms of a harmonious balance of masculine and feminine elements.[81]

Given his preoccupation with harmony it would seem only logical that Pythagoras would come to venerate Orpheus, whose musical abilities were well known. According to Guthrie it was his experiments with music that had given him such an understanding of mathematical ratio.[82] Le Corbusier himself wrote enthusiastically of Pythagoras' forays into 'Mathematica, herself the daughter of the Universe' in his book *Modulor 2*.[83] Evidently Pythagoras' influence upon the development of his system of proportion was decisive.

Plato and the Union of Opposites

Le Corbusier's reading of Schuré also appears to have introduced him to the ideas of Plato. Building on the ideas of Pythagoras, Plato believed that number was central to the process of bringing harmony to the world[84] and that the reconciliation of opposites could be found in music.[85] He wrote in the *Symposium*:

> Harmony is composed of differing notes of higher or lower pitch which disagreed once, but are now reconciled by the art of music for if the higher and lower notes still disagreed, there could be no harmony − clearly not. For harmony is a symphony, and symphony is an agreement; but an agreement of disagreements while they disagree there cannot be; you cannot harmonise that which disagrees. In like manner rhythm is compounded of elements short and long, once differing and now in accord; which accordance, as in the former instance, medicine, so in all these other cases, music implants, making love and unison to grow up among them; and thus music, too, is concerned with the principles of love in their application to harmony and rhythm.[86]

Plato bemoaned man's neglect of Love 'for if they had understood him they would surely have built noble temples and altars and offered solemn sacrifices in his honour; but this is not done, and most certainly ought to be done: since of all the gods he is the best friend of men.'[87] Love, the relationships between people, was fundamentally linked to mathematics. This is where it begins to impinge on the main thesis of this book.

Plato is also significant because of his account of what he called 'the original human nature' to be found in the pages of the *Symposium*:

> The sexes were not two as they are now, but originally three in number; there was man, woman, and the union of the two, having a name corresponding to this double nature, which had once real existence, but is now lost, and the word 'Androgynous' is only preserved as a term of reproach . . . Now the sexes were three, and such as I have described them; because the sun, moon and earth are three; and the man was originally the child of the sun, the woman of the earth, and the man-woman of the moon, which is made up of sun and earth.[88]

This race was 'terrible' in its 'might and strength'. These people began to make attacks upon the gods, believing their rightful place to be in heaven. To punish them for their insolence Zeus developed a plan: 'men shall continue to exist, but I will cut them in two and then they will be diminished in strength and increased in numbers; this will have the advantage of making them more profitable to us'.

Plato then observed that 'after the division the two parts of man, each desiring his other half, came together, and throwing their arms about one another, entwined in mutual embraces, longing to grow into one another'.[89] It thus became the lot of mankind to spend his life in pursuit of his or her other half. Plato recorded what would happen when they actually found one another:

> The pair are lost in an amazement of love and friendship and intimacy, and will not be out of the other's sight, as I may say, even for a moment: these are the people who pass their whole lives together; yet they could not explain what they desire of one another. For the intense yearning which each of them has towards the other does not appear to be the desire of lover's intercourse,

but of something else of which the soul of either evidently desires and cannot tell, and of which she has only a dark and doubtful presentiment.[90]

For Plato this 'desire and pursuit of the whole is called love'. Again he emphasised the importance of praising the god Love 'who is our greatest benefactor, both leading us in this life back to our own nature, and giving us high hopes for the future, for he promises that if we are pious, he will restore us to our original state, and heal us and make us happy and blessed'.[91] This vision of the Platonic androgyne will be seen to have had a profound influence upon Le Corbusier and many others of his set in early twentieth century Paris.

Alchemy

Plato's ideas were also central to the ancient science of alchemy, another interest of Le Corbusier's. Famed for their attempts to transform base matter into gold, the alchemist's true aim was in fact rather more subtle. Experiments were conducted in the spiritual and material world simultaneously since, for the true alchemist, these two realms remained inextricably linked. The alchemical process took place in a series of stages, the last and most difficult of which was the marriage of opposites, man and woman, symbolised by *sol* and *luna*, sun and moon. The transformation took place through the *coniunctio*, symbolised by their sexual union, which culminated in the attainment of the 'philosopher's stone' or *lapis*. The alchemical hermaphrodite became an important symbol of this process. 'He who experiences this transformation has no more desires, and the prolongation of earthly life has no more importance for him who already lives in the deathless' observes Stanislas Klossowski de Rola.[92]

Carl Gustav Jung illustrated the geometrical manifestation of the union of opposites in his groundbreaking work *Psychology and Alchemy* of 1944 with an illustration of the alchemist drawing the 'squared circle' with a giant compass on an ancient wall. In a circle at the centre of the image are the figures of a man and a woman (Fig. 4.3). For the alchemists, the union of opposites, the balance of masculine and feminine, could be represented in the form of geometry, an idea that I will return to in Chapter 6.[93]

Pico della Mirandola

Pico della Mirandola (1463–1494) was amongst a group of Neoplatonists who revitalised the Kabbalah, an ancient form of Jewish theosophy, that went through a rebirth in thirteenth century Provence at the same time that Catharism and philosophical pantheism were being violently attacked by the Church.[94] Le Corbusier described the Kabbalah as 'a profound course of study for anyone willing to risk it!'[95] For the Kabbalists the message of their quest could be found within the Hebrew scriptures, but only the initiated could perceive them. They described the structure of the divine world and suggested ways in which mankind might attain harmony within it.[96] Like that of the Orphics, theirs was a vision that was strongly dualistic and governed by number. The soul, before it entered the world, was male and female united in one being. When it descended to earth the two parts separated and animated different bodies. If a person behaved wisely they would be lucky enough to meet and marry the other half of their soul.[97] If a person used their life badly, their soul, as in Orphism, would return to earth a number of times so that he or she could make amends. Eventually all souls would be united with the highest soul and there would be no more sin, temptation and suffering.[98] In Pico's syncretic view the Kabbalah formed the link between a number of aspects of antique occult thought

Figure 4.3   'Squaring the circle to make the two sexes one whole.' From Maier, *Scrutinium Chymicum* (1687). British Library shelfmark 89.e.24.

Platonism, Neoplatonism, Hermeticism, Orphism, Pythagoreanism and Christianity.[99] Le Corbusier wrote in one of his *Sketchbooks* dated 1957:

> The modern age has carved up physics, chemistry, medicine, the army, mechanics, and even education into categories proportionate to the vastness of the human brain, to the availabilities of [certain kinds of] education. Pico della Mirandola is, as his name implies a miraculandolous [sic], exceptional individual summit . . . If there is somewhere and someday, some Pic [sic[100]] della Mirandola arising on the horizon, he will appear (mirandoling mirandolesque) with his biceps and his head and that's all right! Schools are not turning them out, that's precisely today's great equivocation.[101]

He admired Pico for his ability to bring a number of elements from a number of different religions and philosophies into a unified whole. He was able to utilise both his 'biceps and his head', his body and spirit in doing so.

Summary

From this brief account of the doctrines and ideas of Orphism come a number of important themes: secret knowledge; the symbolic use of number; the use of geometry in the creation of harmony; the union of opposites; love, asceticism and the relationship of body and spirit. Of primary importance for this discussion is the idea that geometry plays a profound role in the relationship between people and things, influencing the ultimate union of opposites, man and woman. Le Corbusier came to see the equality of the sexes as a fundamental law of nature necessary if the desired state of harmony was to be achieved. Such ideas would be confirmed in the artistic milieu that he entered when he moved to Paris.

Orphism and the questioning of sexual roles in early twentieth century Paris

Le Corbusier was not alone in his enthusiasm for Orphism. It would have been fuelled by a number of key figures whom he met when he came to Paris in

1908, when he spent sixteen months working for Auguste Perret, who invited him to some of the Thursday evening meetings that he organised with artists, writers and musicians.[102] He was eventually to make the city his home in 1917, joining forces with the artist Amédée Ozenfant in 1920 to publish *L'Esprit Nouveau*, a wide ranging journal covering topics as diverse as science, art, literature, medicine, alchemy, dance, astronomy, magic and, of course, architecture.

Julia Fagan-King has noted that there was a 'pervasive quasi-religious belief in a high mystical ideal for a new era' among artistic circles in Paris at the beginning of the twentieth century. In her opinion:

> That the arts were a channel to the divine or the Absolute, that the aesthetic creative or appreciative experience was comparable to the ecstasy of mystics or prophets with an equivalent divine power, was a deep rooted belief reaching far back beyond their immediate predecessors, the symbolists, to the mystically orientated exemplars of Michelangelo and Leonardo da Vinci – even to Plato himself.[103]

Simultaneously there was a major re-evaluation of sexual roles in society.[104] Much has been written, for example, on the way male artists such as Marcel Duchamp cross-dressed,[105] in doing so giving an increasingly ironic take on the issue of masculinity.[106] It did not take long for these two strands of thought, the mystical and the sexually questioning, to meet and mingle amongst those of Orphic inclination.

During the early 1920s Le Corbusier came across the ideas of a number of different artists and authors who had a specific interest in the Platonic idea of the mystical androgyne and the role of the feminine in the artistic life of man, for example Joséphin Péladan, Guillaume Apollinaire, André Breton, André Gide and Jean Cocteau (the latter four of whom were acquaintances, if not friends).[107] It is my belief that the work of these men would provide further affirmation for Le Corbusier of his already strong belief in Orphism.

Joséphin Péladan

Joséphin Péladan (1858–1918) was a key figure in the revival of the esoteric arts in Paris when he instigated a series of 'Salons de la Rose + Croix', the rose and cross,[108] which lasted from 1892 to 1897. The cause of Rosicrucianism, to which he was committed, took elements from both mainstream Christianity and Kabbalism. Drawing upon both alchemical and Gnostic philosophies, Péladan's organisation also had links to the ancient craft guilds and to the Freemasons.[109]

A number of notable artists exhibited their work within Péladan's salon, for example Gustave Moreau and Georges Rouault. According to Robert Pincus-Witten, more than 22,600 visiting cards were left at the first Salon de la Rose + Croix which took place in 1892, testament to the interest generated by the event.[110] In an annotation to one of his books on Catharism containing references to the Rose + Croix, Le Corbusier indicated that he had met 'Saar Péladan',[111] but the full extent of his association with Péladan, who died in 1918, is not known.[112]

Whilst being famously misogynist,[113] Péladan was, by all accounts, obsessed by the concept of the mystical androgyne. Mario Praz made a relevant point in his book *The Romantic Agony*:

Part of the seventh treatise in Péladan's *Amphithéâtre des sciences mortes* expounds the theory of the androgyne under the title of *Érotologie de Platon*: here the female androgyne is defined as Martha and Mary in one, combining the active with the contemplative faculty, a perfect fusion of intelligence and voluptuousness . . . The androgyne is the artistic sex par excellence, realized in the creations of Leonardo.[114]

For this reason it would play a significant role in the work of a number of artists, among them Le Corbusier.

Guillaume Apollinaire

In a sketchbook dated October 1951 Le Corbusier made a note to himself to buy a book of poems by Apollinaire, *Ombre de mon amour*.[115] Le Corbusier became an admirer of the poet's work when he first arrived in Paris. It was he who provided Jeanneret and Ozenfant with the inspiration to entitle their journal *L'Esprit Nouveau*.[116] Significantly Apollinaire wrote in the

essay 'L'Esprit nouveau et les poets' that modern poets were prophets for whom Plato was a primary source of inspiration.[117] This does not mean to say that they took on board all his opinions – Plato is thought to have had a repugnance for coitus, and a low view of the female sex in general – instead the modern poets chose to applaud the aspects of his thought that celebrated the propagation of sexual harmony.[118]

In 1907 Apollinaire wrote a collection of quatrains *Bestiare ou Cortège d'Orphée* in which he incorporated the figure of Orpheus as a symbol of the poet and the artist in general.[119] Apollinaire was instrumental in identifying and defining the early twentieth-century art movement known as Orphism,[120] which counted among its adherents Robert Delaunay, Francis Picabia, Marcel Duchamp and Fernand Léger.[121] These artists took inspiration from Orpheus' ability to create harmony through his music.[122] They wanted to achieve a similar state of harmony through painting, using colour and form to affect the emotions and communicate meaning.[123] To this end a collection of Orphist paintings was put on display at the Salon des Indépendants in March 1913.

Apollinaire was very knowledgeable about religion. He developed the ability to combine Christian symbolism with that of alchemy and other Orphic forms of spirituality. He likened his lover, the artist Marie Laurencin, to an alembic, the vessel in which the alchemists conducted their experiments. As such her body was a place of transformation, an idea that I will return to in my discussion of the Chapel at Ronchamp in Chapter 6. Through contact with this woman he was able to bring his own creative talents to fruition.[124] She would enable him to attain the necessary balance of masculine and feminine within his life and within his work to achieve enlightenment, thus woman would have a vital role in the creative processes of man. In admiring the man and appreciating his work, Le Corbusier too must have engaged with such ideas.

André Breton and the Surrealists

Le Corbusier had a brief flirtation with Surrealism at the beginning of his career and was to remain a friend, if distant, of André Breton, the self styled leader of the Surrealists, for the rest of his life. To this end the presence of a copy of Breton's *L'Art Magie* of 1957 in Le Corbusier's personal library in the FLC should be noted.[125] Indeed in one of his 1957 sketchbooks he noted to himself that he needed to regain contact with Breton.[126] The Surrealists took inspiration from both alchemy and mysticism as well as Orphism.[127]

The Surrealists were preoccupied by the image of the androgyne as a spiritual ideal. The Surrealist androgyne had its origins in Plato's description of the third sex, but it also had clear links with the androgyne of alchemy and with late nineteenth century versions of the same theme, presumably including those of Péladan.[128] Breton wrote:

> Chosen perhaps
> From man and from woman . . .
> This meeting
> With everything that from a distance is fatal in it
> This rushing together of two systems considered
> Separately as subjective
> Sets off a series of very real phenomena
> That take part in the formation of a distinct world
> Of a kind to bring shame on what we would
> perceive without it.[129]

Whitney Chadwick writes that 'male Surrealist artists inherited from the late-nineteenth century Symbolists a polarized view of woman embracing both the creative and subversive powers of the love instinct'.[130] For the Surrealist artist the feminine principle governed the creation of the artistic work, a point emphasised by Breton in *Arcane 17*, written in 1944. In it he prophesied that

> The time will come when the ideas of woman will be asserted at the expense of those of man, the failure of which is already today tumultuously evident. Specifically it rests with the artist to make visible everything that is part of the feminine, as opposed to the masculine system of the world. It is the artist who must rely exclusively on the woman's powers to exalt, or better still, to jealously appropriate to himself everything that distinguishes woman from man with respect to their styles of appreciation and volition.[131]

To this end he believed that it was the role of the male artist to regain contact with his inner feminine, his muse, a fact that may explain why Surrealist literature and painting are so dominated by images of women.[132]

Jean Cocteau

Mention should also be made of Jean Cocteau (1889–1963), another figure who inhabited the fringes of Surrealism. Le Corbusier owned one of his books, *Le Grand Écart*, as well as a biography of the artist and author.[133] Famously homosexual, Cocteau contributed an article to Le Corbusier and Ozenfant's journal *L'Esprit Nouveau* in 1920.[134] Le Corbusier wrote in *L'Art décoratif d'aujourd'hui*, 'Cocteau has shown us delightfully how to let off steam; like it or not, there is always space for our curiosity and room for mystery.'[135] He referred to him in a note in his sketchbook dated 1957 suggesting that the flamboyant artist remained in his thoughts.[136]

Cocteau reminisced that his 'development took place in the midst of isms: Cubism, Futurism, Purism, Orphism, Expressionism, Dadaism, Surrealism, and an avalanche of secrets exposed'.[137] He turned his hand to a number of different art forms, most notably cinema, of which his explicitly Orphic films *Orphée* (1949), based on a stage play first performed in 1926, and *Le Testament d'Orphée* (1950), are perhaps the most famous examples.

Cocteau drew images from the realm of myth to express the complexities of his vision, reworking and adapting the stories of ancient Greece and Rome as well as those of the Middle Ages to fit his needs. Like Breton and Péladan he took the mystical androgyne as a model to aspire to, writing in his book *Opium*:

> Art is born of coitus between the male and female elements of which we are all composed, and they are more balanced in the case of artists than of other men. It results from a kind of incest, of love of self for self, of parthenogenesis. It is this that makes marriage so dangerous among artists, for whom it represents a pleonasm, a monstrous effort towards the norm. The 'poor specimen' look which is the mark of so many men of genius arises from the fact that the creative instinct is satisfied

elsewhere and leaves sexual pleasure free to exert itself in the pure domain of aesthetics inclining it also towards unfruitful forms of expression.[138]

Arthur Evans has noted that in certain accounts Orpheus was reputed to have instigated the practice of homosexuality in ancient Greece. In Evans' opinion 'Cocteau would most assuredly find in this portion of the myth a reflection of his own self'.[139] Certainly Cocteau, like many of his contemporaries, was questioning established gender roles and used the myth of Orpheus as a vehicle to do so.

During the 1930s and 1940s Cocteau, André Gide (for whom Le Corbusier also held great admiration) and their friends began to make demands for the liberation of homosexuals and of women.[140] Shari Benstock writes: 'The matriarchal mystery allied itself to a cult of male youth, a metaphorical alliance between the powerless elements of society (women and adolescents) that constituted a radical critique of patriarchal power'.[141] Such was the atmosphere in which Le Corbusier continued to develop his architectural experiments.

Conclusion

The Orphic idea that a harmonious relationship with nature could be achieved through number and geometry was one that developed out of Le Corbusier's early home experiences, receiving affirmation from his reading, his studies and those around him. In the Orphic world in which he lived, harmony and geometry were closely linked to love. The alchemists' ultimate quest, the crystalline, geometrically formed philosopher's stone, would be made possible by the union of opposites – man and woman – an idea that would profoundly influence Le Corbusier who started to see the world in terms of a balance between masculine and feminine elements, incorporating such ideas symbolically into his paintings through what he called the 'marriage of lines'. Le Corbusier observed that 'Tools of unity, of peace making, breakers of walls, tools for the traffic of ideas and objects. The secret of my quest must be sought in my painting'.[142] He repeatedly stressed that his explorations as an artist formed the basis for everything that he did.

Notes

1 Le Corbusier, *My Work* (London: Architectural Press, 1960), p.65.
2 J. Peter, *The Oral History of Modern Architecture* (New York: Harry N. Abrams, 1994), p.138.
3 Ibid.
4 See for example Matila Ghyka, *Nombre d'or: rites et rhythmes Pythagoriciens dans le development de la civilisation Occidental* (Paris: Gallimard, 1931), p.57 in Le Corbusier's own library in the Fondation Le Corbusier (hereafter referred to as the FLC).
5 See annotations to Coincy Saint Palais, *Esclarmonde de Foix: Princesse Cathare* (Toulouse: Privat, 1956), p.27 in FLC.
6 Ibid., pp.28–9.
7 Ibid., p.27 in FLC.
8 Ibid.
9 Le Corbusier, *My Work*, p.19.
10 Le Corbusier commented on his parent's enthusiasm for Rabelais and Cervantes in the draft for his book *Fond du Sac* which was never completed. FLC F2.10.302.
11 Le Corbusier Sketchbooks Volume 4 (Cambridge, MA: MIT Press, 1982), sketch 501.
12 Le Corbusier, *Sketchbooks Volume 3, 1954–1957* (Cambridge, MA: MIT Press, 1982), sketches 85–88.
13 F. Rabelais, *The Histories of Gargantua and Pantagruel* (London: Penguin, 1955), p.26.
14 Ibid., p.24.
15 C. Swietlicki, *Spanish Christian Cabala* (Columbia: University of Missouri Press, 1986), pages 9 and 43.
16 Rabelais. *Oeuvres Complètes* (Paris: Gallimard, 1951), p.641 in FLC. It is important to note the fact that Le Corbusier's own edition of *Gargantua and Pantagruel* contained lengthy explanatory notes indicating these types of link.
17 Le Corbusier, *Sketchbooks Volume 3*, p.10.
18 Ibid., sketch 80.
19 Ibid.
20 Le Corbusier, *Journey to the East* (Cambridge, MA: MIT Press, 1987), p.83.
21 Flora Samuel, 'The Representation of Mary in Le Corbusier's Chapel at Ronchamp,' *Church History*, 68, 2 (1999) 398–416.
22 W.K.C Guthrie, *The Greeks and Their Gods* (Boston: Beacon Press, 1955), p.161.
23 See, for an elaboration of this discussion, Flora Samuel, 'Le Corbusier Rabelais and Oracle of the Holy Bottle', *Word and Image: a Journal of verbal/visual enquiry*, 17, 4 (2001), pp.325–338.
24 Le Corbusier, *The Decorative Art of Today* (London: Architectural Press, 1987), p.198. Originally published in 1925.
25 See for example the discussion of the artist Paul Klee in Robert Rosenblum, *Modern Painting and the Northern Romantic Tradition* (London: Thames and Hudson, 1994), p.154.

26 R. A. Moore, 'Le Corbusier and the *mecanique spirituelle*: An investigation into Le Corbusier's architectural symbolism and its background in Beaux Arts design', unpublished D Phil thesis, University of Maryland (1979), p.317.

27 E. Schuré, *Les Grands Initiés* ((Paris: Perrin, 1908), pp.51–2 quoted in Moore, 'Le Corbusier and the *mecanique spirituelle*', p.317.

28 'Carrying vases', they were described as the 'seekers of Aphrodite'. Schuré, *Les Grands Initiés*, p.240 in FLC.

29 Schuré, *Les Grands Initiés*, p.226 in FLC.

30 Chapter entitled 'Orphée (Le mystères de Dionysos)' in ibid., p.219.

31 Ibid., p.232.

32 Ibid., p.227.

33 Ibid., p.244.

34 Ibid.

35 Ibid., p.264.

36 Ibid., p.272.

37 Ibid., p.549.

38 Ibid., p.546.

39 Letter Le Corbusier to his parents, 31.01.08 in the archives at La Chaux de Fonds (CdF LCms 34, transcription supplied by Mlle Françoise Frey). Quoted by Benton, 'The Sacred and the Search for Truths', in T. Benton (ed.), *Le Corbusier Architect of the Century* (London: Arts Council, 1987), p.239.

40 P. Turner, *The Education of an Architect* (New York: Garland, 1977), p.10.

41 Henry Provensal, *L'Art de Demain* (Paris: Perrin, 1904), p.34 in FLC.

42 P. Serenyi, 'Le Corbusier, Fourier and the Monastery of Ema', *Art Bulletin*, 49 (1967), p.283.

43 S. Benstock, *Women of the Left Bank* (London: Virago, 1994), p.52.

44 Ibid.

45 G. Baker and J Gubler, *Le Corbusier: Early Works by Charles-Edouard Jeanneret Gris* (London: Academy, 1987), p.23.

46 Le Corbusier, *Oeuvre Complète Volume 1* (Basel: Birkhauser, 1995), p.12.

47 Letter Le Corbusier to Wiliam Ritter, 01.03.1911, FLC R3.18.59. Quoted in J. Jenger, *Le Corbusier Choix de Lettres* (Basel: Birkhauser, 2002), p.23.

48 Jenger, *Le Corbusier Choix de Lettres*, p.23.

49 I. Zaknic, *The Final Testament of Père Corbu: a Translation and Interpretation of Mise au Point* (New Haven, CT: Yale University Press, 1997), p.100.

50 Edouard Trouin marvelled at Le Corbusier's knowledge of art history. Rapport du Secrétaire Géneral Edouard Trouin sur nos projets en cours, 8 February 1955, FLC 13.01.390.

51 Le Corbusier, *The Decorative Art of Today*, p.112.

52 Le Corbusier, *Precisions on the Present State of Architecture and City Planning* (Cambridge, MA: MIT Press, 1991), p.60.

53 Le Corbusier, *The City of Tomorrow and its Planning* (London: Architectural Press, 1947), p.75.

54 Le Corbusier, *Modulor 2* (London: Faber, 1955), p.93.

55 Ibid., p.94.

56 Ibid., p.52.

57 Moore, 'Le Corbusier and the *mecanique spirituelle*', p.266.

58 Le Corbusier, *Modulor* (London: Faber, 1954), p182.

59 Trouin, 'Table provisoire', n.d., FLC 13.01.399.

60 W.K.C. Guthrie, *Orpheus and Greek Religion* (London: Methuen, 1935), p.217.

61 Ibid., p.18.

62 G. Filoramo, *A History of Gnosticism* (Oxford: Basil Blackwell, 1991), pp.52–3.

63 Guthrie, *Orpheus and Greek Religion*, p.17.

64 Ibid.

65 Ibid., p.39.

66 Ibid.

67 Ibid., p.41.

68 Ibid., p.114.

69 Ibid., p.41.

70 S. Pomeroy, *Goddesses, Whores, Wives and Slaves* (New York: Dorset, 1975), p.222.

71 Guthrie, *Orpheus and Greek Religion*, p.16.

72 Le Corbusier, *Sketchbooks Volume 3*, sketch 1011.

73 Pico della Mirandola, *On the Dignity of Man* (Indianapolis: Hackett, 1998), pp.30–31. Originally written in 1486.

74 Luca Pacioli was a Renaissance writer, a friend of Piero della Francesca (who Le Corbusier greatly admired), who wrote what Le Corbusier called a 'magnificent book on divine proportion'. Le Corbusier, *Modulor 2*, p.77.

75 Louis César Victor Maurice de Broglie (1875–1960) was an eminent physicist and a pioneer of research into X rays.

76 Zacnic, *The Final Testament of Père Corbu* (New Haven, CT: Yale University Press, 1977), p.44.

77 Le Corbusier wrote 'one day – six centuries before Christ – someone first thought of making music permanently transmissible in another way than from mouth to ear: that is to write it down'. Le Corbusier, *The Modulor*, p.15. It seems likely that he was alluding to Pythagoras who is then mentioned on the next page.

78 Guthrie, *Orpheus and Greek Religion*, p.220.

79 Ibid., p.217.

80 Schuré emphasises the influence of Pythagoras' mother on his developing ideas. Schuré, *Les Grands Initiés*, p.279.

81 Ibid., p.331.

82 Ibid.

83 Le Corbusier also referred to the discussion of Pythagoras at the Milan Triennale of 1951 dedicated to 'de divina Proportione'. Le Corbusier, *Modulor 2*, p.145.

84 Plato, *Timaeus*: 32.

85 Plato, *Symposium*, in S. Buchanan (ed.), *The Portable Plato* (Harmondsworth: Penguin, 1997), p.140.

86 Ibid., p.141.

87 Ibid., p.143.

88 Ibid., p.144.

89 Ibid., p.145.

90 Ibid., p.147.

91 Ibid., p.148.

92 S. Klossowski de Rola, *The Secret Art of Alchemy* (London: Thames and Hudson, 1973), p.22.

93 C.G. Jung, 'The Structure and Dynamics of the Self,' *Collected Works 9, Part II* (London: Routledge & Kegan Paul, 1951), para 355.

94 M. Idel, *Kabbalah, New Perspectives* (New Haven, CT: Yale University Press, 1988), p.251.

95 Le Corbusier, *When the Cathedrals were White: A Journey to the Country of the Timid People* (New York: Reynal and Hitchcock, 1947), p.6.

96 Idel, *Kabbalah*, p.xi.

97 H. Sperling and M. Simon, trans., *The Zohar* (London: Soncino Press, 1933), p.91.

98 *Encyclopaedia Britannica* (Cambridge: Cambridge University Press, 1911), p.620.

99 Swietlicki, *Spanish Christian Cabala*, pages 9 and 43.

100 Pun on 'pic', the French word for peak.

101 Le Corbusier, *Sketchbooks Volume 3*, sketch 1011.

102 A. Ozenfant *Mémoires* (Paris: Seghers, 1968), p.104.

103 J. Fagan-King, 'United on the Threshold of the Twentieth Century Mystical Ideal', *Art History*, 11, 1 (1988), p.89.

104 Wood and Greenhalgh reflect that developments in psychology and sexology that were burgeoning at that time could 'be seen as empirically based attempts to describe, codify and control sexuality and behavioural systems'. G. Wood and P. Greenhalgh, 'Symbols of the Sacred and Profane' in P. Greenhalgh (ed.), *Art Nouveau 1890–1914* (London: V & A, 2000), p.89.

105 It should be noted that several of the artists of early twentieth century Paris were critical of Catholicism yet utilised its symbolism. Marcel Duchamp and Max Ernst are good examples. At the same time there was a revival of interest in Hermeticism, Rosicrucianism and gnosticism which was used to undermine and revivify Catholic themes. See D. Hopkins, *Marcel Duchamp and Max Ernst : the Bride Shared* (Oxford: Clarendon Press, 1997) for a useful discussion of art, religion and sexual roles during that period.

106 A. Jones, ' "Clothes make the Man": The Male Artist as Performative Function', *Oxford Art Journal* 18:2 (1995), p.22.

107 Letters from Apollinaire to Gide, Breton and Cocteau appear in Michel Décaudin, ed., *Oeuvres Complètes de Guillaume Apollinaire, Volume 4* (Paris: André Balland et Jacques Lecat, 1966), p.17.

108 There is an extensive discussion of the 'Allegorie Rose-Croix' in K. Seligmann's *Le Miroir de la magie* (Paris: Fasquelle, 1956), p.388 in Le Corbusier's personal library in the FLC.

109 He also took an interest in the troubadours. Joséphin Péladan, *Le Secret des troubadours* (Paris, 1906).

110 Pincus Witten, *Occult Symbolism in France*, p.58.

111 Péladan raised himself to the rank of Sâr, or high priest, the Rosicrucian version of the Pope. J. Turner (ed.), *Grove Dictionary of Art* (London: Macmillan, 1996).

112 Saint Palais, *Esclarmonde de Foix*, p.175 in FLC. According to Philippe Duboy Le Corbusier met Péladan in the Bibliotheque Nationale in 1915 but unfortunately he gives no source for this information. P. Duboy, *Lequeu: An Architectural Enigma* (Cambridge, MA: MIT Press, 1987), p.95.

113 Jean-Martin Charcot's work on female hysteria would be particularly important for artists, including many of those working with Péladan. Wood and Greenhalgh, 'Symbols of the Sacred and Profane', p.89.

114 M. Praz, *The Romantic Agony* (Oxford: Oxford University Press, 1979), p.334. First published in English 1933.

115 Le Corbusier, *Sketchbooks Volume 2* (London: Thames and Hudson, 1981), sketch 659.

116 Le Corbusier attended the first performance of the Eric Satie's 'Parade' where he heard Apollinaire attempt to calm down the angry audience who were threatening to destroy the interior of the Theatre du Châtelet within which it was held. Here Apollinaire spoke of the 'l'esprit nouveau' wanting to draw the attention of the audience to the fact that 'Parade' marked a new beginning. J. Lowman, 'Le Corbusier 1900–1925: The Years of Transition.' Unpublished doctoral dissertation, University of London (1979), p.93. On 26 November 1917 Apollinaire held a conference on the subject of 'l'Esprit Nouveau'.

117 G. Apollinaire, *L'Esprit nouveau et les poëtes* (Paris: Jacques Haumont, 1946), p.24.

118 W. E. Phipps, *The Sexuality of Jesus* (New York: Harper & Row, 1973), p.81.

119 G. Apollinaire, *Le Bestiaire ou Cortège d'Orphée* in Michel Décaudin (ed.), *Oeuvres Complètes de Guillaume Apollinaire* (Paris: André Balland et Jacques Lecat, 1966), p.17.

120 A. Hicken, *Apollinaire, Cubism and Orphism* (Aldershot: Ashgate, 2002).

121 V. Spate, 'Orphism', in Nikos Stangos (ed.), *Concepts of Modern Art* (London: Thames and Hudson, 1997), p.194.

122 V. Spate, *Orphism: the Evolution of Non-figurative Painting in Paris in 1910–14* (Oxford: Clarendon Press, 1979), p.61.

123 Ibid., p.2.

124 Fagan-King, 'United on the Threshold of the Twentieth-Century Mystical Ideal', p.94.

125 It appears that Le Corbusier kept in contact with Breton on a sporadic basis for much of his life. For example there is a letter of 16.05.49, FLC E109.216 from Breton to Le Corbusier.

126 Le Corbusier, *Sketchbooks Volume 3*, sketch 959.

127 W. Chadwick, 'Eros or Thanatos – The Surrealist Cult of Love Re-examined,' *Art Forum*, 14 (November 1975), p.14.

128 Ibid.

129 Translated from A. Breton 'L'Air de l'eau', *Clair de Terre* (Paris: Gallimard, 1966), p.176.

130 Chadwick, 'Eros or Thanatos – The Surrealist Cult of Love Re-examined,' p.14.

131 A. Breton, *Arcane 17* (Paris: Jean-Jacques Pauvert, 1971), p.66. Originally published 1947.

132 Chadwick, 'Eros or Thanatos', p.46.

133 J. Cocteau, *Le Grand Écart* (Paris: Libraire Stock, 1923). C. Mauriac, *Jean Cocteau* (Paris: Odette Lieutier, 1945). Both books are in the FLC.

134 Jean Cocteau, 'Autour de la Fresnaye,' *L'Esprit Nouveau*, 3 December 1920, pp.321–6.

135 Le Corbusier, *The Decorative Art of Today*, p.167.

136 Le Corbusier, *Sketchbooks Volume 3*, sketch 810.

137 W. Fowlie (ed.), *The Journals of Jean Cocteau* (London: Museum Press, 1957), p.48.

138 J. Cocteau, *Opium* (London: Icon, 1957), p.66. Written 1929–30 in Roquebrune which, as for Le Corbusier, became a holiday place for Cocteau.

139 A. Evans, *Jean Cocteau and His Films of Orphic Identity* (London: Associated University Press, 1977), p.75.

140 W. Chadwick, *Women Artists and the Surrealist Movement* (London: Thames and Hudson, 1985), p.16. Cooper writes that when among friends Cocteau would argue that 'homosexuality was part of a natural order' in which 'nature strove to maintain an equilibrium. E. Cooper, *The Sexual Perspective* (London: Routledge, 1986), p.139.

141 Benstock, *Women of the Left Bank*, p.52.

142 Le Corbusier, *Modulor 2*, p.296.

5 Women in the Art of Le Corbusier

In my drawings and paintings I have always shown only women, or pictures, symbols and genealogies of women.[1]

In the last chapter it was seen that Le Corbusier's primary objective was the achievement of Orphic unity through the union of opposites, including that of men and women. He believed it necessary to promulgate the role of women both within society and within religion in order to bring about the state of harmony that he so desired. It may be for this reason that women would play a particularly important role in his painted and graphic work. It is this, the role of women in the art of Le Corbusier, that is the focus of this chapter.

I will begin by discussing some of the specific ways in which Le Corbusier expressed his ideas about Orphic unity in his work as an artist, for example through colour, geometry and symbolism. This provides the background to all that follows. I will then focus on his treatment of the subject of woman, starting by comparing his ideas with those of certain of his contemporaries. Le Corbusier lived in a lively artistic milieu in which woman was often used as a subject through which certain ideas and values could be expressed. Like many other painters, he was fascinated by the subject of the odalisque. By contrasting his treatment of this subject, the mysterious eastern woman of pleasure, with that of other artists, the particular emphasis of Le Corbusier's representation of women begins to emerge.[2] This emphasis will be brought into greater focus through a discussion of certain themes in his paintings that provide a clear indication of his growing belief in the important role of woman in gaining access to the divine. These themes will be developed further through an analysis of *The Poem of the Right Angle*, the book that, more than any other, reveals the importance that he gave to woman in the life of man.

Tools of Unity

Conveniently forgetting his youthful forays into watercolour, Le Corbusier wrote in *A New World of Space* of his 'first' experiments in painting at the age of thirty-one:[3]

I then recognised that art — broader and deeper than anything else — is the means by which the individual may count completely. Realising how much our world was convulsed by the birth pains of the machine age, it seemed to me that to achieve harmony ought to be the only goal.

Nature, man, cosmos: these are the given elements, these are the forces facing each other.[4]

For Le Corbusier art would play a fundamental role in bringing about that state of unity that he so desired, one in which male and female would, as in nature, be accorded equal roles. In his paintings he would employ a number of strategies to facilitate this process of unification. These would include symbolism, the exploitation of physical response in the pursuit of spiritual change, geometry and colour.

Symbolism

Le Corbusier worked and reworked the same images, carrying piles of old sketches with him whenever he went travelling so that he could improve them if he so desired. He wrote of these as 'exercises on a variety of themes ranging from painting to architecture and urbanism, exercises which spring from logic and the poetic, even from the symbolic'.[5]

For Le Corbusier symbolism was an obsession, 'a yearning for a language limited to only a few words'.[6] This fascination, learnt during his youthful studies of ancient art and architecture, was to remain with Le Corbusier throughout his life although he did, on occasion, deny it.[7] He made it very clear that his work would reveal a great deal if examined closely. In the booming words of a prophet, he intoned:

> What could you not find contained in a canvas if you could obtain the painter's confession? But the canvas goes out alone, making or not making its way, bearing its message. There is a world in a painting or a building as there is also in a work of city planning. Seek, and you shall find. Look into the depths of the work and ask yourself questions. There are illuminations and scenes; there are hours of fullness, agonies, radiant or menacing skies, houses and mountains, seas and lagoons, suns and moons and there are besides all the cries of the subconscious, sensual or chaste, and everything you can imagine . . .[8]

Every project upon which he embarked contains evidence of what he called 'secret labour; of 'profound value'[9] which could be read by those 'with eyes to see'.

Le Corbusier described painting as 'a duel between the artist and himself with the battle taking place within, inside and unknown to the outside world. If the artist relates it he is a traitor to himself'.[10] He told Margaret Tjader Harris that his paintings were made to be read by graphologists, seers or psychiatrists.[11] Like entry into a cult, the experience of art was, for Le Corbusier, one of initiation: 'the mystery is not negligible, is not to be rejected, is not futile. It is the minute of silence in our toil. It awaits the initiate. The initiate is the man of greater strength who will explain . . . one day'.[12] Indeed, he wrote to Edouard Trouin that an 'initiation' was necessary to understand his art properly.[13] 'One understands without words that which is in divine language' responded his client.[14] Significantly Trouin wrote that when Le Corbusier introduced him to this 'plastic sensibility' it awoke in him a consciousness of his own femininity.[15] It is indeed possible that, like the Surrealists, Le Corbusier believed it necessary to establish contact with his feminine muse in order to produce works of inspiration.

Whether his symbolic repertoire was very personal, like that of Jean Cocteau, or whether it was based upon historical discoveries made in the course of his research is not entirely clear. Le Corbusier himself observed that 'there is nothing new under the sun: all things meet again across time and space, a proof of the oneness of human concerns which set men thinking, everywhere, up and down the scale'.[16] Significantly, he made the point that the works of Surrealism were 'very clearly dependent of the products of straightforward conscious effort, sustained and logical, cross checked by the necessary mathematics and geometry'; they were not the arbitrary products of the subconscious that their creators claimed them to be.[17] In his opinion the symbolic language of Surrealism was learnt; it came from books and paintings. His own symbolic language was drawn from similar sources, for example the medieval bestiaries.[18] While being of collective relevance, it also spoke of his personal life and aspirations.

The exploitation of physical response in the pursuit of spiritual change

For Le Corbusier the quest for unity, 'human happiness' would in part be achieved by resolving what he called the 'reason-passion equation', the relationship between body and mind.[19] Art would play a primary role in this process.

As Ozenfant and Le Corbusier were to observe in the pages of L'Esprit Nouveau, 'the complete man is both sensual and cerebral'.[20] Highly conscious of the need to utilise both the instinctual and the intellectual sides of his character, Le Corbusier spent his mornings in his studio painting and dedicated his afternoons to work of a more pragmatic nature, believing that 'the human creative work stands midway between the two poles of the objective and the subjective, a fusion of matter and spirit'.[21] The importance of achieving a balance between mind and body would remain an important theme within his work. For him the 'joys of the body are interdependent with intellectual sensations in a symbolism having strong, sober, even basic roots: physiology and lyricism'.[22]

Le Corbusier expressed an inability to move from representational to abstract art because he needed 'to keep contact with living beings'.[23] As Christopher Green has observed, the architect was 'always willing as figure painter to acknowledge and exploit his sexual responses'.[24] Contained within L'Esprit Nouveau is a series of articles on the relationship between sexuality and art, a theme that was to preoccupy Le Corbusier throughout his career.[25]

Le Corbusier wrote of the ability of a sculpture, flower or fruit to arouse, *émouvoir*.[26] For him painting was a 'miracle' achieved when body and spirit worked in unison.[27] He was very preoccupied with the manner in which the body would respond to art and to architecture. 'I have a body like everyone else, and what I'm interested in is contact with my body, with my eyes, my mind.'[28] He believed that through affecting the feelings at the most base level it was possible to bring about subtle changes in behaviour.[29] In order to do this it was necessary to arouse the body, evoking, if necessary, the female form.

During his Purist period, when he worked in close collaboration with Ozenfant, Le Corbusier usually took simple pure forms as his subject: bottles, jars and so on (Fig. 5.1).[30] At this time the film-maker Jean Epstein went to visit the two artists in their studio. He observed that

> Their pictorial purism was a sort of austere Cubism, traced in a straight line, on a single projection plane. The reverent purist brothers, as they were sometimes known, both equally serious and dressed all in black, in an office where every chair, every board, and every sheet of paper had its strictly determined use, intimidated me terribly.[31]

In spite of the arid atmosphere in which they were conceived, Kenneth Silver observes that the subjects of Ozenfant and Jeanneret's Purist paintings have 'an

Figure 5.1   E. Jeanneret (Le Corbusier), *Nature morte pâle à la lanterne*, 1922.

almost anthropomorphic quality' and even 'an emotive life'.[32] Their love affair with the body is made clear in a passage within the pages of *After Cubism* in which they describe a scene, a possible subject for a painting:

> The wallpaper is quite idiosyncratic and resembles some of Picasso's surfaces; the wood of the table has an interesting matte quality; the sheets of paper give off a rigorously modulated light; the knife gleams, the violin has gentle curves: a classic still life. The potted palm introduces vegetation into the room and the complexity of superior organisms. But the figure is enthroned as queen and reduces the still life to role of décor.
>
> The flesh of the woman's face has a matte quality still more beautiful than that of the wood, the light on her forehead is more beautiful than that on the sheets of paper, the gleam in her eyes is more beautiful than that from the knife.
>
> The human body is organized in accordance with the laws of symmetry as legible as those that determined the construction of the violin; the whole of the room is a lucky anecdote, a fortunate happenstance that would make for a good choice; but a single thing encompasses and exceeds the beauty of the others; the human figure; it is this that promises the highest plastic yield.[33]

Ozenfant and Jeanneret clearly set out their belief in the 'parallel between the analytic methods of science and of art'.[34] They defined a series of laws to which the artist should adhere if the goals of 'harmony' were to be met. These would include 'the mechanism of emotion', beauty, in their belief 'acting like sound waves on a resonator'.[35] 'Anthropocentrism', geometry and the human body were also important themes. Such ideas would have a continuing effect on the work of Le Corbusier long after the two men would cease their relations with one another.

While Le Corbusier continued to create still life paintings following his break with Ozenfant, the simple forms of Purism quickly began to blur together with those of a more figurative and symbolic nature, for example *Femme couchée* of 1929 (Fig.5.2). Included in this painting are a number of what Le Corbusier called 'objects that evoke a poetic reaction', elements that would play an increasingly important part in both

Figure 5.2   Le Corbusier *Femme couchée (Figure rouge)*, 1929.

his art and architecture and key to the resolution of the 'reason passion equation'. Le Corbusier wrote of them in *Talks with Students*:

> I have on occasion used them as themes for my paintings and murals. Through them, characters emerge: male and female, vegetable and mineral, bud and fruit (dawn and noon), every shading (the prism giving off its seven acid colours, or the muted tones of earth, stone, wood), every shape (sphere, cone, and cylinder, and their varied sections). We men and women are plunged in the midst of life. We react with hardened , sharpened sensibilities.[36]

Christopher Pearson has observed that such objects were distributed within Le Corbusier's buildings in order to reinforce their symbolic programme, to highlight, for example, connections between the bodies of women, the earth and the sea.[37] They would also play an important role in the narrative of unity that took place within his painted work.

Geometry

During his long hours as a youth studying in museums, Le Corbusier developed a love for Renaissance art. Thomas Schumacher has written of his fascination with the paintings of Piero della Francesca and the very particular interest that he took in the geometrical layout of his canvases.[38] He would translate such ideas directly into his own painted work. For Le Corbusier, as for Ozenfant, 'everything

can be represented numerically; proportions are the numerical relations constituting a painting. A painting is an equation.'[39] Whilst the subject matter of Le Corbusier's later painted work is very different to that of his Purist phase, it would be created with equal attention to issues of geometry and all that it signified including, as we have seen, the relationships between people and things.

Colour

As within his architecture, over time, colour would gain an increasingly significant role in Le Corbusier's art. Kenneth Silver notes that the palette of the Purist paintings was the same 'Mediterranean palette' that Picasso used for his 'pantheon of classical painters', suggesting that there are clear links between Purism and the classical tradition.[40] More vivid colours would be used with equal care in Le Corbusier's later work. Colour was used both symbolically (blue to signify water, for example) and harmoniously, its strategic use giving an impression of overall unity. Le Corbusier described the colour range that he created for the wallpaper firm Salubra as a 'keyboard . . . each of us will be touched by such or such a harmony'.[41] 'Colour . . . Mister Psychiatrist, is it not an important tool in diagnosis?' he wrote.[42] Colour, it will be seen, could also carry information of a sexual nature. It would contribute to the dialogue of gender taking place within his paintings. 'For me, for twenty years, in my work where colour occupied half of my day, blue commanded me: blue and green in echo'.[43] Both of these colours were for Le Corbusier those of nature and indeed woman.

The artistic representation of women in Le Corbusier's milieu

Whilst little has been written upon the subject, Le Corbusier was evidently influenced by Art Nouveau and the art of the Symbolists prevalent in his youth and a particular influence on L'Eplattenier. For such artists as these, women provided an ideal symbolic vehicle through which to represent their ideas about nature. Ghislaine Wood and Paul Greenhalgh note that 'The positioning of women within the irrational and instinctive realms of nature, and men in the cerebral and intellectual sphere of culture, took on particular resonance in much fin-de-siècle imagery. Naturalist decoration, through the process of metamorphosis, provided a rich area for the depiction of women'. Nature became, in their opinion, 'the site of erotic interchange', a highly loaded subject.[44] Le Corbusier's work must be seen against this very particular backdrop.

Most of the women in his paintings are voluptuous but disturbing. They have the same uncanny quality of women as portrayed by the Symbolists and the Surrealists who took on the Symbolist mantle. In Whitney Chadwick's opinion:

Male Surrealist artists inherited from the late-nineteenth century Symbolists a polarized view of woman embracing both the creative and subversive powers of the love instinct. Simultaneously goddesslike muse and femme fatale, the Surrealist woman was located by the dialectical world view of Hegel and Marx. It was a world view in which the artist could align the polarity of the female with the other contradictions that Surrealists sought to resolve: life and death, the conscious and the unconscious, dream and wakefulness.[45]

Chadwick's description of the male Surrealist viewpoint will be seen to have much in common with that of Le Corbusier.

It has already been mentioned that Le Corbusier was acquainted with the self-proclaimed leader of the Rosicrucians, Sar Péladan. Wood and Greenhalgh observe that for Péladan 'High morality, religious fervour, sexual desire, horror, awe and joy were interchangeable expressions of the spiritual self. In the hands of Rose+Croix artists such as Alphonse Osbert or Alexandre Séon, the Virgin and Aphrodite might fuse or ancient deities might take on a modern form to petrify the bourgeoisie in their urban dwellings.'[46] The poster for the first Rose + Croix salon of 1892 shows two women, one dark haired in a dark dress, the other light haired in a light dress, holding hands. The dark haired woman is holding out a flower to the light haired woman. Looking on from beneath is a water nymph, her hands dripping weed.[47] This type of imagery, involving the juxtaposition of opposing feminine types, would also become prevalent in the architect's work.

Le Corbusier would have been keenly aware of developments in the work of Picasso, whom he

Figure 5.3   Le Corbusier, *Le jugement de Pâris*, 1944.

admired greatly. Silver has documented the development of the female figure in Picasso's work. During the period 1921 and 1924 this was clearly classical in character,[48] his favourite theme being that of *maternité*. Silver notes that this would have been a theme with official sanction at that time because of the need for repopulation.[49] This view is corroborated by Mo Price, who observes the prevalence of the 'maternal subject' in avant-garde art of this period, for example in the work of Fernand Léger, Juan Gris and Gino Severini.[50] Significantly it is a subject that will be seen to be conspicuously rare in the painted work of Le Corbusier.

The implications of representing women in particular ways would almost certainly have been a subject of discussion for Le Corbusier and Ozenfant, who had already discussed within *L'Elan*, the journal that he worked on before he joined ranks with Le Corbusier, the ways in which the female form could be used to represent the aspirations and feelings of a nation. Le Corbusier was to explore this issue in the 1944 painting *Le jugement de Pâris* (Fig. 5.3). Here he appears to play on a classical theme in order to create a representation of an episode that took place before his eyes during the Liberation, one that he recounted in *When the Cathedrals were White*, a very literal judgement of Paris, the city represented by its women.[51] When the American soldiers drove into the city in their armoured cars and trucks the Parisian women climbed up to kiss the soldiers in gratitude. Unused to such impulsive acts of gaiety the American soldiers promptly mistook them for prostitutes. This was the judgement of Paris. The painting is divided into two: one side dark, containing the enigmatic dark figure of a man on a chariot, the other light, depicting naked women, talking together, hands on hips, the archetypal pose of prostitutes touting for business. A further example of what Le Corbusier believed to be repressed American attitudes to sex, on this occasion Americans found Europe 'indecent'. Paris was liberated in August 1944. The date of this painting, also 1944, lends credence to this theory. Whilst the painting is an attack on American prurience, its message could also be one of woman's need to express herself freely without being judged. In using woman to symbolise a nation, Le Corbusier was conforming to a standard topos in French art, one that Silver explores extensively in is book *Esprit de Corps*.

The depiction of women would also have been a likely topic of conversation between Le Corbusier and Léger, who became a good friend of his during the 1920s. The 'artistic alchemy' of Léger's work would be celebrated by Le Corbusier and Ozenfant in an article in *L'Esprit Nouveau*.[52] Charlotte Perriand was to reminisce that, while working in Le Corbusier's office, she, Léger and Le Corbusier would go beach combing in search of material for their paintings.[53] It seems that Le Corbusier learnt a great deal from the artist.

In the opinion of Mo Price, Léger set himself the task of extricating any erotic associations from his representations of the female form. She writes that when Léger arrived in New York in 1935 to promote an exhibition there, a headline appeared in the *New York Herald Tribune* on 5 October: 'Léger advises Painters Not To Use Beautiful Women as their Models'.[54] He explained in the report that 'A painter should not try to reproduce a beautiful thing, but should make the painting itself a beautiful thing'. Price observes that the representation of woman became a real conundrum for Léger 'Locked into a system of conventional ideas about beauty, this motif inevitably interfered with – indeed competed against – the machine aesthetic's concept of beauty making it especially difficult to redraw the lines'.[55] In her opinion Léger acknowledged 'the disruptive effect of traditional constructs of femininity within his aesthetic scheme'.[56] My suggestion is that Le Corbusier too would have been fully aware of the implications of representing women in particular ways.

Women of the East

No discussion of the representation of women in early twentieth-century Paris would be complete without addressing the issue of the odalisque, the woman of the East, the passive battlefield over which different artists fought to assert the supremacy of their representational ideas and values.[57] It has already been seen that Le Corbusier was particularly interested in the women of cultures other than his own. From comments made in *Journey to the East* it quickly becomes evident that the hidden possibilities that lay beneath the drapes of Moslem women provided ample fuel for his imagination

During his 1931 trip to Algiers Le Corbusier was intrigued by the beauty of two girls, one Spanish the other Algerian, whom he sketched both singly and grouped together on 'schoolbook graph paper', possibly because of his interest in proportion.[58] He also acquired a number of postcards showing scantily dressed native women. Colomina makes the point that 'the Algerian sketches and postcards are a rather ordinary instance of the ingrained mode of a fetishistic appropriation of women, of the east, of "the other"'.[59] As Zeynep Celik notes, he was undoubtedly 'immersed in the discourse that attributed a lascivious sexuality to Islamic culture', a standard element of the French colonial view of Algiers at that time.[60] However, I believe that Le Corbusier's approach to the East was not as 'ordinary' as all that. Sibel Bozdoğan observes that the young Le Corbusier is not 'the proud agent of Western civilisation in search of self affirmation in the contrasting image of the alien and the exotic'.[61] It is her belief that he approached the East with an open mind 'his experiential sketches and scribbles, irreducible to pure representation and resistant to consumption as imagery, are informed by what we can call critical inquiry – an exploratory rather than expository task'.[62] His sketches of women were made in an effort to understand rather than objectify them. Romy Golan too notes that while certain of his paintings, especially those developed from postcard imagery, are orientalist in sensibility, others indicate a shift away from this: 'the elaborate corsets, décolletées, and exotic paraphernalia are discarded in favour of a focus on the unadorned body'.[63] It is her belief that Le Corbusier came to such images through his studies of fisherwomen in Arachon rather than through the Orient. Things other than colonialist superiority were uppermost in his mind as he drew.

Le Corbusier made a number of studies after the *Women of Algier* by Delacroix,[64] in Von Moos' opinion the definitive version being one of the murals at Eileen Gray's house.[65] Price writes that 'traditionally, the odalisque signified an erotic, narcissistic, decorative creature of display and the motif continued to function as an object of masculine desire, even when, as in the case of Matisse's contemporary re-framings, it was critically discussed in an expedient post-war rhetoric of sobriety and French colonialism'.[66] Léger too was to play with the odalisque theme in *Le Grand Déjeuner* 1921, bringing to it his particular view of the notion of beauty. Women artists, fully aware of the loaded nature of the subject, would also give it their own particular interpretation. Jacqueline Marval, for example, played down the erotic in her painting *Les Odalisques* 1902–3, admired by Apollinaire.[67] It is not so much the subject, but the treatment of the subject that is key for this discussion. While there is no doubt that Le Corbusier was certainly fascinated by the idea of 'divine, thrilling odalisques ... suffocated from waiting so long in their magnificent cages',[68] his images of women are paradoxical, talking simultaneously of eroticism and women's repression.[69]

While on his 'Journey to the East' Le Corbusier, posed for a photograph disguised as an odalisque, next to his friend Klipstein as a Pacha (Fig. 5.4). The question is whether this photograph was intended as a schoolboy prank or an ironic presentation of this deeply loaded subject.[70] In my view the latter is likely to be the case. A number of images of swathed Moslem women appear in *The Radiant City* under the title 'Witnesses: the "Barbarians" speak' used with evident irony (Fig. 5.5).[71] It is my suggestion that Le Corbusier actually felt some sympathy for these women desiring for them, as he did for women of his own society, a new degree of liberation.

In one of his 1939 paintings, *Les deux mouquères d'Alger*, one woman appears shrouded, her eyes wide and frightened (Fig. 5.6). The other, perhaps her alter ego, bare and painted, stares insolently, aggressively and possibly provocatively at the viewer. As Le Corbusier wrote in *Precisions*, 'the important sign is ... in the eyes'.[72] This painting could be interpreted in a number of ways. It could be Le Corbusier's fantasy of the women behind the veil, or it could be a statement of protest against the veil, one that would fit in with

Figure 5.4   Photograph of Le Corbusier and August Klipstein, with Le Corbusier as the odalisque.

O inspiring image!
Arabs, are there no peoples but you who meditate daily in the splendid sunset hours? Sky, sea and mountains. Beatitudes of space. The power of eyes and mind carries far.

See how, in the European city, the "civilized" people are holed up like rats in the deafening straits of stone!

O inspiring image!
Arabs, are there no peoples but you who dwell in coolness and quiet, in the enchantment of proportions and the savor of a humane architecture?

While the street is a channel of violent movement, your houses know nothing of it: they have closed the walls which face the street. It is within the walls that life blooms.

the key	= the cell
	= men
	= happiness

The street is only the bed for the rushing stream of passers-by.

O inspiring image! Arabs, you are at home within the hospitable and charming house, so clean, so measured, ample and intimate.

Figure 5.5   Photographs of Arab women from Le Corbusier, *The Radiant City*, 1935.

Figure 5.6   Le Corbusier, *Les deux mouquères d'Alger*, 1939.

Figure 5.7   Detail from Le Corbusier, mural Swiss Pavilion, Paris, 1948.

his ideas about the liberation of women through their clothes. It is also a statement of the contradictions that he perceived beneath Algerian society. Such is the complexity of Le Corbusier's thought that it would seem likely that all three interpretations are in some way true.

Mo Price notes that research by Peter Wollen, Kenneth Silver, Romy Golan, Tag Gronberg and others has:

> firmly established the ground for the idea that certain tendencies within French taste – in particular, a passion for the decorative, the exotic, the Oriental – were associated by conservatives with notions of seduction, excess and indulgence and cast both as 'feminine' and unpatriotic: these 'foreign' traits were regarded as threatening to the true (classical) spirit of France – which confusingly, was also usually symbolised as a woman (often in the guise of a maternal figure as 'guardian of the hearth') thus indicating the currency of belief in ambivalent femininities.[73]

It will be seen that in the work of Le Corbusier women straddle the boundary identified by Price. They are exotic, but retain the symbolic ability to represent, not so much the classical tradition, but the Orphic Pythagorean tradition, with its strong links to the East and to a 'purer' past.

The emergence of the numinous woman in Le Corbusier's painted work

A close study of Le Corbusier's painted work reveals the emergence of a number of themes that suggest a growing belief in the importance of engaging with woman and the feminine in order to gain access to the divine. Intimately linked to the role of woman in the life of man, versions of four of these: *Ubu*, *La cathédrale de Sens*, *Icône* and the Siren would be brought together by Le Corbusier in the mural that he painted at the Swiss Pavilion in Paris in 1948 (Fig. 5.7).[74] Before the mural, like an altar, stands a marble table like a Roman cartibulum, waiting for some offering.[75] For Le Corbusier woman was a subject worthy of worship. What follows is an exploration of this aspect of his work.

Union of Opposites

I have already discussed the fact that Le Corbusier saw his work as an artist as a means by which to attain his

Figure 5.8 Le Corbusier, *Deux figures, soleil et lune*, 1928.

Figure 5.9 Le Corbusier, *Divinité marine*, 1933.

Figure 5.10
Le Corbusier,
*Composition
spirale
logarithmique
(Composition figure
d'homme)*, 1929.

Figure 5.11 Le Corbusier, *Sculpture et nu*, 1929.

Figure 5.12
Le Corbusier, *La Lanterne
et le petit haricot*, 1930.

Figure 5.13
Le Corbusier, *Nature morte
géométric*, 1930.

desired state of Orphic unity. In his 1928 painting *Deux figures, soleil et lune* he depicted a man and a woman as if joined, a version of the classical alchemical union of opposites (Fig. 5.8)[76] a theme that would recur in his work – for example, in the 1933 painting *Divinité marine* (Fig. 5.9). Here the figures are flanked by two circles, one light and one dark, sun and moon, masculine and feminine in alchemical terms.

Even during his Purist phase Le Corbusier had been fascinated by mathematics and proportion. All his canvases are carefully composed, and mathematical forms like that celebrated in *Composition spirale logarithmique* (1929) (Fig. 5.10) appear and reappear. It has already been seen that he enjoyed playing with what he called the marriage of lines, the contrast between curved and rectilinear forms, for example in *Sculpture et nu* (1929), (Fig. 5.11) and in *La Lanterne et le petit haricot* (1930), (Fig. 5.12) where a sharded crystalline form contrasts with the curved glass beside it. This theme is repeated in another 1930 painting *Nature morte géométric* (Fig. 5.13) and becomes an important characteristic of his work during the early 1930s, most specifically in the series entitled *Harmonique périlleuse* which appears to culminate in the 1931 painting *Nature morte à la bohémienne (à Von)*, (Fig. 5.14).

Hovering at the top of this canvas are two organic stone or bonelike forms.[77] If Richard Moore is to be believed, Le Corbusier used stones as a form of self-portrait, representing imperfect base matter.[78] This means that the painting is actually another version of the union of opposites, this time that between the artist and Yvonne, whose face appears on the one on the left. It is associated with the curving cross visible below the horizon line of the painting. This form (Fig. 5.15) reappears in the Milieu section of *The Poem of the Right Angle* above the following words:

> Erect on the terrestrial plane
> Of things knowable you
> Sign a pact of solidarity
> With nature: this is the right angle
> Vertical facing the sea
> There you are on your feet[79]

Beneath the words are two footprints facing one another. One large like a man's and one smaller, like that of a woman.

Beneath the two hovering shapes is a pentagon. The pentacle form found in the cross section of an apple was based on the symbol of the earth goddess Kore and was worshipped by the Pythagorean

Figure 5.14   Le Corbusier, *Nature morte à la bohémienne (à Von)*, 1931.

Figure 5.15   Detail from Le Corbusier, *Le Poème de l'angle droit*, A3, Milieu.

mystics. Whilst the exact meaning of this intriguing painting remains obscure, it evidently suggests that Le Corbusier displays a continuing thread of interest in the links between woman and man, the union of opposites, revelation, harmony and nature.

Nature morte à la bohémienne (àVon) would seem to have a particular relationship with the following highly significant quotation taken from the *Modulor*:

> The spirit of geometry produces tangible shapes, expressions of architectural realities: upright walls, perceptible surfaces between four walls, the right angle, hallmark of balance and stability. I call it *spirit under the sign of the set-square*, and my description is confirmed by the traditional name of 'allantica' given to Mediterranean architectural art, for *allantica* means antique, based on the set-square.
>
> Or else the sprit of geometry produces brilliant diagrams, radiating out in all directions, or folded in upon themselves in triangles or other polygons, source of spatial amplitude as of subjective and abstract symbols. I call it spirit under the sign of the triangle and the pentagon, star-shaped or convex, and of their volumetric derivations: the icosahedron and the dodecahedron. Architecture under the sign of the triangle, called during the Renaissance '*allagermanica*'.
>
> In the one, strong objectivity of forms, under the intense light of a Mediterranean sun: *male* architecture. In the other, limitless subjectivity rising against a clouded sky: *female* architecture . . . I believe it to be natural that an inner law should animate the work created by a human being.[80]

Le Corbusier's creations would be animated by this 'inner law'. It is, in a sense, a law of nature. Within this quote Le Corbusier makes his fascination with the idea of architecture and, indeed, art as a manifestation of the relationship between the sexes totally explicit.

Woman and the sea

Le Corbusier had already begun to dwell upon the subject of woman and water as early as 1912, for example in one of his pre Purist gouaches *Femmes sur la plage* (Fig. 5.16). It was a theme that he would develop further in the 1920s. Pearson notes that 'Le Corbusier often made a conceptual association of

women with large bodies of water' hence their frequent juxtaposition in his painted work. He would also introduce paintings and sculptures of women into waterside positions within a building, as was seen in the mural paintings of Eileen Gray's E.1027 on the shores of the Mediterranean.[81] A similar effect would be achieved nearby in Le Corbusier's Cabanon where the inner linings of the shutters are adorned with female figures. They would thus replace the view of the sea, with which they were intimately linked, when the shutters were closed (Fig. 5.17).[82]

It was during the early 1930s that Le Corbusier began to experiment with the combined themes of woman, ropes and boats. It is my belief that this thread in his work has a specifically Christian underpinning, reflecting his burgeoning interest in the roots of religion. He would have known of Christ in the

Figure 5.16   Le Corbusier (Charles Edouard Jeanneret), *Femmes sur la plage,* 1912.

Figure 5.17   Cabanon, interior of shutter.

symbol of the fish from a very large and impressive volume that resides within his collection of books, *Les Catacombes de Rome: Histoire de l'art et des croyances religieuses pendant les premiers siècles du Christianisme.*[83] Given his evident interest in symbolism, he would have been fully aware of the connection between the boat, the womb, Mary and many other pagan goddesses.

Woman and the shell

Le Corbusier's fascination with shells is no secret. He observed:

> I have had a weakness for seashells ever since I was a boy. There is nothing as beautiful as a seashell. It is based on the law of harmony, and the idea behind it is very simple. It develops in a spiral or it rays out, both in the interior and exterior. You can find these objects everywhere. The point is to see them, to observe them. They contain the laws of nature and that is the best instruction.[84]

In *Le Corbusier before Le Corbusier* Françoise Ducros gives three examples of the way in which he linked woman with the cockleshell in a number of paintings dating back to 1917, including a reworking of Boticelli's *Birth*

of *Venus.*[85] According to traditions of symbolism the shell came to represent Venus who, in turn, was linked to Mary Magdalene – a figure of great importance to Le Corbusier, as we will see in the next chapter.[86]

In a 1928 painting *Le Déjeuner au phare* (Fig. 5.18) the sun is seen above the horizon and the moon as a plate with a sickle shadow. Connections with the feminine sea, perhaps the most potent symbol of Le Corbusier's oeuvre, begin to appear, not only with the lighthouse but also with the hand-like shell, a specifically feminine symbol[87] with interesting links to another 1928 painting *Pêcheuse d'huîtres* (Fig. 5.19), the first of a fisherwoman series. It was in this year that, according to Richard Moore, Le Corbusier started to symbolise 'aesthetic matters of vision through a representation of the water balance in the inner ear which, combined with the open hand, represented the giving and receiving of sound'. The use of realistic anatomical detail of the inner ear dissolved into a representation of the womb of the 'archetypal woman', her fertility tied to the tides, and thus to the moon.[88] Le Corbusier cast his associations back to ancient symbolic traditions in which the sea, moon, women and water are firmly linked. Such was his interest in the subject that he even ruminated on the way in which women's menstrual cycles were governed by its cycles.[89]

Figure 5.18   Le Corbusier, *Le Déjeuner au phare*, 1928.

Figure 5.19   Le Corbusier, *Pêcheuse d'huîtres,* 1928.

Woman and music

With 1926 began another important thread in Le Corbusier's painted work, that of women and music, exemplified by the work *Joueuse d'accordéon* (Fig. 5.20). The link of woman with music harks back to an image included in *L'Esprit Nouveau* of a naked woman sitting on a chair in a verdant place playing the lute. The caption reads 'Nature' (Fig. 5.21).[90] It is my thesis that Le Corbusier believed women to have a special role in the propagation of harmony, giving men access to nature. The woman with the accordion forms part of this tradition, as do the many women who dance through his canvases, for example those in *Deux Danseuses et banderolles* of 1940 (Fig. 5.22). Richard Moore observed that for Le Corbusier 'the female figure is an incarnate acoustical symbol in the curving and expansive, resonant mobility of her archetypal form'.[91]

Le Corbusier returned to the theme of the lighthouse in 1929 with his painting *La Fille du gardien de phare* (Fig. 5.23). Her presence is strong and totemic: her face like a mask to the right of the canvas; her staring eyes mesmerising. Next to her there are musical instruments, linking her back to nature and to numerical harmony, as do the shells and spirals that inhabit the canvas elsewhere, the end of the violin

Nature

Figure 5.21   Image included in Jeanneret and Ozenfant's *L'Esprit Nouveau* 19 entitled *Nature*.

Figure 5.20   Le Corbusier *Joueuse d'accordéon*, 1926.

Figure 5.22   Le Corbusier, *Deux Danseuses et banderolles*, 1940.

Figure 5.23   Le Corbusier, *La Fille du gardien de phare*, 1929.

transmuting into one such organic form. The theme – the lighthouse – gives a clue as to the meaning of the painting: light being linked with inspiration and the divine in Le Corbusier's mind. It is also highly likely that he would have been aware of the phallic masculine attributes of the lighthouse form. Once again, at base level, the subject of the canvas appears to be the union of opposites, the staring lighthouse keeper's daughter forming part of a tradition of uncanny all seeing and sinister females that populate Le Corbusier's canvases. They evoke the wild uncontrollable side of nature that often seems so far removed from his harmonious vision.[92]

All seeing woman

The large eyes of the women that inhabit Le Corbusier's canvases suggest some uncanny and other-worldly knowledge, a particular case being *La Femme à la Cléopâtre* (1937) where his subject, the woman, takes on something of the air of an Egyptian deity (Fig. 5.24). This theme is continued in *L'Horreur surgit* of 1940 (Fig. 5.25), a very disturbing painting suggesting some deep depression on Le Corbusier's part, its date, at the very beginning of the war, giving it a particular poignancy. Mogens Krustrup believes that this painting has an interpretation that is very personal to Le Corbusier. He sees it as an image of Yvonne sitting in a doorframe with a second person lying before her with his head on her knees. Krustrup's theory is that the second figure is Le Corbusier, in spite of its 'feminine character'.[93] Either way, the painting seems to indicate a crisis point in

Figure 5.24   Le Corbusier, *La Femme à la Cléopâtre*, 1937.

Le Corbusier's life, which indeed it was, his brief flirtation with the Vichy regime leaving him disillusioned and disgraced.

Ubu

Le Corbusier retreated to Ozon, where he continued to work, paint and think, a period of isolation which, as has already been mentioned in an earlier chapter, Yvonne found very difficult. His paintings of this period have a peculiarly rough and abstract quality (perhaps because of the poor availability of art materials). It was during this time that he worked on the Ubu series. Ubu was a figure of indeterminate sex, the brainchild of Alfred Jarry, the 'progenitor' of Dadaism, who wrote 'absurdist' plays and novels at the turn of the century. These revolved around the 'grotesquely vulgar, scatologically inclined' figure of Père Ubu[94] with whom Le Corbusier seems to have identified. The Ubu form (Fig. 5.26) also seems to include elements of Yvonne as she is depicted in the painting *Vonvon* of 1943 (Fig. 5.27). *Ubu bois* (1944) is crowned with a horizontal mask that appears in the early work *Composition spirale logarithmique* of 1929 with which the Ubus seem to have some kinship (Fig.

Figure 5.25 Le Corbusier, *L'Horreur surgit*, 1940.

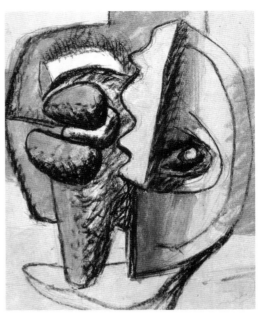

Figure 5.26 Le Corbusier, *Ubu forms*, pastel on paper, ca. 1940.

5.10). Von Moos writes that the role of these masks is to reveal instinctual and demoniac reflexes.[95] There would seem to be some truth in this suggestion as Le Corbusier came to associate Ubu with Rabelais' creation Panurge, both trickster and teacher.

Panurge was to remain such a significant a figure for Le Corbusier that in 1961 he became the subject of a series of lithographs.[96] Alice Gray Read has traced the development of the Ubu figure in the architect's work from a series of early sketches in 1946 to the redefined Ubu Panurge of the 1960s. In her opinion he exemplifies what she calls 'an embodiment of the guts of human presence':

> the Ubus strike a blow against idealist thinking. His forebears: Père Ubu, L'Eternal, the inverse cripple, Panurge and Obus are material beings that each in turn parody, dismember, lampoon and explore the 'higher' ideals of a platonic intellect as Zarathustra denied a transcendent God.[97]

Figure 5.27 Le Corbusier, *Vonvon*, 1943.

In Le Corbusier's late work the mouth of Ubu Panurge is open 'as if to speak', as Gray Read puts it. He has knowledge to give if we can only hear. Given that similarity in form between the Ubu paintings and *Vonvon* it appears that Le Corbusier is here making connections between Ubu and his Rabelaisian, trickster wife who seems to have seen it as her role to prevent Le Corbusier from becoming too serious and idealistic.

La Cathédrale de Sens

A 1931 canvas, *Saint Sulpice* (Fig. 5.28) appears, as its name suggests, to depict the interior of a building, at once in plan and in cross section. The theme of this painting appears to be developed in *Nature morte à la cathédrale de Sens* (Fig. 5.29) in its bipartite format and cross hatching. In this 1940 painting one side is devoted to a network of geometrical lines, the other to amorphous shellfish forms, a clear rendition of the union of opposites. Its title refers to the cathedral of Sens, a town in the Bourgogne area of France, halfway between Paris and Dijon. Whilst it has a cathedral, there would seem to be no special reason for its important role in Le Corbusier's symbolic repertoire beyond its name, 'sens' meaning senses. It is my suggestion that, with his usual fondness for wordplay, it is Le Corbusier's intention to blur two meanings *la*

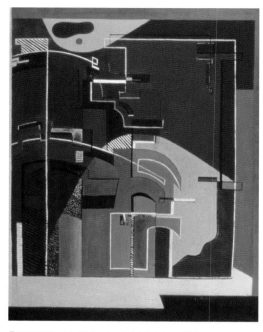

Figure 5.28   Le Corbusier, *Saint Sulpice*, 1931.

Figure 5.29   Le Corbusier, *Nature morte à la Cathédrale de Sens, 1940.*

Figure 5.30   Le Corbusier, *Portrait de femme à la cathédrale de Sens (l'ange gardien du foyer II),* 1944.

cathédrale de Sens, the cathedral of Sens and *la cathédrale des Sens*, the cathedral of the Senses.

This painting is connected, very largely through its name, to another painting, *Portrait de femme à la Cathédrale de Sens (l'ange gardien du foyer II)* of 1944 (Fig. 5.30). Early in the war Le Corbusier had made a sketch of Yvonne sitting at a table with a glass, with her hands before her. This image finds its way into the foreground of the 'Cathedral of the senses' painting. The link to Yvonne, 'the guardian angel of the hearth', is made clear in the title. Behind her the canvas is given depth. It is as though her body is the cathedral and she is the guardian of that space. Horizontally beneath her hands is seen what looks like the chamfered side of a door, reinforcing the idea that the painting is the depiction of a point of entry. The words 'cathedral', suggestive of spirituality and 'senses', suggestive of something very different, contain a message that I believe to be at the heart of Le Corbusier's philosophy, that of the need to engage with the spirit through the body, in partic-ular the body of woman. The underlying theme and form of this painting would be translated into the *Icône* series, making explicit the links that Le Corbusier per-ceived between woman and the divine.

Siren

The eminent historian Emile Mâle wrote of twelfth century representations of a centaur with a siren in which the siren was not represented as a woman fish but as a woman bird, 'a tradition long followed by the Bestiaries'.[98] He described the siren as a 'tradition of antiquity, for the Greeks never represented sirens in any other way'. She was borrowed by the Greeks from the art of Egypt as a means to symbolise the soul separated from the body, the relationship of the two being a preoccupation of Orphism.[99] Apollinaire linked the siren with Orpheus in two verses of his *Le Bestiaire ou Cortège d'Orphée*.[100] According to Provensal, Plato believed that the soul had an important role in mediating between the terrestrial and the divine.[101] She can be seen, as if copied from a Greek vase paint-ing, in the pages of one of Le Corbusier's sketchbooks (Fig. 5.31);[102] indeed, she occupied an important role in his painted work. In 1946 he drew a series of sketches of the siren, the woman bird, entitled 'Protect my wing in your hand'[103] (Fig. 5.32), studies for the eventual cover of *Poésie sur Alger*.[104] In one version Le Corbusier drew the image on top of a collage made out of newspaper cuttings. One cutting, deliberately ripped, was from a section devoted to woman's hair-styles (Fig 5.33). It is as though Le Corbusier was making a connection between the role of the siren and that of modern woman.[105] Given Mâle's inter-pretation of the woman bird, it is in fact, a depiction of a hand sheltering the soul, the wings symbolic of its connection with the heavens. The hand is encour-aging the soul to act as an intermediary between body and spirit.[106] Such is the role that Le Corbusier envi-sioned for woman in the life of modern man.

Taureau/Icône

Whilst on holiday in Cap Martin during the summer of 1952 Le Corbusier made a number of studies of the bull, *Taureau*.[107] 'One fine day the discovery of a bull on my canvases came to light quite out of my control' he wrote.[108] The horned head of the *Taureau* series of paintings emerges out of the 1952 painting *Métamorphose du violon* (Fig. 5.34), a clear melding together of orphic themes, the horned head of Dionysus and the musical instrument. In such paint-ings as *Taureau 1* (Fig. 5.35) the bull can be read as male or female, or both, the opposing dark and light circles at the heart of the painting simultaneously reading as breasts and/or the sun and moon, to be seen in Le Corbusier's earlier paintings. Testicles and penis appear in stylised opposition to the breasts

Figure 5.31   Le Corbusier, sketch of siren.

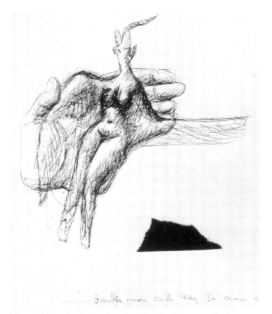

Figure 5.32 Le Corbusier, sketch, 'Gardez mon aile dans ta main', 1946.

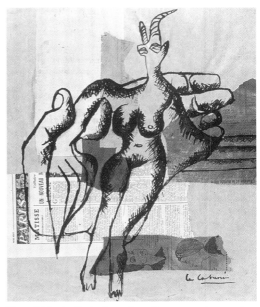

Figure 5.33 Le Corbusier, collage, *Femme cornée avec des ailes*.

Figure 5.34 Le Corbusier, *Métamorphose du violon*, 1952.

Figure 5.35 Le Corbusier, *Taureau 1*, 1952.

Figure 5.36 Le Corbusier, *Taureau IV*, 1959.

creating an androgynous whole. By the emergence of *Taureau IV* (Fig. 5.36) the woman is clearly horned like her sister the siren.

Le Corbusier wrote of the development of the *Taureaux* paintings that they were intimately connected to his relationship with his wife:[109]

> These *Taureaux* = total and intimate confession Corbu-Yvonne my constant, sick, dying, dead wife = the *Taureaux*!! Incitement! From whom? Subconscious acts! Yes. Divinings, uplifting of the heart and spirit. Yes![110]

Together they formed a unit 'Corbu-Yvonne', like that described by Plato, their lives and fates entirely intertwined.

The year 1955 saw the beginnings of the *Icône* series (Fig. 5.37), one that quickly merged with that of the *Taureau*, the 'icon' herself being based on the aforementioned 'cathedral of the senses' paintings. It is no coincidence that the birth of this series coincided with the serious deterioration of Yvonne's health. She is the icon at the heart of Le Corbusier's work, the focus of the 'iconostasis' of *Le Poème de l'angle droit*, The Poem of the Right Angle.

Figure 5.37   Le Corbusier, *Icône 1,* 1955.

The Poem of the Right Angle, 1947–1953

Le Corbusier wrote of *The Poem of the Right Angle* that it contained matters that were not only at the base of his character but were also at the bottom of his work whether built or painted.[111] A combination of paintings and text, Le Corbusier arranged the key, or contents page of *The Poem* into what he called an iconostasis, a sequence of panels in the form of a tree (Fig 5.38). In *Journey to the East* he wrote of an 'intoxicating' iconostasis that he saw in a church that 'shone twenty-nine icons from their golden heavens and the halos of their saints'.[112] Traditionally the iconostasis was linked to the icons of Christ and Mary; Le Corbusier's own version appears to allude to his love for Yvonne who is depicted in the guise of Icône at its centre.[113] The exact meaning of *The Poem of the Right Angle*, a 'pact of solidarity' with nature, still remains very unclear although it has been subjected to much scrutiny from Krustup, Becket Chary and others.[114] Each layer, like each stage in the alchemical process, is allied to a particular colour and theme. In this analysis I will dwell in particular upon layers, C 'Flesh', D 'Fusion' and E 'Character' as these, I believe, specifically address the issue of man's relationship to woman.

The iconostasis has seven layers. Given his evident interest in the subject it seems likely that Le Corbusier used Pythagorean number symbolism in the way in which he structured *The Poem*.[115] The eminent historian Louis Réau wrote, with reference to the numerological laws of the medieval cathedral builders, that seven was a number that was 'particularly august'.[116] It could be obtained by adding three, symbolic of the Trinity, and four, symbolic of earthly concerns (such as the seasons and the elements). Thus it was expressive of the relationship between the earth and sky, body and spirit – the right angle, as Le Corbusier called it. Seven could also be significant because it refers to the number of colours in the spectrum,[117] as well as the seven notes of the musical scale and indeed the seven strings of the lyre of Orpheus.[118] According to the art historian Émile Mâle:

> The number seven, regarded by the fathers as mysterious above all others, intoxicated the mediaeval

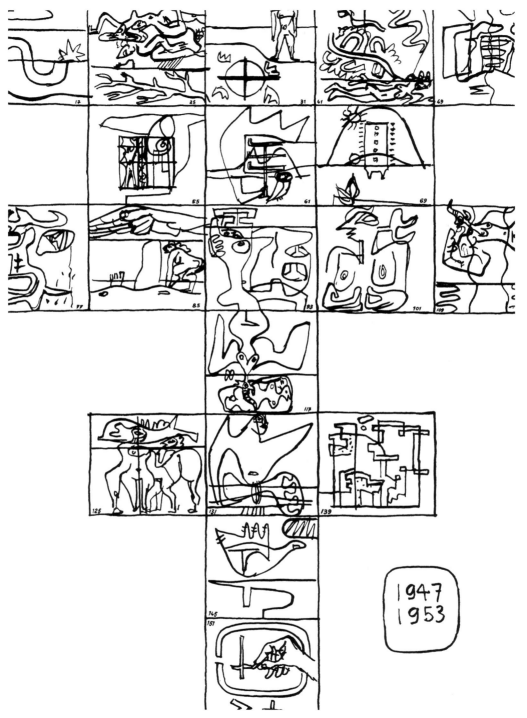

Figure 5.38   Iconostasis from Le Corbusier's *The Poem of the Right Angle.*

mystic. It was observed first of all that seven – composed of four, the number of the body, and of three, the number of the soul – is pre-eminently the number of humanity, and expresses the union of man's double nature . . . The number seven thus expresses the harmony of man's nature, but it also expresses the harmonious relation of man to the universe. The seven planets govern human destiny, for each of the seven ages is under the influence of one of them. Thus seven invisible threads connect man with the scheme of the universe.[119]

The number seven thus represented the order of the universe and the union of body and spirit, one of the central themes of *The Poem*.

At the top of the iconostasis layer A, 'Milieu' consists of five squares corresponding to the five squares on the third level down, C, devoted to the theme of 'Flesh'. 'Milieu' is a complex word expressive of nature in its raw, original, sense. 'Environment' is not an adequate translation of this term. Both 'Milieu' and 'Flesh' have five squares. According to Réau, in Christian art the number five corresponded to the five senses.[120] This would seem to be appropriate if Le Corbusier was trying to emphasise the links between these layers and the body. Layer B, in between 'Milieu' and 'Flesh', which is devoted to 'Spirit', has three squares corresponding, as Réau would have it, to the Trinity. The top three layers of *The Poem of the Right Angle* are thus devoted numerically to the relationship of spirit and matter, as is the whole iconostasis through the use of the number seven.[121]

One square is allotted to each of the layers devoted specifically to the cause of unity: 'Fusion' an image of the alchemical union of opposites; 'Offering', an image of Le Corbusier's symbol of the 'Open Hand', signifying giving and receiving of love and 'Instrument' into which the whole *Poem* is summarised. According to Réau the number one was, for the medieval builders, symbolic of unity and of God.[122] By giving each of these layers just one square Le Corbusier emphasised their importance. Thus, through the use of number symbolism, the architect used the structure of the iconostasis to reinforce its message, that of the coming together of the spirit and the flesh in the pursuit of the divine. Woman would

play a vital role in this process. Hence perhaps his concerted effort to send copies of *The Poem of the Right Angle* to so many of his women friends.[123]

Le Corbusier was profoundly influenced by Adolf Loos' well-known essay 'Ornament and Crime' (1908) in which he affirmed his belief that decoration was primitive and amoral:

> The first ornament that was born, the cross, was erotic in origin. The first work of art, the first artistic act which the first artist, in order to rid himself of his surplus energy, smeared on the wall. A horizontal dash; the prone woman. A vertical dash: the man penetrating her. The man who created it felt the same urge as Beethoven, he was in the same heaven in which Beethoven created the Ninth Symphony.[124]

The Poem retains a vestigial trace of this, man's 'first work of art'.

Sun and sea, man and woman

On the first page of *The Poem* Le Corbusier writes of the influence of the sun in the life of 'our' earth. In Fig. 5.39, Le Corbusier's body is shown as a rocky landscape extending out into the sea. The image, based on an experience Le Corbusier had of his body as an archipelago in a bath in a hotel room in London in 1953,[125] serves to blur the difference between the earth and the body, a central theme of the poem. The sun brings life to the earth as the sun, spirit and light bring life to the body.[126] Each is subject to natural laws that rule throughout the cosmos.

Figure 5.39   Detail from 'milieu' section of Le Corbusier's *The Poem of the Right Angle*.

Having discussed the role of the sun, Le Corbusier moves on to a discussion of the sea, 'daughter of droplets and mother of vapours'.[127] In *The Radiant City* Le Corbusier wrote of the relationship of sun and water, man and woman and of the way in which each could not exist without the other. Here, whilst ostensibly writing of the water cycle, of the patterns in nature, he is also commenting on the interdependence of man and woman.

Flesh

The reliance of man and woman on each other is explicitly addressed in layer C of the iconostasis.

> Woman always somewhere
> At crossroads proves
> That love is a question of fate
> Of number and chance
> Where the accidental even
> Inexorable meeting of two roads is suddenly marked
> With amazing joy.[128]

Woman is 'always somewhere at crossroads'. She plays a fundamental role in the uniting of the 'two roads', the vertical and the horizontal, the result being 'amazing joy'.[129] Le Corbusier made an image of a woman's face with a version of the right angle superimposed suggesting her fundamental role in the process of which he is writing (Fig. 5.40), although her face is anything but joyful.[130]

Within section C3, at the centre of the layer devoted to 'Flesh', Le Corbusier describes the loving relationship between the hand and the seashell. The text is accompanied by a drawing of a seashell that metamorphoses, first into intertwined hands, and then into the hands of a woman, one holding her own breast and the other reaching out towards the reader. The text is breathless and excited. Unlike any other part of *The Poem* it comes in short staccato bursts, suggestive of arousal. The subject paradoxically is God incarnate, in the flesh, a peculiar blurring of the sexual, the spiritual and the mathematical.

In what we are speaking of here
An absolute sublime accomplishment
Intervenes it is the harmony
Of tense the penetration of
Forms proportion – the ineffable
In the end precludes
the control
of
reason
carried beyond
all
diurnal
reality
admitted
to the heart
of an
illumination
God
incarnate
in
the illusion
the perception
of truth
perhaps
indeed.[131]

Figure 5.40   Detail from the 'characters' section of Le Corbusier's *The Poem of the Right Angle*.

This passage is of immense importance in drawing together a number of themes. God incarnate, in the 'flesh' literally, appears as 'illumination', light upon the penetration of two forms in harmony, a not so covert allusion to the sexual act. In the right conditions for Le Corbusier this could be the source of a profound enlightenment, but in order 'to attend ones own wedding' it would be necessary to be 'down to earth' and 'alert'.[132]

Like the Greek goddess Baubo, the women of the 'Flesh' section appear to perceive the truth of nature in the most instinctual way, through their erect nipples. The tension between spirituality and eroticism expressed in Le Corbusier's writing is perfectly embodied in Bernini's famous altarpiece in Sta Maria della Vittoria in Rome (circa 1644), in which Saint Teresa of Avila can be seen in a state of religious ecstasy. A discussion took place in pages of L'Esprit Nouveau on the exact nature of her experience and whether indeed Bernini's sculpture constituted erotic art.[133] Significantly, the answer seems to have been negative.[134] Although her body was implicated, her ecstasy was profoundly spiritual.

Fusion: male and female

In one of his sketchbooks Le Corbusier described the experience of seeing men and women like 'Fish in an aquarium criss cross, sliding by each other, never touching'. In this way, he felt 'man's fate is not played out'.[135] Like Plato, he believed that it was 'man's fate' to connect to his or her other half, as can be seen from the following extract from The Poem:

> Men tell of
> woman in their poems
> and music
> Their sides eternally rent
> from top to
> bottom. They are but
> half, and feed
> life but by half
> And the second half comes
> to them and binds
> And good or evil come
> to all those
> who encounter each other![136]

Krustrup has referred to one of Le Corbusier's sketches for the cover of the 'Fusion' section of The Poem as a self-portrait.[137] It can be seen as a derivative of a hermaphrodite figure representing the marriage of opposites (Fig. 5.41). The figure has two heads, a square and a circle. These are replaced in the final version of the drawing by one head, clearly male, and one clearly female (Fig. 5.42). While this image repre-

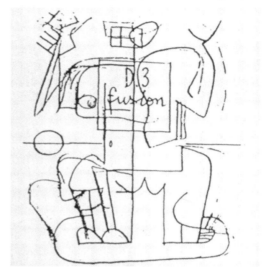

Figure 5.41   Le Corbusier, sketch for cover of 'Fusion' section of his The Poem of the Right Angle.

Figure 5.42   Cover of 'Fusion' section of Le Corbusier's The Poem of the Right Angle.

sents the balance of masculine and feminine within a couple, I would also suggest that it may represent a balance of masculine and feminine forces within Le Corbusier himself.

'Fusion', the culmination of love, the union of 'Spirit' and 'Flesh,' occurs on the fourth layer down of the iconostasis. It occupies just one square, which is divided horizontally by a horizon line. Below the horizon a couple can be seen in the act of sexual union; Krustrup has demonstrated that this type of image was based on Le Corbusier's reworkings of an image of the union of opposites taken from an alchemical text (Figs 5.43 and 5.44).[138] The theme of fusion, union, sexual balance and unity is reiterated within *The Poem* in a number of different ways.

Body and spirit

Above the horizon line of the 'Fusion' square Le Corbusier's winged siren, symbolic of the soul separated from the body, can be seen.[139] Not only is the square a celebration of the union of man with woman, it is also a celebration of the union of the soul with the body. Plato wrote of the 'soul which is ever longing after the whole of things both divine and human'; in this image the siren is head down, her horn, a phallic element penetrating the image of the two lovers below.[140] The siren inhabits both the celestial and the earthy sides of life, and in doing so she links the lovers with the divine. It seems very

strange that Le Corbusier should portray the siren thus upside down unless we refer to the words of Pico della Mirandola who, as has been noted, was much admired by Le Corbusier. Pico wrote that it was a saying of Zoroaster that the soul had wings and when her feathers fell off she was 'borne headlong into the body' and that when they sprouted again she flew back up into the 'heights'.[141] In other words, the soul gained sustenance from the body, in this case through the act of making love.

Woman and enlightenment

The layer below 'Fusion', devoted to 'Characters', has three squares, again a Trinity, suggesting that it is in some way concerned with the spirit. At its centre, the centre of the whole iconostasis, is Yvonne as Icône, familiar from Le Corbusier's paintings of that same name. She appears to cup a flame in her hands which can be read simultaneously as light and vulva, her reading changing according to the viewer's interpretation of this ambiguous element[142] which takes the form of the *vesica piscis*, used by the early Christians to represent the mystery of God's union with his mother bride, as Le Corbusier well knew (Fig. 5.45).[143] The symbol opens up the possibility of a multiplicity of interpretations. *Icône* can be interpreted simultaneously as the Virgin holding the divine light of God within her body; as mother, guardian of the home or as the lover who offers herself to the viewer – three different forms

Figure 5.43   Le Corbusier's reworking of the alchemical union of opposites.

Figure 5.44   Union of Opposites from *Rosarium Philosophorum* in the collection of C.G. Jung.

Figure 5.45   Le Corbusier's sketch of the *vesica piscis*.

of giving. Through love of such a woman it would be possible to gain access to the divine.

Mary

Mary appears in the *Poem of the Right Angle,* thus cementing her role in Le Corbusier's cosmos (Fig. 5.46). Significantly she is surrounded by red, Le Corbusier's colour for 'fusion' or physicality, 'force' or 'violence' as she is at Ronchamp.[144] Red is also the traditional colour for the cloak of Mary Magdalene, the Virgin Mary herself being more often depicted in blue. In an earlier sketch Le Corbusier's Mary (Fig. 5.47) is depicted with a halo, as she is in a Crucifixion scene at Santa Maria Antigua in Rome, which is, as Krustrup has illustrated, the likely source for the image,[145] but in *The Poem* she appears on the beach, her halo gone. Careful inspection of the Mary figure reveals that she is not one but two draped women, one facing towards us and one facing away: a two sided Mary, at once Magdalene and Virgin. Overleaf, next to a full colour image of Icône appear the words:

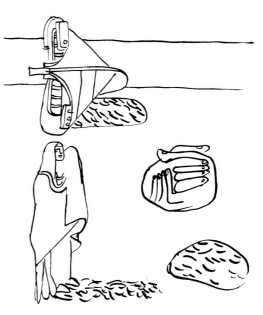

Figure 5.46   Detail of 'Mary' from the 'Characters' section of Le Corbusier's *The Poem of the Right Angle.*

> who made her thus where does she come from?
> She is rightness child of
> limpid heart present on earth
> close to me. daily acts of
> humility vouch for
> her greatness[146]

While obviously referring to his wife Yvonne, these words link the Mary on the beach with the humble Mary Magdalene who washed Christ's feet with her hair. Jencks writes that 'several French acquaintances'

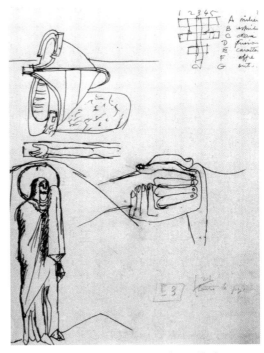

Figure 5.47   Sketch of Mary from the Carnet Nivola.

have said that Yvonne 'was more than a woman of easy virtue', another possible reason for Le Corbusier associating her with the Magdalene.[147]

Love

It has been seen that in the *Symposium* Plato bemoaned the neglect of the god of Love[148] as he would play an important role in the creation of Orphic harmony. Le Corbusier was to take up this theme in the section of *The Poem* entitled 'Flesh', discussed above, and also in the square entitled 'Offering'. This contains an image of Le Corbusier's symbol of the Open Hand, its theme being the giving and receiving of love. The enlightened soul who had experienced the other earlier layers of the iconostasis would understand the true importance of this message.

Conclusion

From this brief overview of Le Corbusier's painted work a number of themes relating to the role of woman in the life of man have emerged. Woman is receptacle, like a shell; 'cathedral of the senses', she is to be worshipped as icon and guardian of the light within her body. She is central to Le Corbusier's view of the relationship between the body and the spirit. She is also muse, associated with music and dance, with special access to nature.

The writings of the priest and palaeontologist Pierre Teilhard de Chardin, much admired by Le Corbusier,[149] are of particular use in deciphering the meaning of Le Corbusier's thoughts on this subject. For Teilhard:

> Woman stands before [man] as the lure and symbol of the world. He cannot embrace her except by himself growing, in his turn, to world scale. And because the world is always growing and always unfinished and always ahead of us, to achieve his love man is engaged in a limitless conquest of the universe and himself. In this sense Man can only attain woman by consummating a union with the universe. Love is a sacred reserve of energy; it is like the blood of spiritual evolution. This is the first revelation we receive from the sense of the earth.[150]

The attraction of the feminine, in her human form, was the concentrated form, destined to expand, of cosmic attraction, the force that would inevitably bring man and nature together in unity.[151] Women would thus play a crucial role in the attainment of harmony.

Within his work as an artist Le Corbusier intertwined personal, mythical and religious subjects with some abandon. He attributed to Yvonne in particular a connection to the wild, to the instinctual and the anarchic but vital forces of humour. In this way she carried a very important source of knowledge and illumination. Whether Yvonne, who was apparently appalled by some of Le Corbusier's more graphic nudes, could really live up to this role is another matter.[152] Drew was to observe that although Le Corbusier spoke continually of the 'Poetry of Life' in actual fact 'the poetry of affection escaped him'.[153] In the next chapter it will be seen that Le Corbusier chose to make links between the women whom he loved and examples of feminine divinity, believing them to be re-enacting, at a small scale through their lives, archetypal cosmic roles.

Notes

1 Le Corbusier quoted in H. Weber (ed.), *Le Corbusier the Artist* (Zurich: Editions Heidi Weber, 1988), pages not numbered.
2 Krustrup makes a comparison between Le Corbusier's version of this theme and that of Picasso in M. Krustrup, 'The women of Algiers', *Skala*, 24/25, (1991), pp.36–41.
3 He actually started painting far earlier. This date corresponds to the beginnings of his experiments with Ozenfant. Le Corbusier, *A New World of Space* (New York: Reynal and Hitchcock, 1948), p.10.
4 Ibid.
5 Le Corbusier, *Modulor* (London: Faber, 1954), p.80.
6 Le Corbusier, *Journey to the East* (Cambridge, MA: MIT Press, 1987), p.62.
7 'I am artist enough to feel that there are extensions to all material things, but I halt at the threshold of metaphysics and symbolism, not because I disdain them but because the nature of my mind does not incite me to cross the threshold . . . All this has been so important in the past (and perhaps is even in the present)'. Le Corbusier, *Modulor 2* (London: Faber, 1958), p.83.
8 Le Corbusier, *A New World of Space*, pp.13–14.
9 Le Corbusier, *My Work* (London: Architectural Press, 1960), p.197.

10 Le Corbusier, *Sketchbooks Volume 4, 1957–1964* (Cambridge, MA: MIT Press, 1982), sketch 506.

11 Letter Le Corbusier to M. Tjader Harris, 21.3.39 in J. Jenger, *Le Corbusier Choix de Lettres* (Basel: Birkhauser, 2002), p.258.

12 Le Corbusier, *The Decorative Art of Today* (London: Architectural Press, 1987), p.181.

13 Letter Le Corbusier to Trouin, '30 ou 31' May 1945, Fondation Le Corbusier (hereafter referred to as FLC) 13.01.9.

14 Letter Le Corbusier to Trouin, 17.07.59, FLC 13.01.179.

15 Letter Trouin to Le Corbusier, January 1951, FLC 13.01.53.

16 Le Corbusier, *Modulor 2*, p.33.

17 Le Corbusier, *The Decorative Art of Today*, p.187.

18 Le Corbusier, *Sketchbooks Volume 2, 1950–1954* (London: Thames and Hudson, 1981), sketches 702, 707 and 937. See also Le Corbusier, *Sketchbooks Volume 3, 1954–1957* (Cambridge, MA: MIT Press, 1982), sketch 426.

19 Le Corbusier, *Precisions* (Cambridge MA: MIT Press, 1991), p.68.

20 A. Ozenfant and C.E. Jeanneret, 'Destinées de la peinture', *L'Esprit Nouveau*, 20 (New York: Da Capo Press, 1969), pages not numbered.

21 Le Corbusier, *The Radiant City* (London, Faber, 1967), p.i.

22 A. Rüegg (ed.), *Polychromie Architecturale: Le Corbusier's Colour Keyboards from 1931 to 1959* (Basel: Birkhäuser, 1997), p.101.

23 Le Corbusier, *A New World of Space*, p.21. See D. Neagele, 'The Image of the body in the Oeuvre of Le Corbusier' in *Architecture Landscape and Urbanism 9, Le Corbusier and the Architecture of Reinvention* (London: AA Publications, 2003), pp.16–39.

24 C. Green, 'The Architect as Artist' in Tim Benton (ed.), *Le Corbusier Architect of the Century* (London: Arts Council, 1987), p.126. Shinar accuses Le Corbusier of using a 'specifically male vocabulary of virility and sexual potency'. M. Shinar 'Feminist Criticism of Urban Theory and Design, Case Study: Le Corbusier', *Journal of Urban and Cultural Studies*, 2, 2, 1992, p.32.

25 C. Lalo, 'L'Esthétique sans amour' in two parts. *Esprit Nouveau*, Nos. 5 and 6, (New York: Da Capo Press, 1969), pages not numbered.

26 Le Corbusier, *Oeuvre Complète Volume 6, 1952–1957* (Zurich: Les Editions d'Architecture, 1995), p.11.

27 Le Corbusier, *A New World of Space*, p.14.

28 Le Corbusier, *The Final Testament of Père Corbu: a Translation and Interpretation of Mise au Point by Ivan Zaknic* (New Haven, CT: Yale University Press, 1997), p.120.

29 Le Corbusier, *The Decorative Art of Today* p.167.

30 It should be noted that in 1926, while working on this ascetic repertoire, Le Corbusier painted a series of 50 decidedly unascetic watercolours for his friend Marcel Levaillant on the theme of the music hall in which the figure of woman features repeatedly. A. Rüegg, 'Marcel Levaillant and "La Question du Mobilier"' in S. Von Moos, & A. Rüegg (eds.), *Le Corbusier Before Le Corbusier* (New Haven, CT: Yale University Press 2002), p.125.

31 J. Epstein, *Ecrits sur le cinéma, 1921–1953, Volume 1* (Paris: Cinéma Club/Seghers, 1974/75), p.42 quoted in F. Ducros, From Art Nouveau to Purism', in Von Moos & Rüegg (ed.), *Le Corbusier Before Le Corbusier*, p.138.

32 K. Silver, *Esprit de Corps: The Art of the Parisian Avant-Garde and the First World War, 1914–1925* (Princeton: Princeton University Press, 1989), p.230.

33 Originally published in 1918. Reprinted in C. S. Eliel (ed.), *L'Esprit Nouveau: Purism in Paris* (New York: Harry N. Abrams, 2001), pp.157–8.

34 Ibid., p.154.

35 Ibid., p.156.

36 Le Corbusier, *Le Corbusier Talks with Students* (New York: Princeton University Press, 1999), p.71.

37 C. Pearson, 'Integrations of Art and Architecture in the work of Le Corbusier. Theory and Practice from Ornamentalism to the "Synthesis of the Major Arts"' (1995). Unpublished PhD thesis, Stanford University, p.298.

38 T. Schumacher, 'Deep Space Shallow Space', *Architectural Review*, vol. CLXXXI, no. 1079, 1987, p.41.

39 Eliel (ed.), *L'Esprit Nouveau: Purism in Paris*, p.162.

40 Silver, *Esprit de Corps*, p.385.

41 From the essay 'Architectural Polychromy' by Le Corbusier, in Rüegg (ed.), *Polychromie Architecturale*, p.137.

42 Ibid., p.107.

43 Le Corbusier 'polychromie architecturale', unpublished preface for the Claviers Salubra, 1932, FLC B1(18), 1, 4. Cited in L.M. Colli, 'La Couleur qui cache, la couleur qui signale: l'ordonnance et la crainte dans la poètique Corbuséenne des couleurs' in *Le Corbusier et La Couleur* (Paris: Fondation Le Corbusier, 1992), p.22.

44 G. Wood and P. Greenhalgh, 'Symbols of the Sacred and Profane' in Paul Greenhalgh (ed.), *Art Nouveau 1890–1914* (London: V & A, 2000), p.84.

45 W. Chadwick, 'Eros or Thanatos, The Surrealist Cult of Love Re-examined', *Art Forum*, 14 (1975), p.46.

46 Wood and Greenhalgh, 'Symbols of the Sacred and Profane', p.78.

47 Ibid.

48 Pearson suggests that the 'motif of the female nude' connotes Le Corbusier's 'nostalgia for an idealised classical past'. Pearson, 'Integrations of Art and Architecture in the work of Le Corbusier', p.170.

49 Silver, *Esprit de Corps*, p.282.

50 M. Price, 'The missing méchanicienne: gender, production and order in Léger's machine aesthetic' in V. Mainz, and G. Pollock (eds), *Work and the Image II* (Aldershot: Ashgate, 2000), p.97.

51 Le Corbusier, *When the Cathedrals were White: A Journey to the Country of the Timid People* (New York: Reynal and Hitchcock, 1947), p.xii.

52 Maurice Raynal, 'Fernand Léger', *L'Esprit Nouveau* (1920), 4, pp.427–434.

53 C. Benton, essay to accompany the exhibition, *Charlotte Perriand: Modernist Pioneer* at the Design Museum, London, 24 October 1996 to 13 April 1997.

54 Price, 'The missing *méchanicienne*', p.91.

55 Ibid., p.92.

56 Ibid., p.105.

57 Wood and Greenhalgh observe that images of women 'were often mediated via the East' as it was an 'an exotic and hedonistic realm where women became fantasy creatures de-clawed and subsumed into alternative religions and practices'. Wood and Greenhalgh, 'Symbols of the Sacred and Profane', p.86.

58 S. Von Moos, 'Le Corbusier as painter', *Oppositions* 19–20 (1980), p.89.

59 B. Colomina, *Privacy and Publicity* (Cambridge, MA: MIT Press, 1994), p.84.

60 Z. Celik, 'Le Corbusier, Orientalism, Colonialism', *Assemblage*, 17 (1992), p.72.

61 S. Bozdoğan, 'Journey to the East: Ways of Looking at the Orient and the Question of Representation', *Journal of Architectural Education*, 41, 4 (1989), p.38.

62 Ibid., p.45.

63 R. Golan, *Modernity and Nostalgia: Art and Politics in France between the Wars* (London: Yale University Press, 1995), p.111.

64 Von Moos, 'Le Corbusier as painter', p.89.

65 S. Von Moos, S., *Le Corbusier: L'architecte et son mythe* (Paris: Horizons de France, 1971), p.260.

66 Price, 'The missing *méchanicienne*', p.102.

67 G. Perry, *Women Artists and the Parisian Avant-Garde* (Manchester: Manchester University Press, 1995), p.34.

68 Le Corbusier, *Journey to the East*, p.83.

69 In the opinion of both K. Frampton and Jencks, the forms of the Algerian women whom he studied and sketched found their way into the city plan for Algiers, the plan Obus (appropriately names the shell) of 1932. C. Jencks, *Le Corbusier and the Continual Revolution in Architecture* (New York: Monacelli Press, 2000), p.202.

70 M. Krustrup, 'Les Illustrations de Le Corbusier pour l'Illiade' in G. Viatte (ed.), *Le Corbusier et la Méditerranée* (Marseilles: L'Université de Provence, 1991), p.106.

71 Le Corbusier, *The Radiant City*, p.230.

72 Le Corbusier, *Precisions*, p.107.

73 Price, 'The missing *méchanicienne*', p.99.

74 This mural receives a detailed analysis in R.A. Moore, 'Le Corbusier and the *mecanique spirituelle*: An investigation into Le Corbusier's architectural symbolism and its background in Beaux Arts design'. Unpublished D Phil thesis, University of Maryland (1979), pp.300–317.

75 J.G. Davies, *The Early Christian Church* (London: Architectural Press 1952), pp.17–18.

76 See M. Krustrup, *Porte Email* (Copenhagen: Arkitektens Forlag, 1991), p.128.

77 'I am an architect. I work in planes, profiles, and sections. Well, a bone gives you all that. A bone is an admirable object.' Le Corbusier quoted in J. Peter, *The Oral History of Modern Architecture* (New York: Harry N. Abrams, 1994), p.149.

78 Moore, 'Le Corbusier and the *mecanique spirituelle*', p.290.

79 Le Corbusier, *Le Poème de l'angle droit* (Paris: Editions Connivance, 1989), A3, Milieu.

80 Le Corbusier, *Modulor*, pp. 223–4.

81 Pearson, 'Integrations of Art and Architecture in the work of Le Corbusier', p.298.

82 Ibid., p.320.

83 T. Rollet, *Les Catacombes de Rome: Histoire de l'art et des croyances religieuses pendant les premiers siècles du Christianisme, vol. 2* (Paris: Morel, 1881), illustrations not numbered, in FLC.

84 Peter, *The Oral History of Modern Architecture*, p.149.

85 C. E. Jeanneret, *Nature morte au coquillage* (Still life with shells), 1917, pencil and gouache on paper, FLC. Charles-Edouard Jeanneret, *La Naissance de Vénus* (The Birth of Venus), after Boticelli (Carnet 10), 1917, pencil and watercolour on paper, FLC. Charles-Edouard Jeanneret, *Femme et coquillage sur fond bleu* (Woman and Shells against a Blue Background), 1915–16, oil on canvas, FLC.

86 See S. Haskins, *Mary Magdalene* (London: HarperCollins, 1994), pp.236–240 for an account of her transformation into Venus in the sixteenth century.

87 See for example Le Corbusier, *Le Poème de l'angle droit*, C3, Flesh.

88 R. A. Moore, 'Alchemical and Mythical themes in the Poem of the Right Angle 1947–65', *Oppositions* 19/20 (1980): 111.

89 Krustrup, *Porte Email*, p.80.

90 Ozenfant and Jeanneret, 'Nature et Création', *Le'Esprit Nouveau*, No. 19.

91 Moore, 'Le Corbusier and the *mecanique spirituelle*', p.198.

92 See Colli, 'La Couleur qui cache, la couleur qui signale', pp.23–24 for a discussion of the more sinister side of nature and its relationship with Le Corbusier's work.

93 Krustrup, 'Les Illustrations de Le Corbusier pour l'Illiade', p.112.

94 R. Ingersoll, *A Marriage of Contours* (Princeton: Princeton Architectural Press, 1990), p.13.

95 Von Moos, *Le Corbusier: L'architecte et son mythe*, p.261.

96 H. Weber (ed.), *Le Corbusier, das Grafische Werk* (Zurich and Montreal, 1988), pp.48–49.

97 A. Gray Read, 'Le Corbusier's Ubu Sculpture: Remaking an Image.' *Word and Image* 14, 3 (1998), p. 225.

98 E. Mâle, *Religious Art in France: the Twelfth Century* (Princeton: Bollingen, 1978), p.333.

99 Ibid., pp.336.

100 G. Apollinaire, *Le Bestiaire ou Cortège d'Orphée* in Michel Décaudin (ed.), *Oeuvres Complètes de Guillaume Apollinaire* (Paris: André Balland et Jacques Lecat, 1966), pp.40–41.

101 H. Provensal, *L'Art de Demain* (Paris: Perrin, 1904), p.70 in FLC.

102 Le Corbusier, *Sketchbooks Volume 3*, sketch 257.

103 'Garder mon aile dans ta main'. These words are from a poem by Mallarmé. E. Billeter, *Le Corbusier Secret* (Laussane: Musée Cantonal des Beaux Arts, 1987), plates 121–132.

104 Le Corbusier, *Poésie sur Alger* (Paris: Editions Connivances, 1989). Originally published in 1950.

105 *Femme cornée avec des ailes.* Billeter, *Le Corbusier Secret*, plate 132.

106 'A later series of drawings is entitled: "Garder mon aile dans ta main". Here the famous "Open Hand symbolism of Le Corbusier, extolled by modernist critics in a rapturous acclamation of Le Corbusier's infinite love of humanity, reveals a different, ominous face. A goat-headed, helpless-looking woman is held in a large powerful male hand: the ultimate woman-beast redeemable only by dominant and protective man'. Shinar 'Feminist Criticism of Urban Theory and Design', p.37.

107 Le Corbusier, *Sketchbooks Volume 3*, sketch 662.

108 Letter Le Corbusier to Ronald Alley, 25.06.1958 quoted in J. Coll, 'Le Corbusier. Taureaux: An Analysis of the thinking process in the last series of Le Corbusier's Plastic work', *Art History* 18, 4 (1995), p.562.

109 Salvador Dali experimented with writing his name in conjunction with that of his muse, suggesting the full extent of her role in his creation. It is possible that Le Corbusier was alluding to a similar belief.

110 Le Corbusier, *Sketchbooks Volume 4*, sketch 690.

111 Letter Le Corbusier to M. Levaillant, 21.04.1954 in Jenger, *Le Corbusier Choix de Lettres*, p.376.

112 Le Corbusier, *Journey to the East*, p.62.

113 Le Corbusier drew a sketch of the iconostasis. At the centre he wrote the word 'Von'. Le Corbusier, *Sketchbooks Volume 4*, sketch 41.

114 Le Corbusier, *Le Poème de l'angle droit*, A3, Milieu.

115 Ghyka wrote 'In Pythagorean Number-Mystic, seven was the Virgin-Number'. M. Ghyka, *The Geometry of Art and Life* (New York: Dover, 1977), p.21. Originally published in 1946.

116 L. Réau, *Iconographie de l'art Chrétien Volume 1* (Paris: Presses Universitaires de France, 1955), p.68.

117 Le Corbusier, *Le Corbusier Talks with Students*, p.71.

118 E. Schuré, *Les Grands Initiés* (Paris: Perrin, 1908), p.244.

119 É. Mâle, *The Gothic Image* (London: Fontana, 1961), p.11.

120 Réau, *Iconographie de l'art Chrétien Volume 1*, p.68.

121 According to Balkrishna Doshi Le Corbusier was very superstitious and would not go anywhere without a particular talisman that was given to him in Brazil. Carmen Kagal, 'Le Corbusier: the Acrobat of Architecture. Interview with Balkrishna Doshi, 1986', *Architecture and Urbanism*, 322 (1997), pp.168–183. It may be because of these superstitions that, when flying, he chose to sit in seat number 5. 'Zurich. March 3, 1961 at 1.30pm we take off in AIR INDIA my usual seat Number 5' Le Corbusier, *Sketchbooks Volume 3*, sketch 688.

122 Réau, *Iconographie de l'art Chrétien Volume 1*, p.68.

123 Le Corbusier letters to various female friends, FLC F2.20.366–388.

124 Adolf Loos, 'Ornament and Crime' in U. Conrads, *Programmes and Manifestos on Twentieth Century Architecture*, (London: Lund Humphries 1970), p.19.

125 Le Corbusier, *Carnet Nivola*, p.25.

126 Le Corbusier, *Le Poème de l'angle droit*, A1, Milieu.

127 Ibid., A2, Milieu.

128 Ibid., C2, Flesh.

129 Krustrup writes that the couple Aphrodite and Ares are like Yvonne and Le Corbusier. These two signs of the zodiac feature on the iconostasis on the third line, 'Flesh', separated by 'autobiographical' designs. Krustrup, 'Les Illustrations de Le Corbusier pour l'Illiade', p.113.

130 Le Corbusier, *Le Poème de l'angle droit*, E2, Caractères.

131 Ibid., C3, Chair.

132 Ibid.

133 In the *Phaedrus*, Plato described what Guthrie called the 'four chief kinds of mania . . . that of prophets and seers, that of the authors of rites of purification and initiation, that of poets and that of lovers. The object of the passage is to show that 'the greatest of all good things come to us through mania' and that the word does not mean madness in the ordinary sense, but divine inspiration or possession.' W.K.C. Guthrie, *Orpheus and Greek Religion* (London: Methuen, 1935), p.240.

134 Lalo, 'L'Esthétique sans amour', *Esprit Nouveau*, Nos. 5 and 6, pages not numbered.

135 Le Corbusier, *Sketchbooks Volume 1*, 1914–1948 (London: Thames and Hudson, 1981), sketches 616–620.

136 Le Corbusier, *Le Poème de l'angle droit*, C4 Chair.

137 M. Krustrup, 'Poème de l'angle droit,' *Arkitekten*, 92 (1990), pp.422–432.

138 Krustrup, *Porte Email*, p.128.

139 Réau, *Iconographie de l'art Chrétien Volume 1*, p.121.

140 Plato, *The Republic V* in S. Buchanan (ed.), *The Portable Plato* (Harmondsworth: Penguin, 1997), p.507.

141 G. Pico della Mirandola, *On the Dignity of Man* (Indianapolis: Hackett, 1998), p. 16.

142 J. Coll, 'Structure and Play in Le Corbusier's Art Works', *AA Files*, 31 (1996), p.10.

143 Le Corbusier, *Sketchbooks Volume 3*, sketch 516.

144 From the essay Architectural Polychromy by Le Corbusier, in Rüegg (ed.), *Polychromie Architecturale*, p.115.

145 Krustrup, *Porte Email*, p.143.

146 Le Corbusier, *Le Poème de l'angle droit*, p.130.

147 C. Jencks, *Le Corbusier and the Tragic View of Architecture* (London: Allen Lane, 1973), p.100.

148 Plato, *Symposium*, in Buchanan (ed.), *The Portable Plato*, p.143.

149 F. Samuel, 'Le Corbusier, Teilhard de Chardin and the Planetisation of Mankind' *Journal of Architecture*, 4 (1999), pp.149–165.

150 P. Teilhard de Chardin, *On Love* (London: Collins, 1972), p.14.

151 H. de Lubac, *L'Éternel Féminin: étude sur un texte du Père Teilhard de Chardin* (Paris: Aubier 1968), p.24.

152 Von Moos, *Le Corbusier: L'architecte et son mythe*, p.302.

153 J. Drew interview with M. Garlake, 20–21 May 1995. National Life Story Collection, British Library, F823.

6 The Cult of Woman and the Religious Architecture of Le Corbusier

Mon Père, quelle est la différence entre vous et moi? – je donne ma langue au chat, Madame LC. – Eh bien, voila: vous, vous êtes un consacré, tandis que moi, je suis un sacré con! Yvonne Le Corbusier to Father Couturier.[1]

At the beginning of this book it was noted that, when first starting work on the project for the chapel at Ronchamp, Le Corbusier turned, in pursuit of inspiration, to the pilgrim manual for the old church that stood upon the site. When he came to a passage describing the 'cult of Mary' he underlined it and wrote next to it the word 'feminism'.[2] As was seen in the last chapter, Mary occupied a very special place in *The Poem of the Right Angle* and a central part in Le Corbusier's thinking. It seems that he believed the veneration of Mary would play a specific role in redressing the imbalance that he perceived between the sexes. Like Edouard Schuré he seems to have believed that female as well as male figures of veneration should be brought into the fold if religion was to be made relevant once more. This chapter will contain a detailed examination of Le Corbusier's view of the role of woman in religion revealed through a study of his religious architecture. I will focus on two case studies: the first, the Basilica and City at La Sainte Baume (1945–1960) which was designed around the grotto of Mary Magdalene, a figure of central importance to Le Corbusier; the second, the Chapel of Notre Dame du Haut Ronchamp, consecrated in 1955, dedicated to the Virgin Mary.

The young Le Corbusier gave his view of the religion into which he was born in *Journey to the East*. In his opinion:

Protestantism as a religion lacks the necessary sensuality that fills the innermost depths of a human being, sanctuaries of which he is hardly conscious and which are part of the animal self,

or perhaps the most elevated part of the subconscious. This sensuality, which intoxicates and eludes reason, is a source of latent joy and a harness of living strength.[3]

Le Corbusier's scheme for Ronchamp would embrace that sensuality which he believed to be an intrinsic part of the Catholic Church, experienced by him at first hand at the monastery to the Virgin at Mount Athos in the form of 'A fantastic vision of the sanctuary of the Virgin'. Here he felt in his 'limbs' the 'awe of the sacred ritual' and the 'overwhelming delirium of this moment and place', an experience which he never forgot; testament to the possibility of creating an architecture that affects the emotions at both a physical and spiritual level.[4]

Le Corbusier's enthusiasm for a monastic existence is well known. He emulated the life of a monk, spending long hours in retreat, both before and after his marriage to Yvonne. However, there was one aspect of monastic life to which he could not succumb: sexual abstinence. He does not appear to have valued this latter virtue which, in his view, was both unnatural and unsustainable.[5] In one particularly cryptic passage of *Journey to the East*, Le Corbusier refers to the 'secretly coquettish . . . Brother "Gold Flower"' that he encountered at the monastery of Mount Athos and writes:

ah, I've had enough of all the sweetness of that nature, swollen with sap, damp with joy, quivering with abundant vines . . . Not a single woman is to be seen; thus everything is missing here in the East where only for the sight of her woman is the primordial ingredient . . . all are lonely males, and if not consumed by anguish, then devoid of any noble martial feeling. What are they then? . . . Then should I remain, no! I must flee the sacred mountain and its disquieting sweetness . . . because in the evening hands dangling between the thighs, eyes guided by thoughts, would be cast . . . on the brothers, ah torment . . .[6]

Here he can only be referring to the problems of priestly sexual abstinence and the resultant 'depressing hypocrisy' of pretence.[7]

While feeling a powerful attraction to what he perceived to be the sensuality of Catholicism he had strong reservations about the religion and its implications. For example, when travelling across South America he observed:

What the . . . hell did the . . . curés come here for; we are on the violent red earth of the Indians, and these people had a soul. From my catechism I still remember this saying of Jesus Christ: 'if someone offends one of these little ones who believes in me, it were better to attach a stone to his neck and throw him into the sea.[8]

This passage is significant, not only because Le Corbusier sides himself with pagan religion, but also because it reveals the way in which he was able to turn Biblical imagery to his own ends. He would develop this ability through discussions with enlightened members of the Church, such as Father Couturier and his colleagues at L'Art Sacré, while he gathered together ideas for La Sainte Baume and Ronchamp.

Le Corbusier was loath to discuss his religious convictions, believing that they would be used against him by journalists, for whom he held a profound mistrust. However, contrary to popular misconception, he was a deeply spiritual man, quick to replace the Protestantism of his early youth with a belief in the powers of nature and mathematics, 'the earth mother of the golden section' as a means to regain contact with the divine.[9] It may seem slightly perverse to look to his religious buildings to provide evidence of Le Corbusier's interest in women and sex, but it is here that his opinions become most explicit as the buildings embody a critique of contemporary Catholicism, mediated through the twin issues of gender and sexuality.

Through the design of the chapel Le Corbusier expressed a profound nostalgia for what he perceived

to be the pure roots of this ancient religion. He spoke proudly of the fact that it contained 'not a sign, not an artificial tool created by centuries of decadence'.[10] In one of his *Sketchbooks* a note, dated 4 June 1955, reads: 'I discover in Catholicism the continuation of the most ancient, the most human rites, (human scale, and pertinent).'[11] Le Corbusier would exploit the ambiguities inherent in the iconography of the Virgin Mary and Mary Magdalene to put forward a rather different interpretation of the Bible than that of the Catholic Church. Building upon ideas introduced in the last chapter, I will argue that he believed these two Marys to be fundamentally linked, seeing them as two sides of an all encompassing feminine divinity with strong links back to the pagan past.

It has been seen that Le Corbusier was highly critical of what he perceived to be the Church's hypocritical attitude to love and sex, sentiments echoed by Rabelais, who used what he perceived to be its gluttony, greed and lasciviousness as a favourite subject of derision. Within Rabelais' first book *Gargantua* he described the founding of the Abbey of Thélème,[12] a religious order which was to operate 'in an exact contrary way to all the others'.[13] Here he mocked contemporary opinion that men should be kept separate from women who, like Eve, were perceived as being essentially weak and corrupt. At Thélème no man would be allowed in a room unless women were also present. The community envisaged by Rabelais was, in certain ways, reminiscent of those of the Albigensian Cathars and indeed of the community which Le Corbusier and his client and friend Edouard Trouin hoped to build at La Sainte Baume.

La Sainte Baume

In Le Corbusier's opinion La Sainte Baume formed part of a 'a brilliant landscape, an architectural site, a place of meditation for meetings, capable of allowing you to enjoy its real value, the spirit which reigns over the area', that of Mary Magdalene.[14] Work on this 'marvellous undertaking', an underground Basilica, housing complex, museum and theatre, continued from 1945 into the early 1960s. Although never built, it provides an important part of the backdrop for a number of other schemes on which Le

Corbusier worked during that period, most notably the Chapel of Ronchamp and the Unité in Marseille.

Le Corbusier and Trouin thought of Mary Magdalene as Christ's female counterpart. In emphasising her role they would bring back that element of sexual balance that was noticeably missing within religion. Such an idea would be in keeping with Le Corbusier's Cathar sympathies. Krystal Maurin writes that it was thought by the 'Neo-Catharists' of the 1940s and '50s that the Cathars had ascribed a far more central role to women than did the Catholic Church.[15] In one book that Le Corbusier owned on Catharism, Coincy Saint-Palais' *Esclarmonde de Foix: Princesse Cathare*, he marked the line: 'One knows the importance that the Cathars gave to women' and wrote next to it 'MM', presumably standing for Mary Magdalene, a figure of veneration for this heretical sect who believed her to be Christ's concubine.[16] Further on in the book there is mention of the subterranean churches of Ornolac, Ussat and Bonan as well as the immense 'Lombrives, the future Cathar cathedral'. Le Corbusier underlined these words and in the margin he wrote 'Trouin and LC',[17] indicating that he envisaged the basilica at La Sainte Baume to be just this, essentially a Cathar cathedral. This seems all the more likely if we consider that the project was situated on the site of the grotto of the Magdalene herself, a place of veneration for both Catholics and heretics alike.

Le Corbusier traced his own ancestry to the *perfecti* of the Languedocian Cathars whose religion allowed women into its inner sanctum, conferring upon them the sacrament of ordination, the *consolamentum*.[18] A tiered system, the highest level of Cathar spirituality belonged to the *parfaits*, or perfect ones, some of whom were women. Richard Abels and Ellen Harris write that 'once the postulant had been baptized in the spirit through the impositions of hands, her soul which had been imprisoned in matter, was reunited with the holy Spirit, and she became a wholly new creature'. In this way she would become a *perfecta*, in every way the equal of a *perfectus*, an exalted status in Cathar terms. Sexual difference was deemed to be based on matter. It would therefore play no role in the life of the spirit.[19] If indeed Le Corbusier believed this to be the case, it is not surprising that he promulgated the role of woman within religion.

Like Le Corbusier's interpretation of Rabelais' great work, the network of ideas at the heart of the programme for La Sainte Baume is essentially Orphic. This can be seen from a sketch plan of a book entitled *La Ste Baume and Marie Magdalene* the 'city according to Rabelais' that Trouin sent to Le Corbusier in 1945, in which he described La Sainte Baume as the 'Orphic City'. Chapter titles include 'Jesus = son of the mountain (like Orpheus)' and 'Mary Magdalene = orphic (phallic and ascetic)'.[20] Jesus was like Orpheus in that he had returned from the Underworld, whilst Mary Magdalene, the fallen woman who repented, was 'orphic', both sexual and spiritual, with, as will be seen, a particular connection to geometry.

Background to the project

In 1946 Trouin, the owner of much of the land at La Sainte Baume, went to Paris to look for an architect for his project, an underground basilica. He was, according to Le Corbusier, a 'geometer': that is to say a surveyor, a significant occupation in Le Corbusier's terms because of its connection to geometry.[21] An opportunist, he quickly infiltrated the intellectual circles in which Le Corbusier moved. Auguste Perret initially produced a scheme for the site, but it was Le Corbusier who would develop the scheme because he evidently felt a real affinity for the project.[22]

Together with Father Couturier they developed a plan for an underground Basilica, housing for both permanent and transitory members of the community, a museum of Mary Magdalene iconography and a theatre. Le Corbusier was to become a close friend of his client, the duration of his involvement in the scheme and the warmth of his letters to Trouin testifying to the degree of his emotional investment in the project.

During one of the dips in their tempestuous relationship, Le Corbusier sent a copy of the fifth volume of the *Oeuvre Complète*, including a relatively lengthy section on La Sainte Baume, to Trouin who wrote back: 'I received your trilingual book and couldn't stop myself from crying'.[23] Le Corbusier responded to Trouin's emotional outburst with a curt letter including a small footnote in which he emphasised the importance of La Sainte Baume and indicated the pages that Trouin should read. In this offhand way he indicated the extent of his feelings for both Trouin and his project.[24] The extensive notes that Le Corbusier made for the section on La Saint Baume in the *Oeuvre Complète* can be seen in the Fondation Le Corbusier.[25]

The site

La Sainte Baume is situated in Provence in the South of France 40 kilometres to the east of Marseilles. Mary McLeod has noted that for the Regional Syndicalists, a group with which Le Corbusier was involved, the Mediterranean sun represented 'the essence of France's classical heritage; both rational thought and spiritual joy'.[26] The Mediterranean thus became a symbol of France's connection with ancient Greece. In his book *Provençal Regionalism*, written in 1954, Alphonse V. Roche noted the recent growth of a movement that he referred to as Pan-Latinism, characterised by the writings of Jean Desthieux and Nicolas Rubio:

> They pictured the peoples inhabiting the shores of the Mediterranean as united by a mysterious poetic element emanating from the sea itself, and strengthened by their common enjoyment of sea, sun, and breezes murmured in pine woods on coastal hills . . . when the Greek and Roman elements merged with the population of the Western Mediterranean seaboard, a particular spirit arose which must be called Latin, as this term refers to a common mentality and shared emotional and cultural outlook that was brought about by the expansion of the 'the Latin federation,' and the spread of 'the Latin viewpoint' to all the west.[27]

According to Rubio it was possible for a historian to treat all the peoples of the Mediterranean as one, united by 'our sea'.[28] Although it is not known whether Le Corbusier and Trouin were familiar with the work of these men, it appears that they held a similar belief about the unifying role of the Mediterranean. This may explain in part Le Corbusier's attitude to this sea, which bordered on veneration. In particular he was to retain a great affection for Provence, where his wife Yvonne was born.[29]

The La Sainte Baume Massif is the highest of the Provençal mountain ranges, reaching 1148 metres above sea level at its highest point. It extends 12 miles from east to west. The grotto of Mary Magdalene, a popular site of pilgrimage, is set into a limestone outcrop to the north side of the ridge, 700 metres above sea level. The Massif contains many caves, like that of the grotto at La Sainte Baume below which the northern face of the ridge is shrouded in forest, consisting largely of beech, lime and maple trees. Because of its altitude La Sainte Baume is also markedly different in climate from other areas in the Midi; in contrast to its hot and dusty surroundings it is almost Scandinavian in character.[30]

Mary Magdalene

Mary Magdalene is usually associated with the sinful woman who washed Jesus' feet with her hair as a sign of her humility and repentance. Although there are only a few brief and inconsistent references to her in the New Testament gospels of Matthew, Mark, Luke and John, there is some consensus on certain important issues. Firstly, they agree that Mary Magdalene was indeed one of Christ's female followers and that she was present at his crucifixion. Secondly, they agree that she was a witness to his resurrection and that she was the first to receive his message and the first to spread his word to the people. There are a number of different versions of the Provençal legend of the Magdalene, the best known being that she travelled to France by boat in the company of Saint Maximin.[31]

The master carpenter Antoine Moles, an acquaintance of Le Corbusier,[32] gave a further version of the story of the Magdalene in his book on the cathedral builders of the Middle Ages, the birth of the guilds and of Masonry, *Histoire des Charpentiers*, within which he dedicated an entire chapter to La Sainte Baume.[33] Le Corbusier owned a copy of this book containing a dedication by Moles, according to whom Mary Magdalene arrived in Provence in the company of the first 'campagnons bâtisseurs', forebears of the guilds of master craftsmen, who came from the plateaux of Asia. The suggestion is that together they brought with them to Europe the knowledge of geometry developed by the ancient Greeks and Egyptians. Mary

Magdalene was in some way seen as the protectress of their knowledge. It was for this reason that she was held in great respect by the 'Compagnons du Tour de France', a guild of master craftsmen who were to be involved in the development of the Basilica scheme.[34] Le Corbusier seems to have believed that the builders of the medieval cathedrals had knowledge of Pythagorean, and hence Orphic, thought.[35]

The first two pages of the section in Le Corbusier's *Oeuvre Complète*, devoted to La Sainte Baume, are dominated by images from Trouin's collection of Magdalenic iconography (Figs 6.1 & 6.2).[36] Here Le Corbusier wrote admiringly of the way in which his client covered the walls and even the ceiling of his garret room with images of the Saint.[37]

Next to the images of the Magdalene in the *Oeuvre Complète* Le Corbusier gave his version of her legend:

Half-way up this massive vertical rock face is the black hole of a cave: here lived Mary Magdalen, the friend of Jesus, who came from Palestine in a small boat, with the other Marys. Every morning angels came to the cave and carried her 200 metres up to the summit of the mountain called 'Le Pilon', where she used to pray. From there the mountain falls away as far as Toulon and the Mediterranean. The legend has made La Sainte Baume a divine place, which today is guarded by the Dominicans. On the plain at the foot of the hills is The Basilica of St Maximin, where the beautiful head (skeleton) of Mary Magdalene is kept in a golden casket.[38]

It is significant that Le Corbusier referred to the other Marys, fully aware of the blurring of boundaries between the various saints of that name and indeed

Quelques illustrations de la Maquette établie par Trouin sur l'iconographie de Marie-Madeleine

An astonishing and perhaps marvellous undertaking: inspired by Edward Trouin whose family have been geometers in Marseilles since 1780. He, the last of them, is fifty years old, and is descended from seamen and pirates of St-Malo, and from peasants of Provence. He is a geometer, that is to say that he is devoted to architecture, construction, the management of the land, the countryside and to geometry. He speaks with a Marseilles accent, has the energy of the ''thunder of God'', as they say in Marseilles, and possesses by chance a million square metres of uncultivated and unproductive land at La Sainte-Baume. He decided to make some use of it. Week-end hunters came and asked him to sell them pieces here and there, but Trouin did not wish to sell, he wanted to realise a noble idea, to save the countryside of La Sainte-Baume from the speculative builder, who had already invaded Le Plan d'Aups. Then began the long search for an architecture worthy of the countryside.
La Sainte-Baume—''a High Place'', a formidable wall of rocks on the edge of half a plate (Le Plan d'Aups), the other half, slightly raised, looking to the north as far as

Marie-Madeleine, amie du seigneur

26   **La Sainte-Baume**

Dans la grotte de la Ste-Baume

Figure 6.1   A selection of Edouard Trouin's collection of Magdalenic iconography included in Le Corbusier's *Oeuvre Complète Volume 5*, including a detail from Mary Magdalene as a hermit, by the Magdalen Master (c.1280).

the Virgin herself. By examining his own version of the story of the Magdalene, I will try to identify the attributes of the Saint that were of particular interest to him; attributes that he and Trouin then tried to emphasise through the design for the scheme at La Sainte Baume.

The medieval theologian Jacobus de Voragine described in his *Legenda Aurea* how every day 'at the seven canonical hours she [Mary Magdalene] was carried aloft by angels and with her bodily ears heard the glorious chants of the celestial hosts'.[39] It seems likely that Le Corbusier may have been drawing from this account of her legend in his version of the story. According to Voragine, Mary Magdalene could be symbolised through light.[40] Like the figure of Icône in Le Corbusier's paintings, the Magdalene was the bringer of illumination. Her presence could therefore be implied through the careful manipulation of radiance,[41] as will be seen in the Basilica scheme.

Le Corbusier and Trouin placed emphasis upon the Magdalene's role as hermit and penitent, Le Corbusier himself having long been fascinated by the possibilities of an ascetic existence. For Trouin the Magdalene was a 'perfect symbol',[42] a woman who, with her hair, wiped the perfumed oil from the feet of 'a God' to whom she gave her own life.[43] In his opinion her heart was 'not that of a lamb nor of an innocent person'; it was a 'paragon of knowledge'.[44] It seems that Trouin did not believe the Magdalene's love for Jesus to be entirely spiritual: 'Renan wrote that the vision of this woman in love gave the world a resurrected god and that the church called him the "APOSTLE of APOSTLES". Not at all bad for an ex-prostitute'.[45] Trouin was referring to the nineteenth century writer Ernest Renan's highly controversial description of the Resurrection in which the Magdalene, crazed by love, had a vision of Christ, a vision that then became the foundation of the Christian religion. From the number of annotations made by Le Corbusier in Renan's *La Vie de Jésus* it is evident that this work also occupied a special position in his own collection of books.[46] Given the importance of this book to the two men it seems that they must have agreed with Renan's view that the Christian religion was not founded solely upon faith; it was founded on knowledge, *gnosis*, and upon love.

the mountain Sainte-Victoire, already made memorable by Cézanne. Half-way up this massive vertical rock face is the black hole of a cave: here lived Mary Magdalen, the friend of Jesus, who came from Palestine in a small boat, with the other Marys. Every morning angels came to the cave and carried her 200 metres up to the summit of the mountain called "Le Pilon", where she used to pray. From there the mountain falls away as far as Toulon and the Mediterranean. The legend has made La Sainte-Baume a divine place, which to-day is guarded by the Dominicans. On the plain at the foot of the hills is La Basilique de St-Maximin, where the extremely beautiful head (skeleton) of Mary Magdalen is kept in a golden casket.
In about 1946, Trouin went up to Paris, and there he saw everybody including the academicians. He engaged each to make a special project for the Val d'Aups at the foot of the Rocks which would establish in this lordly landscape a place of architecture, a place of meditation, a meeting place which would make possible the appreciation of the full value of the spirit which reigns there. He got his project, but when, after some years, the first enthusiasm for

his ideas had died down, he found himself left alone with only one architect remaining faithful to him—Le Corbusier. The Basilique was a remarkable architectural enterprise, invisible, enormous effort expended on the interior destined to move only those souls capable of understanding. The building was entirely within the rock, partly artificially and partly naturally lit, it ran from one side of the rock at the entrance of the cave of Mary Magdalen, to the other, opening suddenly on the blinding light and the distant sea.
The plans show first the conception of the Basilique with its inclined ways, and vertical and horizontal rooms which receive the light of day through wells, or from the ends of the galleries. In some places electric light would have been used.
The corollary of the enterprise was the search for a modern form of hotel, of hospitality, for a clientèle desirous of solitude and thought, or simply for people who might come to stay a week-end or more permanently.
The scheme for La Sainte-Baume comprises the Basilique, cut in the rock, the two ring-shaped hotels, and the Permanent City on the other side of the plateau. Near the Per-

manent City there lies by chance an old ruined sheepfold which might serve as a museum of Mary Magdalen, where Trouin's talent would be able to manifest itself as much in the exceptional iconographical collection as in the manner of displaying it, intense and moving.
Because of adverse opinions about the enterprise and the changes it would make in the landscape, Trouin made the drafts for two books, astonishing works which still exist and are: one a history of architecture, set out according to a new method, the other an iconography of Mary Magdalen. For some years Trouin lived in Paris in a garret the walls of which he covered with plans, drawings and paintings. When the walls were covered he began to fill the ceiling as well. It is a pity that this extraordinary room was never photographed.
After several years the affair was at a standstill. One might have thought that our modern world was unsuited for such an enterprise, the object of which was to touch the very foundations of the human soul: sin and pardon, weakness and grandeur, magnanimity and courage, simplicity and humility. There was nothing of the banal in it; all was in deference to the landscape, modulated by and even expressive of the landscape. The means employed were those at the disposal of people who desire to do something, but have only the resources of the unfortunate. The Permanent City had been designed in the humblest possible manner, to be built in pisé (rammed earth within wooden shuttering), as the basic structure.
With such an architecture the noblest and greatest town plans can be achieved, deprived of emphasis but with inherent grandeur. Life in these pisé buildings can have great dignity and regain for man in the machine age a sense of the fundamental human and natural resources.
But circumstances allowed the use of another material; the firm of "French Aluminium" listened to our proposals, and the result was that an aluminium architecture was conceived, to be built alongside the pisé, in that most exact and the most modern of metals.
The illustrations here show only a miserable portion of all that was made, thought and designed for La Sainte-Baume. At present silence reigns after the hatred and scorn have raged. But Trouin like Le Corbusier can raise his head, satisfied to have attempted, in this age when no one works except for financial or utilitarian ends, an enterprise destined to touch the bottom of the human heart.

La Sainte-Baume   27

Figure 6.2   Detail of Mary Magdalene from Mathias Grunewald's, *Isenheim Altarpiece* (c.1513–15) , part of Trouin's collection of Magdalenic iconography included in Le Corbusier's *Oeuvre Complète Volume 5.*

For Renan Christ was resurrected through Mary Magdalene. Once again, woman plays a vital role in giving man access to the divine.

In his book *Les Grands Initiés*, so very influential upon Le Corbusier, Schuré made the point that Mary Magdalene was the most 'ardent' of Jesus' disciples. It was his belief that Christ focused upon her in particular with the aim of reinforcing the position of women within religion. This is a very important point, one that Le Corbusier seems to have taken to heart. For Schuré Christ was 'the liberator of women', his ideas distorted and spoilt by Saint Paul and the Fathers of the Church.[47] It was Schuré's belief that religion should encompass a harmonious balance of masculine and feminine elements. It was for this reason that he, like Le Corbusier, promulgated the role of the Magdalene.

As the 'prostitute saint' Mary Magdalene embodied the coming together of the physical and spiritual, the message at the heart of *The Poem of the Right Angle*. In such standard works of Catholicism as the Rev. Alban Butler's *The Lives of the Fathers, Martyrs and other Principal Saints*, the Magdalene is presented as a repentant sinner. In a rather misogynistic way she is used to represent the evils of the flesh.[48] Le Corbusier and Trouin play down this image; she was instead to be admired for using her knowledge of the body to reach a higher spiritual state.

As a specifically Provençal saint, Mary Magdalene had a very particular role in bringing the Christian religion of the East to France. Trouin wrote:

> She was the first to reach Europe, in other words, she was universalism, and she was the first to attach to it here on this rock the new Prometheus, the non-vibrant symbol of the freeing of the man of the Sky, but of man by Man; of the Far East breaking into the West (the rise of the Gauls).
>
> If there is a human saint, it is Mary Magdalene.[49]

In bringing the knowledge of Jesus across the Mediterranean to Europe she united orient and occident, one of the main ideas behind the Basilica scheme.

Mary Magdalene was significant to Le Corbusier because she connected with a number of his key interests: Catharism, enlightenment, paradox, knowledge, geometry, asceticism, sexual balance and the Mediterranean. He would use the Saint as a vehicle through which to promulgate his message. As was seen in the last chapter, she was also linked in his mind with his wife Yvonne.

The Basilica

The first design for the Basilica, influenced heavily by St Teresa's book *The Interior Castle* (a fascinating exploration of mystical space and Kabbalistic knowledge) was largely by Trouin (Fig. 6.3).[50] I am going to focus here on the version designed by Le Corbusier (Fig. 6.4) that seems to have been based upon one of his favourite symbols, the sign for the 24 hour day (Fig. 6.5) used, for example, on the entrance stone of the Unité apartment blocks at Marseilles and Nantes-Rezé (1952). He wrote: 'If, in the course of the mutation of the machine civilisation, I have been able to contribute something, as a person with some rationality and intelligence, as a technician, as a thoughtful man, it will be this sign'. It provided him with the means to discover again the 'lost Paradise'.[51]

In Le Corbusier's scheme the pilgrim would climb the wooded foothills of the mountain and enter the Basilica through the grotto of Mary Magdalene herself. In a sense he would re-enact her story. He or she would then travel down into a lower dark chamber (evocative of the Magdalene's life of bodily excess) before moving on to an upper chamber (evocative of the sun coming up and indeed the presence of Jesus in the life of the Magdalene). The whole complex would be proportioned in accordance with the Modulor, Le Corbusier's system of proportion. In *Precisions* Le Corbusier observed that

> Architecture is a series of successive events . . . events that the spirit tries to transmute by the creation of relations so precise and so overwhelming that deep physiological sensations result from them, that a real spiritual delectation is felt at reading the solution, that a perception of harmony comes to us from the clear-cut mathematical quality uniting each element of the work.[52]

Light, sound, colour, rhythm and space would be used to introduce the body to a sense of geometric

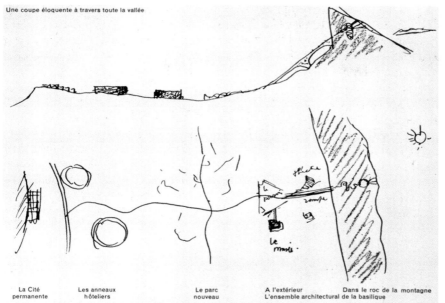

Une coupe éloquente à travers toute la vallée

La Cité permanente   Les anneaux hôteliers   Le parc nouveau   A l'extérieur L'ensemble architectural de la basilique   Dans le roc de la montagne

Figure 6.3
First version of the Basilica at La Sainte Baume, designed by Edouard Trouin.

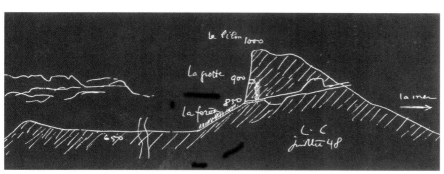

Figure 6.4
Le Corbusier's design for the Basilica at La Sainte Baume.

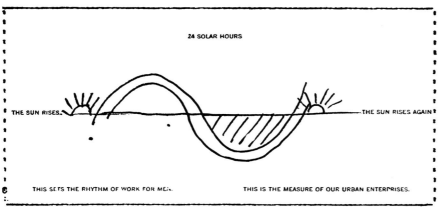

24 SOLAR HOURS

THE SUN RISES.   THE SUN RISES AGAIN

THIS SETS THE RHYTHM OF WORK FOR ME.   THIS IS THE MEASURE OF OUR URBAN ENTERPRISES.

Figure 6.5
Le Corbusier's sign of the 24 hour day.

The Cult of Woman and the Religious Architecture of Le Corbusier

harmony resulting in a state of spiritual transformation.[53] At the end of this disorientating trip, likened by Trouin to an initiation, the neophyte would journey to the top of the mountain, emerging on the plateau above where he or she would be greeted by a sparkling view of the Mediterranean and the sun to the south, climax and focus of the spiritual journey. In this way the neophyte would re-enact the journey of the Magdalene, retracing her steps to a perfect knowledge of a God simultaneously pagan and Christian.

The design for the Basilica at La Sainte Baume evolved over the years 1946 to 1948 when, much to Le Corbusier's disgust, it was rejected as an idea by the Church.[54] Undefeated, he and Trouin set about reusing some of the ideas developed for the Basilica in their scheme for the Permanent City where the Magdalene would play a similarly exemplary role.

The Permanent City

The Permanent City at La Sainte, a small housing development to be built on the other side of the plateau of La Sainte Baume, with direct views across the valley floor to the grotto itself, was envisaged as a 'radiant community' (Fig. 6.6). The scheme, which went through a number of permutations, was based on the idea of a North African casbah.[55] It would, like the Magdalene herself, be the very embodiment of the melding of orient with occident.

Built of rammed earth, the vaulted houses would be cave-like, dark and cool within. Roofed with grass they would be evocative of a tomb or a cave like that of the Magdalene across the valley (Fig. 6.7). It was Le Corbusier's belief that materials could influence

the lives of those that lived within his buildings.[56] By building in earth he was trying to encourage those who lived within to live in accordance with nature. Simple in detailing, the buildings would encourage those who lived within the houses to adopt an ascetic way of life, like that of the Magdalene herself. Built out of the 'most fantastically simple materials', the dwellings would contain 'a radiant spirit'.[57]

The materials of houses would be taken from the site itself, literally of the land, to encourage this sense of connection with all that it meant.[58] Built to Modulor proportions the houses would be in harmony with nature, the use of geometry evoking the Magdalene's special links to this realm.

The Museum

Within what Le Corbusier and Trouin referred to as the 'forum' of La Sainte Baume would be constructed a museum of Mary Magdalene, occupying the particular position in a Roman town that would usually be given to a temple (Fig. 6.8).[59] Trouin and Le Corbusier started to discuss building a museum of the iconography of Mary Magdalene as early as 1948. Indeed it seems that for the two men the museum, allied to a chapel, would have a religious role. In their eyes it was a sacred space.[60]

The museum would house Trouin's collection of images of the Magdalene, the aim being to show how this paradoxical figure had been interpreted in a number of different ways over the years. It was to be situated in an old sheep fold, consciously evoking the stable in which Christ was born. The simple rubble building would be left as plain and cavelike as

Figure 6.6   Le Corbusier, elevation of Permanent City at La Sainte Baume.

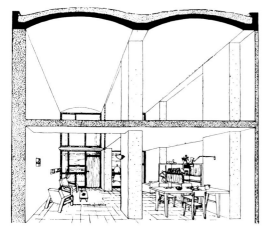

Figure 6.7 Perspective section of interior of house within the Permanent City at La Sainte Baume.

possible, again to evoke the ascetic existence of the Magdalene. Within it would be a table, a raw block of stone. Glass tiles set within the roof would allow beams of light to penetrate the space as if from a crevice in a roof of rock (Fig. 6.9).

The museum would be closely linked to a theatre where the story of the Magdalene would be re-enacted and the latest technology would be used to optimal effect to heighten the sense of her mystery.[61] The Museum and the Theatre would form an important event on the route up to the grotto.

That Le Corbusier took a particular interest in the Museum can be seen from a letter to Trouin of October 1951 in which he reminded his client of its importance for the scheme as a whole:

You have the book on M[arie] M[agdalene] to complete. You ought to devote yourself to that work of making the iconography accessible and feasible (I can help you with that).

You can and must, without moment's delay, bring about the realisation of the M[ary] M[agdalene] museum in the Sheepfold. I am going to revise the plans; the next time I go to Marseilles I shall take Bertocchi to La Sainte Baume. We shall make the necessary enquiries as to technical matters, setting up the building site etc . . .

The Museum of M[ary] M[agdalene] in the sheepfold can become an extraordinary tool of tourism, an extraordinary demonstration of the iconography of art. By means of absolutely dazzling photographic methods we will use the fantastic documentation that exists on this theme in the history of the arts. You will be the painter of certain parts, the sole painter to the exclusion of any other including me. The museum in the Sheepfold is such a living thing that I insist on doing it for you, with you, and there you will put the bell around the neck of the Basilica and all the rest too.[62]

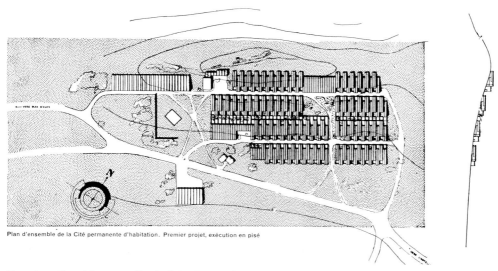

Plan d'ensemble de la Cité permanente d'habitation. Premier projet, exécution en pisé

Figure 6.8 Plan of Permanent City, La Sainte Baume. The museum is the one building set on the diagonal.

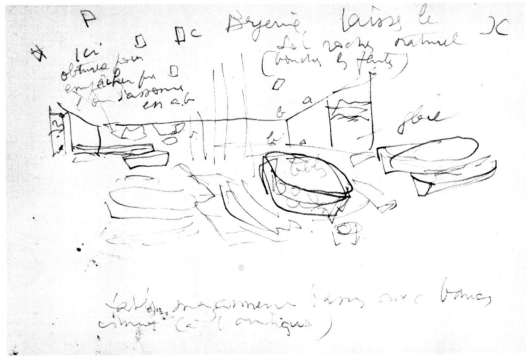

Figure 6.9   Sketch of interior of 'Bergerie' museum, La Sainte Baume.

Le Corbusier wanted to be fully involved in the choice of images to be used within the museum: 'I would like to take part in the collaging of the photo-murals of Mary Magdalene and in the polychromy' he wrote to his client. 'The poorer it is the better it will be' he observed, thus emphasising the ascetic nature of the project.[63]

It was Trouin's hope that the collection in the Museum would follow 'a previously undreamed of classification which the MEMORIAL with its modern and authentic works will perpetuate'.[64] These would be:

Works of art such as only twelve or thirteen photographers in the world are capable of bringing about; enlargements or FACSIMILE according to each case; the work photographed as a whole or in details, from lengthily studied angles, restoring to the object its power to strike . . .[65]

Believing that many important images of the Magdalene were hidden away in the storerooms of museums, Trouin wanted to look all over the world in a 'search for absolutely unknown artworks' which would 'go beyond the imaginary museums of Malraux[66] or others'.[67] At La Sainte Baume he wanted to bring together a collection of Magdalenes of every sort:

We shall put in the main works inspired by our Sainte Magdalene (the anonymous mediaeval ones – Provençal, French, Italian and German – Giotto – Donatello – Durer – Brea – Lucas Moser – El Greco – Goya – La Tour – Daumier, and a few others. And this won't keep us from including all the others, on revolving wall panels, or projections. There will be rather odd perspectives, for example a grouping of all the 'flesh' Magdalenes, daughters of those by Titian. Or of all the theatrical

Magdalenes descendants of the Swabian and the Flemish – or of all the Magdalenes said to be naïve.[68]

He wanted her to be seen in every possible light, reflecting the multitude of possibilities, saintly and heretical, spiritual and erotic, symbolised by this one, eloquent woman. According to Trouin's belief, 'only the iconography of the Virgin' could 'excel that of the Magdalene at La Sainte Baume'.[69]

The Theatre

Late in his career Le Corbusier became increasingly interested in performance.[70] He began to see performance spaces as integral to museums, both of which would serve what was at a fundamental level an essentially spiritual purpose. The aim of an event such as *The Electronic Poem* that took place within the Philips Pavilion at the Brussels World Fair in 1958, a synthesis of 'colour, imagery, music, words and rhythm',[71] was to immerse visitors in a total experience of harmony. Through the use of flashing images and disorientating effects Le Corbusier was attempting to affect people at the most subliminal level (Fig. 6.10).[72] Le Corbusier was profoundly influenced by the ideas of his friend the art historian Elie Faure in this matter.[73] Each of those who witnessed *The Electronic Poem* at the Brussels World Fair of 1958 would be thrown into 'a torrent, a mass, a depth of sensations, showing, demonstrating, and perhaps proving something'.[74]

At La Sainte Baume there was to be a theatre built in conjunction with the museum that would provide just such an experience. This part of the scheme came to be known as the Provisional Theatre. It would become the temporary receptacle for all their aspirations for the site. Le Corbusier and Trouin ruminated at length on the exact nature of the performance that would take place there. In November 1955 Le Corbusier had came back from Japan where he was most impressed by 'Noh theatre, the ancestor of Kabuki'[75] and suggested to Trouin that they should create a Noh theatre at La Sainte Baume. Le Corbusier would already have known about this type of theatre from a 1954 edition of *L'Art Sacré* to which he

Figure 6.10 Interior of Le Corbusier's Pavilion for the Brussels World Fair, showing part of the performance of *The Electronic Poem*.

subscribed on a regular basis.[76] Noh is a traditional form of Japanese drama evolved from the rites of Shinto, an ancient and pantheistic religion, based on the worship of ancestors and of nature. It is possible that Le Corbusier saw certain parallels between it and Orphism.[77]

Trouin took up Le Corbusier's suggestion to create such a theatre at La Sainte Baume, writing: 'thus Noh theatre becomes Magdalenean, like everything else that I manage to assimilate'.[78] It was his plan that the actors in his theatre would work with the sun behind them so that they would appear in silhouette, thus drawing more attention to the movements of their mime than to their faces.[79]

Trouin was constantly dogged by financial problems as well as difficulties with planners. As a result a far more modest scheme was eventually produced for the theatre at La Sainte Baume than was originally intended. The Provisional Theatre (Fig. 6.11), a vaulted structure similar in many ways to one of the houses for the Permanent City, was built as an extension of Trouin's own home. It is the only part of the La Sainte Baume scheme to be built, apart from a combined garage and atelier of indeterminate origins. One of Le Corbusier's main contributions to the

Provisional Theatre was to help Trouin with the colour scheme for the building.[80] It seems to have taken almost two years to complete the decorations, so they were evidently complex.

In July 1959 Trouin wrote to Le Corbusier asking him to come and give the building 'the final touch'.[81] It has since been whitewashed so it is difficult to ascertain what the colours would have been like.[82] Le Corbusier wrote of a photograph of the scheme that the project was 'quite pretty thanks to the blackness of the arcades. What I see on the photos are glaucous greens and blues, pale as tubercular patients!'[83] Evidently it was a poor print as certain visitors to the scheme had described the colours as 'criardes' or gaudy.[84] Trouin himself believed that the Provisional Theatre had an 'insolent beauty'.[85] It seems very likely that Le Corbusier was thinking of the polychromy of brightly coloured classical temples when he chose to paint the building in such strong colours; after all, this was a building where a sacred story would be re-enacted and where sacred artefacts would be kept.

The building was to serve a number of purposes, the most important being to represent the life of the Magdalene, although it could also be used for dances and other more prosaic purposes.[86] Trouin wrote to Le Corbusier:

As you have suggested, we must settle on a single show (like the Oberramergau Passion) which we will put on with the old texts conforming to the St. Mary Magdalene of St. Germain or Bastille or the rue Bouterie, who becomes the naked saint of Christian eroticism.[87]

His plan was to tell the drama of the Magdalene on his walls, which he described as 'a book of 2000m³'.[88] Trouin bought an epidiascope to project images from his iconography onto the walls of the main room where he was also planning to put a cinema screen.[89] He also proposed to produce a booklet to accompany the performance.

Trouin spent much time cogitating over the problem of who would be suitable to play the Magdalene in his performance. He wrote to Le Corbusier:

I am going to offer you a scenario for the play of the whore saint, human, not literary, as soon as I know exactly what auditory and visual means we have . . . we must have Brigitte Bardot who I've seen at St. Tropez, sweetly sad and seeming to seek the role of a great naked mystic such as only La Sainte Baume could authorise her to play. How can I get in touch with Bardot?[90]

His choice of Brigitte Bardot, recently established as a famous sex symbol for her performance in Roger Vadim's film *And God Created Woman* (1956), as the Magdalene is illuminating. His Magdalene was not to be wizened and ascetic; she would be overtly sexual.

Trouin's attention then turned to the way in which the Magdalene should be represented in the theatre. 'Do I dare to say that I see a Magdalene with vengeful retorts like Yvonne's? Without however falling into the extremes of a Marion Delorme by Hugo' he asked Le Corbusier.[91] Then Trouin made a point which, more than any other, explains the importance of the Magdalene to the project and, I would suggest, to Le Corbusier's oeuvre:

In the last analysis, the Magdalene: woman, man's damp link with the earth, with original plasma. Christ himself, son of woman, bases his religion on Woman (avoid coming down on the side of Auguste Comte's Clothilde de Vaux).[92]

For Trouin the Magdalene, as representative of woman, made a link between man and the earth.

Figure 6.11   Exterior of the Provisional Theatre at La Sainte Baume as it looked in 1999.

He described her as 'humid', damp, flowing like water, like plasma, the fluid part of blood that carries suspended within it other active particles.[93] Further, she was 'original' having been present at the beginning, and was therefore associated with the past; indeed, in Trouin's opinion, Christ had based his religion on woman. In words that evoke the winged spirit in Le Corbusier's paintings, Trouin observed that 'the mind beating broken wings in the vacuum of the sensual universe catches on to Woman'.[94]

For Trouin, Yvonne was an 'eternal avenger of the intrinsic value of the individual', symbolic of Le Corbusier's 'puritanical protest against Society's formalism'.[95] Yvonne provided a constant reminder to Trouin and Le Corbusier of the power and presence of the individual. She challenged the assumptions of the two men and forced them to be more realistic. They had to consider a world in which the individual as well as the collective could find fulfilment. Yvonne provided their inspiration, because she had changed their way of thinking; she, like the Magdalene, acted as a Muse. As Eric Dodds observed in his 1951 book *The Greeks and the Irrational*:

> For Plato, indispensable to the production of the best poetry is a type of divine madness defined as possession by the Muses. It was a Muse who took from Demodocus his bodily vision and gave him something better, the gift of song, because she loved him. Epic tradition represented the poet as deriving supernormal knowledge from the Muses . . . The gift . . . of the Muses . . . is the power of true speech.[96]

Yvonne, it appears, occupied such a role in the life of Le Corbusier.

In the opinion of Henriette Trouin 'Le Corbusier, like my husband, venerated woman as the complement of man'.[97] Certainly Trouin came to see his own wife in this way. He wrote in a letter to Le Corbusier:

> She gave herself to me in my burning countryside, like all the women I have had, the day after or the very day of our meeting; for they feel the strength. She gave herself to me in my burning countryside, like a Siren of earth and empty sky who leaps into

the sea . . . Never have I felt such cosmicity [the cosmic] as in those days. I wanted to marry the anonymous, but I have at once my female individual and universality.[98]

Through passionate intercourse with his wife, Trouin felt a sense of connection with the cosmos. He became complete in the manner described by Le Corbusier in *The Poem of the Right Angle*. It seems that in his relationship with his wife he believed himself to be enacting at a small scale some larger cosmic drama. As Le Corbusier wrote in one of his sketchbooks: 'The drama becomes internalised'.[99]

In 1956 Trouin began to refer to the Museum as 'le Museon', a word with significant associations.[100] It was a place of education, dedicated to the Muses, which was attached to a Greek temple much as the Museum at La Sainte Baume was to be attached to the chapel.[101] It is also possible, given his enthusiasm for word play, that in choosing the word 'museon' Trouin was alluding to the presence of Musaios, a figure who appears in connection with Orpheus, for example in the work of Plato.[102] In the opinion of Guthrie 'many of the writings attributed to Orpheus (himself the son of a Muse) were addressed to Musaios'.[103] Whether this was the case or not the Museon would be dedicated to Mary Magdalene as Muse, a source of inspiration and the bringer of harmony.[104]

The Park

Together, through a series of letters and drawings, Le Corbusier and Trouin developed ideas about the reforestation of the site and the planning of the park on it.[105] Through its design the two men would be able to extend the message implicit within the architecture of the City, that of the importance of woman in the spiritual life of man, out into the countryside.

Much has been written of Le Corbusier's 1930 project for the city of Algiers and its similarity in form to the women in Le Corbusier's paintings.[106] It seems that a similar effect was intended for La Sainte Baume. From a reading of Trouin's letters it becomes evident that both he and Le Corbusier enjoyed making analogies between the landscape and the contours of the human body. According to Vincent Scully such a practice was common in ancient Greece, where the forms of the land were used to evoke the body of Mother Earth.[107] For Trouin the landscape was 'vocal'; it could speak to those who came there.[108] In ancient Greece, the Muses were honoured in grottos and in what Marie Luise Gothein referred to as 'philosopher's gardens'.[109] These would contain a particular message for the initiated. Le Corbusier and Trouin may have had a similar idea in mind for the park at La Sainte Baume.

At La Sainte Baume the main attraction both for pilgrims and walkers alike is to climb the leafy path up past the grotto of Mary Magdalene to the top of the ridge above, from which viewpoint the flat valley floor below can be seen almost like a flat canvas. It may have been for this reason that Le Corbusier chose to approach the design of the landscape below almost as he would a painting.[110] Here the contours of the plateau would be translated quite literally into the form of the Magdalene's body. Trouin wrote of Le Corbusier's plan:

> As for Saint Magdalene, she remains from you with the first ring for her head, for wings, the two great leafy plateaux, for her lap the cedar plateau and for her stellar tail the most South-Easterly cedars.
>
> And a second figure of Magdalene superimposes itself on the first and has for its head the second ring, for chest, the central leafy plateau and for buttock and suggestion of thigh the Eastern plateau . . .[111]

Within the park, Le Corbusier wanted to create two figures of the Magdalene, one overlapping the other. Given that Trouin wrote of her as the prostitute saint, it would seem likely that Le Corbusier would associate one Magdalene with the spirit and one with the body. Further evidence for this supposition is provided by the fact that one of the figures would have wings. In this way he would make a connection between the contours of the site, the Magdalene and a much older form of feminine divinity, Mother Earth, for whom he felt a profound nostalgia.[112]

For Trouin, La Sainte Baume was linked with ancient Greece; he liked to refer to it as the 'French Delphi'. Apparently Le Corbusier was in agreement with him on this matter.[113] In *The Earth, the Temple and the Gods*, Scully describes Delphi in some detail.[114] Like the grotto of the Magdalene it was a cave, housing Greece's oldest and most famous oracle, the place in which Mother Earth was worshipped under the name of Delphyne. The word Delphi was synonymous with 'womb'.[115] Le Corbusier himself was to write of the 'admirable form . . . of the omphalos of the temple of Apollo in Delphi'.[116] The Delphic Oracle went through a number of transformations, sometimes being dedicated to the goddess of the sea and at others to the goddess of the moon, both variants on the same theme of the primordial mother.[117] It was Trouin's desire to create at La Sainte Baume 'a beauty worthy of Delphic framework'. He wrote emphatically 'Delphi is dead. La Sainte Baume lives'.[118]

Summary

Mary Magdalene, the 'spirit' of La Sainte Baume, was deeply significant for both Le Corbusier and Trouin. They were interested in her for a number of reasons. Firstly, she was a specifically Provençal saint, uniting aspects of the orient and occident. She was an ascetic saint who had come to knowledge through descent into sin and the body and through a simple life within nature. As the prostitute saint she was a paradoxical figure combining elements of the bodily and the spiritual. She was, in a sense, Jesus' muse: through her his knowledge was brought to the attention of the world. She was also a muse in that, like the Muses of ancient Greece, she was a keeper of harmony and for the Masons, a custodian of the knowledge of the ancient use of number.

Le Corbusier and Trouin tried to evoke Mary Magdalene in a number of ways: by creating a route of initiation through her mountain in passing through which the visitor would re-enact her story; through the use of geometry; through the use of simple materials to create spaces evocative of her cave; and by drawing attention to the rich symbolism of her story within the Museum. Lastly, as if the connection between the Magdalene and the landscape was not already clear enough, they would design a park in the form of her body. To enter the grotto would thus be to enter the very body of the Magdalene. In this way Le Corbusier and Trouin would reassert the role of woman within religion, an important step towards the achievement of harmony. Whilst they stressed her importance in the life of man, their paradoxical Magdalene has few of those passive characteristics normally associated with the 'feminine'. An adventurous creature, her main attribute is a profound and exemplary form of knowledge.

Ronchamp

Le Corbusier initially refused the commission for this project saying that he did not want to work for 'a dead institution', possibly because of the bitterness that he felt about the Church's rejection of the Basilica at La Sainte Baume.[119] His assistant André Wogenscky recorded a conversation in which the architect told Couturier that he had no right to work on the scheme and that they should find a Catholic architect instead. According to Wogenscky:

> Father Couturier explained to him that the decision to ask Le Corbusier had been taken in full consciousness of the situation, in the knowledge that he was not religious. Eventually he said: 'But Le Corbusier, I don't give a damn about your not being a Catholic. What we need is a great artist . . . You will achieve our goal far better than if we asked a Catholic architect: he would feel bound to make copies of ancient churches'. Le Corbusier was pensive for a few seconds, then he said: 'all right, I accept'.[120]

It is likely that Couturier was eventually able to persuade him to accept the commission because Le Corbusier realised that it would at last give him the opportunity to put into practice so many of those complex ideas that were developed whilst working on the Basilica for La Sainte Baume.

Perched on a ridge, the chapel of Ronchamp is visible as a white beacon to the approaching pilgrim (Fig. 6.12). Perhaps the most iconic building of the twentieth century, it needs little introduction. Few of its walls are orthogonal. They undulate inwards and outwards in both dimensions, simultaneously

inviting in and repelling the surrounding landscape. Le Corbusier recounted:

> I had burned stones left from the church before the war. They couldn't carry anything, but I didn't want to get rid of them. I made curved walls so that they could hold them. This curve is useful for acoustics. It is an acoustic of space that receives the four horizons, all different from each other.[121]

The building has three towers and three doors, the one to the east providing access to the exterior chapel used for mass congregations on days of pilgrimage. Within the atmosphere is cave-like, the floor and walls sloping towards a climax at the altar end of the chapel. Colour is injected into the cool white interior by means of painted windows punctured into the thick south wall.

The scheme at Ronchamp was, according to Le Corbusier, the result of 'meticulous research', involving the continual adjustment of a 'thousand factors . . . which no-one ought or would wish to speak of'.[122] His sketchbooks contain evidence of the amount of careful thought that went into the theological programme of the building. Indeed the symbolic programme of the building is so complex that Mogens Krustrup has devoted an entire book to unravelling the meaning of just one door.[123]

Governed by the Modulor, Le Corbusier wrote that the form of Ronchamp was generated in order to stir 'the psycho-physiology of the feelings', not to fulfil the requirements of religion.[124] As in the Basilica at La Sainte Baume it was Le Corbusier's intention to imbue each visitor to Ronchamp with a sense of the transforming and restorative power of harmony, as manifested through colour, sound and form in the

Figure 6.12 Ronchamp exterior

belief that it was possible to change behaviour through affecting the feelings.[125]

Sound would play an important role in bringing about a sensation of harmony. It was Le Corbusier's intention that here

> They will be able to make incredible music, an unbelievable sound when they have twelve thousand people outside with amplifiers. I said to the priest, 'you should get rid of the kind of music played by an old maid on an old harmonium – that's out of tune – and instead have music composed for the church, something new, not sad music, a loud noise, an unholy din'.[126]

Music would play a paramount role in the Chapel's conception, 'music and architecture' in Le Corbusier's view 'being two arts very close in their highest manifestations'.[127]

Given the evidence presented in Chapter 4, it seems very likely that the Modulor was linked in Le Corbusier's mind with the geometry of the philosopher's stone, the marriage of opposites, male and female, culmination of the alchemical process. By challenging us to find the Modulor at Ronchamp, he was challenging us to find the union of opposites within ourselves, the result being a kind of visionary experience, that of l'*espace indicible* or ineffable space.[128] The lines are blurred between the Modulor as a form of measure and the Modulor as a form of experience. As Le Corbusier was to write: 'I have not experienced the miracle of faith, but I have often known the miracle of inexpressible space, the apotheosis of plastic emotion'.[129] He quoted a passage from L'*Espace Indicible*[130] in his book *Modulor*.[131] He then quoted it again in *Modulor 2*, thus underscoring its importance.[132]

> For a finished and successful work holds within it a vast amount of intention, a veritable world, which reveals itself to those who have a right to it: that is to say, to those who deserve it.
>
> Then a fathomless depth gapes open, all walls are broken down, every other presence is put to flight, and the miracle of inexpressible space is achieved.[133]

Here he describes a moment of mystical revelation achieved through the use of mathematics as the 'key' to the 'door of miracles', a fact that did not escape the priests of the *L'Art Sacré* movement with whom he worked closely and one which in part explains their enthusiasm for his work.

Building and body

Christopher Pearson makes the fascinating point that within Le Corbusier's domestic architecture a work of art was intended, amongst other functions, to act as a 'carefully sited anthropomorphic presence within the building, which could dramatise . . . the visitor's relationship to and participation in the architectural space by the creation of a sympathetic bond between visitor and sculpture'.[134] Le Corbusier would hence assimilate anthropomorphic forms into the architecture of the chapel in order to maximise their psychological impact on the visitor.

In the opinion of Jaime Coll the plan of Ronchamp (Fig. 6.13) is derived from a 1946 sketch from the Ubu series (Fig. 6.14).[135] Certainly the similarities are striking. I would also suggest that the plan, and indeed the whole building, retains elements of the *Icône* series of paintings, a fact that seems to justify the suggestion that certain parts of the building might be compared with elements of a woman's body. As well as sharing in the form of the *Icône* paintings, it is my contention that Ronchamp shares in their meaning (Fig. 5.37).

The building invites touch. Lucien Hervé, who worked closely with Le Corbusier to photograph the building, makes the connection between building and body perfectly clear by juxtaposing Le Corbusier's statement 'I believe in the skin of things, as in that of women',[136] with an image of the southeast wall of Ronchamp, which looks uncannily like skin seen at close range.

> Tenderness!
> Seashell the Sea in us has never
> ceased to wash its wrecks of
> laughing harmony upon the shore
> Hand kneading hand caressing
> hand brushing. the hand and the
> seashell love each other.[137]

The imprint of Le Corbusier's own fingers can be seen in the plaster of the wall by the figure of the Virgin Mary.[138]

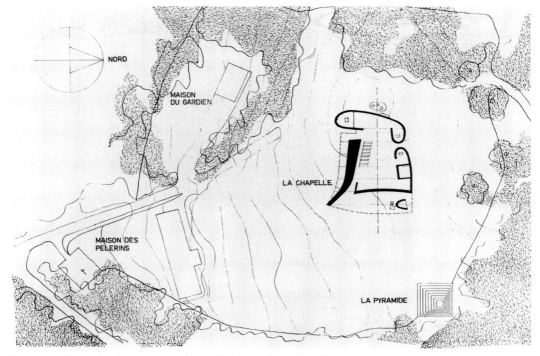

Figure 6.13   Plan of Ronchamp in context from Le Corbusier's *Oeuvre Complète*.

Water being in short supply on the top of the hill, it was required that Le Corbusier build into the church a cistern where rainwater could be collected. Water, Mary and the moon being symbolically linked, such a requirement provided a help not a hindrance to the architect's conception of the building. Water cascades off the crab shell roof,[139] through a gargoyle shaped like an abstracted pair of breasts (Fig. 6.15) and down into a cistern, womblike in form (Fig. 6.16). As if to emphasise this uterine quality, the wall of the church curves out at this point as if in emulation of the stomach of a pregnant woman (this protrusion encloses the confessionals). The cistern itself contains a trinity of sculptural objects which are, like Rabelais' Holy Bottle described in Chapter 4, half immersed in water.

When we enter into the body of the church, through its highly physical curves we enter the womb of the Eternal Feminine in her guise as Mary – again ambiguously chaste and sexual. The chapel is, in the opinion of Dominique Lyon, 'a womb, a belly, represented by the swellings of the concrete veils. It is no less than the Virgin's belly. Ronchamp shows the point

Figure 6.14   *Acoustic forms*, pastel on paper, New York 1946.

Figure 6.15   Photograph of gargoyle, Ronchamp.

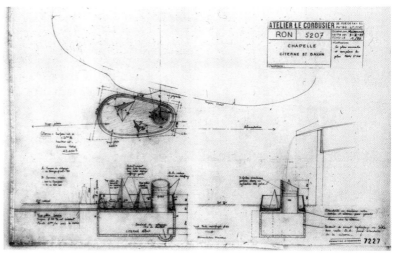

Figure 6.16   Le Corbusier, sketch plan of water cistern, Ronchamp.

where nature and the divine mingle'.[140] We should remember the connection that was made between the spiral, the ear, acoustics, balance, water level and woman in the last chapter. In Ronchamp Le Corbusier created 'an acoustic of space that receives'.[141] Like the ear, like the womb, it is a place where sound/water waves meet in balance and a harmonious state is achieved.[142]

The ear

At this point it is worth repeating Panurge's words to Bacbuc in the Oracle of the Holy Bottle, as they provide a clue to the symbolism of the towers at Ronchamp:

> O Bottle great
> with mysteries
> with one ear do
> I listen:
> for the proffered word to sound
> the Holy Bottle.[143]

Le Corbusier describes the lighting in the towers of Ronchamp as 'very special', I would suggest because of a link between light and sound, erotic and spiritual revelation.[144] Gregory of Nyssa (d. 394) posited the idea that Mary conceived Jesus on hearing the words of the

angel.[145] This idea quickly gained a 'literal stamp' and was celebrated by many medieval poets resulting in the notion that the Virgin was impregnated through her ear. Le Corbusier may be alluding to this belief. Certainly he seems to have believed in the power of musical harmony to bring us closer to the divine. Through its earlike form the tower acts as a receiver of sound. The word of God enters Mary's body in the form of light. The tower is simultaneously ear and vagina, open to spiritual or erotic connotations. At a different level light, symbolic of sound, would penetrate the body through the earlike form of the chapel, bringing to the pilgrim, as it did to Panurge, a greater under-standing of the revelatory power of harmony.

The vase

Julia Kristeva writes of the representation of Mary:

> of the virginal body we are entitled only to the ear, the tears, and the breasts. That the female sexual organ has been transformed into an innocent shell which serves only to receive sound may ultimately contribute to an eroticization of hearing and the voice, not to say of understanding. But by the same token sexuality is reduced to a mere implication. The female sexual experience is therefore

anchored in the universality of sound, since the spirit is equally given to all men, to all women.[146]

In doing so she unwittingly draws together a number of Corbusian themes.

Both Mary and Mary Magdalene are traditionally represented through vessel symbolism, the Virgin through her womb and the Magdalene through the Myrrophone, the jar of funerary oil that she carries with her. Together they preside over the realms of birth, death and love. As vessels, holy bottles, they are embodied in the form of the chapel which Le Corbusier significantly described as 'a vase of silence, of sweetness. A desire.'[147]

Evoking Rabelais' Oracle of the Holy Bottle, Le Corbusier described Ronchamp as 'a vessel of intense concentration and meditation'.[148] The imagery of the vessel haunts Le Corbusier's work, receiving its most clear expression in the scheme for the church at Firminy Vert (1960), where the congregation floats in a literal interpretation of an alchemical alembic, the site of transformation (Fig. 6.17). The church takes the form of a kind of squared cone, itself a union of orthogonal and curved geometries. It is raised on a platform as though there were a fire beneath. The light pours in from the top as if through the mouth of a bottle. At the same time its slightly lopsided form evokes the hooded women of Le Corbusier's paintings and indeed the towers of Ronchamp.

In the *Timaeus* Plato tried to explain the origins and the structure of the universe, in so doing gendering the explanation. Form he described as male, the father

of and model for the material object. Chora is female, a kind of womb for material existence, the place or space which functions as receptacle, mother and nurse. It is a term which 'eludes definition or bounding' as Jennifer Bloomer observes.[149] As males were superior to females, Plato believed abstract ideal Form to be superior to the mere container that was the Chora. Whilst, to my knowledge, Le Corbusier makes no specific reference to such ideas, something similar seems to be implicit in his work. Contrast, for example, his enthusiasm for 'pure'[150] Platonic solids expressed in *Towards a New Architecture* with the nebulous and womblike spaces of Ronchamp. In his early work he makes explicit reference to ideal forms, but his later more chthonic work seems rather to allude to the Chora as a key reference. It seems no accident that Le Corbusier chose to build a pyramidal war memorial next to Ronchamp. The pure pyramidal form, in many ways a monument to the sun, would act as a perfect foil to the watery vessel that is Ronchamp.

In *Space, Time and Architecture* Le Corbusier's friend Siegfried Giedion was to comment upon the similarity of the form of the towers of Ronchamp to those of an ancient neolithic tomb (Fig. 6.18).[151] John Alford, who wrote about Ronchamp at the time of its construction, was to make a similar observation. In his opinion there were remarkable similarities

344a. Stele at the neolithic monumental "Tomb of the Giants" in Sardinia.

344b. LE CORBUSIER. Pilgrimage Chapel of Notre Dame du Haut, Ronchamp, 1955. View from the west. A Mexican architect, R. Barragan, pointed out the secret affinity of the towers of Ronchamp with a prehistoric cult structure in Sardinia.

Figure 6.18   Page from Siegfried Geidion's book *Space, Time and Architecture* in which he compares an image of the towers at Ronchamp to the forms of ancient neolithic French tombs.

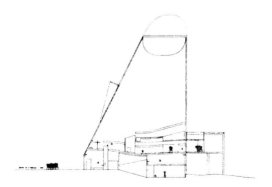

Figure 6.17   Section through Le Corbusier's scheme for the church at Firminy.

between the shapes of its forms and those of the neolithic mortuary sculptures of Brittany characterised by the imposition of a rectilinear and circular geometry on the human figure.[152] Le Corbusier seems to be making a connection between Mary and these primitive death goddesses who preside over the process of transformation in their womblike tombs.

Annotations to the Pilgrims Manual at Ronchamp suggest that Le Corbusier was interested in a more pagan Mary, one with roots back to the distant past, to the origins of religion.[153] An illustration in *Le Livre de Ronchamp* makes the connection between Mary and some more primal feminine deity very clear (Fig. 6.19). A circle of people sit in the dark around a fire in front of the exterior chapel, as if re-enacting some ancient ritual, while Mary looks on from the shadows. The Virgin, and her counterpart the Magdalene, continue the tradition of the Great Mother, whose fertility was less primly portrayed in archaic times. As Le Corbusier was to observe, 'Ronchamp lies beyond Rome, gets, without having sought it, in touch with the origins'.[154]

The Marys

Mary's symbolism can perhaps be seen most clearly in the painted glass of the south wall. Le Corbusier was fully aware that according to traditional Catholic symbolism Mary was associated with blue.[155] She is the water, the sea, and the moon. Her name Marie, painted on to the glass, evoked that of his own mother. While working on the scheme for Ronchamp, Le Corbusier was particularly impressed by the vision of the woman of the Apocalypse 'clothed in the sun, the moon at her feet'.[156] So interested was he in all aspects of her story that when he passed an insignificant train station called Labergement Sainte-Marie he made a note to himself to find out more about the word '*labergement*'.[157] His profound interest in iconography has already been noted in the discussion of the museum at La Sainte Baume.

One aspect of Marian symbolism in which Le Corbusier took a particular interest was the Catholic topos of three Marys. Significantly he chose to include in the refectory of the Pilgrim House at Ronchamp a reproduction of a medieval painting showing the dead Christ surrounded by a trinity of Marys: the Virgin, the Magdalene, and Mary of Egypt (Fig. 6.20). The same theme found its way into the pages of his book *The Radiant City* in the form of a statue of Jesus with his arms around three women taken from the cathedral of Chartres. Beneath it the caption reads

Figure 6.19   Photograph of the exterior altar at Le Corbusier's Ronchamp at night from *Le Livre de Ronchamp*.

Figure 6.20   View of interior of refectory in Pilgrims House, Ronchamp, showing painting of Jesus and three Marys.

'eternally permissible product: the work of art, final end of human nature', suggesting the enduring significance of this story.[158]

According to the gnostic *Gospel of Mary*, all three Marys of the canonical books were interchangeable.[159] That Le Corbusier appears to have been fully aware of the multiplicity of possibilities embodied in this one name is indicated by his use of the word 'Marys' in plural in his account of the life of the Magdalene in the *Oeuvre Complète*.[160] Given what we know of Le Corbusier so far it seems highly unlikely that he would have taken much interest in the standard virtuous Mary, so virtuous that she managed to conceive without losing her virginity. As an impossible model for women, her perfect image would only serve to outlaw the sexual act. It is my suggestion that Le Corbusier saw the Marys as different aspects of a greater divinity, and he used a generalised Marian figure to embody extremes of physicality and spirituality in order to create the kind of balance of which he was so fond.

I was first alerted to the possible presence of a two-sided Mary at Ronchamp when writing a paper on the very deliberate way that Le Corbusier composed photographic images to convey certain meanings.[161] In the *Oeuvre Complète* there is an image of the exterior chapel (Fig. 6.21) where the figure of the Madonna, installed in her niche, can be seen half in sun and half in shade. Attention is drawn to her by the spike of an open umbrella. 'Observe the play of shadows' writes Le Corbusier.[162] Working drawings indicate that it was his specific intention that she should be bisected into zones of light and shadow (Fig. 6.22). By representing her like this Le Corbusier seems to be suggesting that Mary has a dual aspect, a notion that is given further substance when we consider that the statue of the Virgin is fixed on a pivot in the niche, so that she can be turned around to reveal either of two sides, to face outward, toward nature, or inward, toward the church.

Jaime Coll has convincingly linked Le Corbusier's painted representations of Yvonne to the figure of Ariadne as she appears in André Gide's version of *Theseus*, which Le Corbusier read in 1951. Coll identifies certain important aspects of Ariadne's figure: she has two sides, one positive and one negative; she is also a lunar deity represented by the presence of the moon and the sea. Interestingly, all such symbolism

Figure 6.21   Photograph of exterior of chapel on the east side of Le Corbusier's Ronchamp on a pilgrimage day, from Le Corbusier's *Oeuvre Complète*.

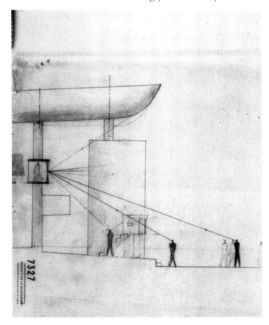

Figure 6.22   Le Corbusier's working drawing showing section through box containing the figure of Mary above the altar.

is equally applicable to the Virgin. This is not, perhaps, so surprising when we consider that it has been argued that the figure of the Virgin was derived from a reworking of more ancient religious ideas.[163]

In the last chapter it was noted that the Mary/Magdalene/Yvonne figure that inhabits the 'Fusion' section of *The Poem of the Right Angle* appears to have two heads, one in profile and one that looks into the page. The relationship between the two heads is remarkably similar to the relationship between the two smaller hooded chapels at Ronchamp, adding weight to the argument that, in line with his Symbolist leanings, Le Corbusier saw Mary not as one woman, but as two.

Robin Evans has drawn attention to the intimate associations that Le Corbusier brought to Ronchamp, suggesting that he named its three towers after the Virgin Mary, his mother Marie (to whom he was devoted), and Yvonne.[164] In Chapter 1 it was seen that Le Corbusier portrayed his mother as a divinity, a giant sphinx flanked by the sun and the moon. Her tower, painted white inside, may represent the maternal aspect of the feminine, while Yvonne's, painted red, may represent the sexual. Together, they are dominated by the larger white tower representing the Virgin herself.

When the building was consecrated on 25 June 1955 the archbishop presiding over the proceedings spoke of the importance of Le Corbusier's mother to its conception. Le Corbusier was to relay this information to Marie Jeanneret, indicating that it was indeed true.[165] It is my belief that Krustrup is correct in making the 'tentative' suggestion that the Chapel at Ronchamp represents a homage to Le Corbusier's mother as well as to the mother of God, to whom it is consecrated.[166] In addition I would argue that it also encompasses a tribute to his wife, closely associated with the Magdalene in Le Corbusier's mind.

The east door

That Le Corbusier worked closely with his photographers to create highly contrived images of his buildings has already been mentioned. In the photograph of the east end of the chapel interior (Fig. 6.23), our view is on axis with the Virgin in her glass niche. If the photograph is divided in two horizontally, the inner corner of the seating platform is at its exact centre. At this point, we are immediately aware of the two conflicting geometries at work: one leading us to the altar (via lines in the concrete of the floor), and one leading out of the east door into nature (via the seating platform). The image is described thus by Le Corbusier in the *Oeuvre Complète*:

> The main altar is situated in the nave (the axis of which is delineated in the flooring by a simple concrete band) where the ceiling is the highest, being 10m high at the mid-point of the altar wall and only 4.78 high at its lowest point . . .[167]

There is, however, something wrong with this statement. The ceiling is not highest above the altar: it is at its highest and most well lit above the concrete door that leads out to the exterior chapel on the east side of the building.

Le Corbusier seems to have been slightly ambivalent about the importance of the central altar. By his own admission, he found its organisation a very difficult piece of design, which perhaps explains its omission on the site plan in the *Oeuvre Complète*, in spite of the inclusion of the three smaller chapels.[168] 'I put the cross in a very significant place. At first it was in the wrong place. It was in the axis, it looked solemn. No, it looked silly'.[169] It was here that he seems to have had the most difficulty in balancing the demands of the Church with his own thinking. In the end Le Corbusier positioned the cross 'on the side like a witness', observing that 'when you think that they

Figure 6.23   Interior of the main altar of Le Corbusier's Chapel at Ronchamp.

crucified someone on it, that is dramatic'.[170] In its new position the cross appears on the right hand side of the altar below Mary, both of which draw the eye towards the east door beneath. It is my suggestion that Le Corbusier was actually more interested in arranging the composition of Mary, the cross and the east door than in the static altar itself.

Occupying the position beneath the zenith of the great roof, the east door at Ronchamp is obviously a site of great importance. Formed in concrete, a perverse but highly intentional choice of material, it is more than reminiscent of the stone that the angel rolled away from the entrance of Jesus' tomb on the third day, the day of his resurrection. As Le Corbusier was to write: 'sometimes there is a door: one opens it – enters – one is in another realm, the realm of the gods, the room which holds the key to the great systems. These doors are the doors of the miracles.'[171]

The handle of the door itself appears to take the abstract form of a woman's body (Fig. 6.24). It is juxtaposed with an imprint of a cockleshell, linked with woman, to Venus and to the Magdalene in the art of Le Corbusier.[172] In The Radiant City, Le Corbusier juxtaposed an image of a cockleshell with a pine cone next to the word 'harmonies' (Fig. 6.25).[173] The pine cone, being a traditional symbol of masculine creative force, combines with the cockle to create sexual balance. The pine cone appears in the pages of The Poem

Figure 6.25   Image of cockle shell and pine cone from Le Corbusier, The Radiant City.

pointing directly towards the groin of a naked woman on the opposing page accompanied by the words 'to make architecture is to make a creature' (Fig. 6.26).[174] In alchemical terms the pine cone is the Roman symbol of Jupiter, associated with tin which combines with copper (associated with Venus), to make the bronze of the handle itself. Whether this was intentional, one can only speculate, although we do know that the architect was interested in the concept of alchemical metal symbolism and the possibility of bringing down beneficent forces from the planets through their use.[175]

Working drawings showing the door handle in plan reveal its uncanny likeness to a pair of breasts (Fig. 6.27), a fact that could not have escaped Le Corbusier, who wrote 'try to look at the picture upside down or sideways. You will discover the game.'[176]

According to Krustrup, Le Corbusier associated Yvonne with the figure of Venus[177] who, in turn, has long been associated with that of Mary Magdalene, who also has a place in the symbolism of this door.[178] Here, once again, Mary Magdalene is offered up as an exemplar, but she is now admired for her knowledge, not for her shame. As we have seen, she came to the tomb on the third day, and was the first witness to Christ's resurrection, carrying away with her his message to which she gave new life. Oriented to the rising of the sun, the door seems to symbolise the death and resurrection of Jesus. Simultaneously, in an alchemical sense, it represents petite morte of sexual union, the relinquishing of the body and subsequent spiritual rebirth.

Figure 6.24   Detail of the east door. Photograph by Lucien Hervé.

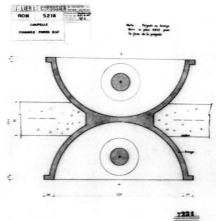

Figure 6.26   Detail of woman and pine cone, from Le Corbusier's *The Poem of the Right Angle*.

Figure 6.27   Working drawing showing handle of east door in plan.

The shell and the handle of the door represent the feminine side of a union of opposites. Here in Le Corbusier's gender balanced world the masculine is significantly absent. It is my suggestion that the visitor to the building is encouraged to take on this particular role. Le Corbusier wrote of Ronchamp 'the drama is designed, installed. For you living men, to live the drama as well.'[179] Here the male visitor to the chapel is encouraged to engage with the building in a very physical way. What the female visitor should do remains unclear. It may be that Le Corbusier intended her to project herself into the Marian role, as generations of Catholic women have done.

Le Corbusier wrote in *Towards a New Architecture*: 'All great works of art are based on one or other of the great standards of the heart: *Oedipus*, *Phaedra*, the *Enfant Prodigue*, the Madonnas, *Paul et Virginie*, Philemon and Baucis.'[180] He himself appears to have modelled his life upon perhaps the greatest 'standard of the heart', the story of Jesus and Mary, at once Virgin and Magdalene.

The same door handle appears in another large door, this time set into the exterior wall of Heidi Weber's house in Zurich. Here the stark white enamel square bears an illustration of Taureau/Dionysus, man, woman and bull in an embrace (Fig. 6.28). Late in life, in this secular setting, Le Corbusier felt able to create a door of initiation, one that was at last explicitly Orphic in character. Its message is the same as that of the door at Ronchamp, though couched in rather different terms.

Figure 6.28   Exterior door, Heidi Weber house, Zurich.

Summary

In a medieval painting which adorns one of the walls in the Pilgrim House at Ronchamp, Jesus and Mary are pictured together as equals sitting at a table. An image of this painting is included in Le Corbusier's book *Modulor 2* (Fig. 6.29).[181] In a 1959 photograph of Le Corbusier in his bedroom, a painting by the naïve painter André Bauchant can be seen above his marital bed (Fig. 6.30).[182] It appears to be a version of the standard Roman Catholic image of Christ crowning the Virgin Mary. Above the heads of the two figures looms a God crowned with two horns in the form of two tiny angels. Around them, in a Bacchic celebration, frolic further angels. Whilst this image

Figure 6.29   Photograph of medieval painting of Mary and Jesus in Le Corbusier's Pilgrims House at Ronchamp.

Figure 6.30   A 1959 photograph of Le Corbusier in his bedroom at 24 Rue Nungesser et Coli.

ostensibly depicts a Christian scene, the Orphic elements (for example the horns and the grapes) indicate that it can be read in another way. It is possible to interpret the painting as an image of the union of opposites, the androgynous unity described in Plato's *Symposium*, with which Le Corbusier and many of his circle were so preoccupied. To place such a painting above his own bed was a sign of his personal commitment to a God at once Christian and Dionysiac and his belief in the parallels between his own relationship with his wife and that of Mary (Virgin or Magdalene) and Jesus.[183] The painting makes his bed an altar, the site of his union with Yvonne, with woman (in Teilhard's terms), with the earth. From the bed the couple share, through the window beyond, a panorama of the sky, sun and clouds, paramount constituents of Le Corbusier's radiant world.

In the opinion of the Gnostics, the troubles of mankind had been brought about when Eve separated from Adam thus destroying the primal androgynous unity found in Genesis 1:27: 'so God created man in his own image; in the image of God he created him; male and female he created them.' For the Gnostics the alliance of Christ and the Magdalene would bring once again that perfect state of unity that was lost in the Garden of Eden.[184] Whether Le Corbusier adhered to this belief is not known. It does, however, seem that he saw his relationship with his wife as a vital step in his own pursuit of mystical harmony, a cause that he sought to promulgate through the architecture of Ronchamp.

Conclusion

The architecture of the chapel at Ronchamp is open to two rather different interpretations: one pertaining to the tenets of the Catholic Church and one looking back to more ancient forms of nature worship, Gnosticism and alchemy, the former embracing chastity, the latter sexuality. Central to the conflict is the figure of Mary, as Virgin and as Magdalene, chaste or sexual. Le Corbusier delicately traces a line in between. When, after the success of the scheme, he was asked to produce yet more churches he wrote in his sketchbook:

I did one taking 1[sic] risk the big risk. It's done.
I possess a sense of the unknown, of the immense

space left to man before his imagination, his possible choice between good and evil. Define the one and the other? A single light: discern and opt.[185]

It seems very likely that Le Corbusier became so interested in the figure of Mary Magdalene the 'prostitute saint' because she embodied those tensions, between spirit and body, at the heart of his spiritual programme. In the opinion of Susan Haskins, the figure of Mary Magdalen was used 'as a vehicle to explore ideas about sexuality, love and sin' throughout the nineteenth century.[186] Like his Romantic forebears, Le Corbusier appears to be an adherent of this tradition. Nevertheless, the figure of Mary Magdalene is also representative of strength, courage and faith; she is not passive in the traditional 'feminine' sense. She has equal access to God. Through her Le Corbusier attempted to reassert the role of the feminine within religion, because he believed it to be a natural law and an important step in the pursuit of harmony.

The Virgin Mary was impregnated through hearing the word of God and gave birth to Christ. The Magdalene, according to Renan, heard the word of Christ and, in a sense, gave birth to Christianity.[187] Both became physical containers of divine knowledge, waves of sound, linking the realm of the spirit to that of the body. In this way they literally embodied that recurring set of themes, central to Le Corbusier's painted work: sound, water, balance and harmony, Ronchamp itself serving a very similar function.

Although Le Corbusier's portrayal of the feminine and the female is not without its problems, he should be given credit for attempting to reassert the role of women within the Church, seeing this process as having wider ramifications for society as a whole. Indeed, it should be noted that the discussion that has taken place here belongs to a much wider discourse on gender that was highly topical in France at that time, and even within the Catholic Church as a whole. It is no coincidence that in 1950 the Vatican decided to make it an article of faith that the Virgin Mary was assumed into heaven, thus consolidating her role as a figure of veneration.[188]

Jaime Coll has discussed Le Corbusier's preoccupation with the story of Theseus and the Labyrinth and its place in the architect's work.[189] It is a story analogous with that of Orpheus' journey in to the

Underworld.[190] In 1951 Le Corbusier read André Gide's *Thésée* (1945) with great interest. He read it again in 1958.[191] Here Gide recounted the story of Theseus who went to fight the Minotaur, a monster, mothered by Pasiphae, the queen of Crete, and fathered by a bull. Pasiphae is evocative of the figure of *Icône* who merged together with the bull in Le Corbusier's *Taureau* series of paintings.[192] The Minotaur was housed in a Labyrinth,[193] built by Daedalus according to the rules of Egyptian mathematics and geometry and haunted by the spirit of his son Icarus.[194] In a long monologue Daedalus mused upon the nature of the world:

> Who began it: man or woman? Is the eternal feminine? From the belly of what great Mother did you emerge, multiple forms? And what fathering principle fertilized your womb? Inadmissible duality. In this case, God is the child. My spirit refuses to divide God. As soon as I admit the existence of the division there is conflict. Whoever has gods has war. There are no gods but there is one God. God's reign is peace. Everything is absorbed and reconciled in Unity.[195]

Thus, Daedalus, the architect, poses the essential question that seems to have preoccupied Le Corbusier for much of his life. For Le Corbusier, God was neither male nor female, but both.

Whilst it would be foolish to attempt to give a precise account of Le Corbusier's private theogony, certain themes do emerge. Like Gide's Daedalus, I sense that Le Corbusier wanted to believe in a unified God at once male and female, present in the interaction between the sexes at all scales in the cosmos. He does, however, give repeated emphasis to feminine divinity. Male divinity receives little mention. At one level woman is, as Trouin puts it, plasma, the primal matrix out of which everything emerges, but lurking paradoxically in the shadows is the divine force of man, the sun, whose precise role is never made clear.

Notes

1 Although 'con sacré' would nowadays translate as 'the real thing', 'sacré' indicating emphasis and 'con' meaning thing, I am informed that three generations back it is likely to have carried the meaning 'sacred cunt' which makes sense in this context. Here Yvonne makes a very risqué pun on the word consecrated. 'Je donne ma langue au chat' is the traditional answer used by children for riddles or jokes for which they do not know the answer.

2 M. le Chanoine Belot, Curé de Ronchamp, *Manuel du Pelerin* (Lyons: Editions Lescuyer, 1930), p.22 in Fondation Le Corbusier (hereafter referred to as FLC).

3 Le Corbusier, *Journey to the East* (Cambridge, MA: MIT Press, 1987), p.162.

4 Ibid., pp.202–3.

5 '. . . my life is more or less exactly that of a Trappist or any other kind of monk of your choosing (except for the vow of chastity).' Letter Le Corbusier to Sigismond Marcel, 28.01.1925, FLC, Dossier La Roche, doc.131. Quoted and translated by T. Benton 'The Sacred and the Search for Myths', in T. Benton (ed.), *Le Corbusier Architect of the Century* (London: Arts Council, 1987), p.243.

6 Le Corbusier, *Journey to the East*, p.206.

7 Le Corbusier, *Precisions on the Present State of Architecture and City Planning* (Cambridge, MA: MIT Press, 1990), p.29.

8 Ibid., p.11.

9 Le Corbusier quoted in R.A. Moore, 'Le Corbusier and the *mecanique spirituelle*: An investigation into Le Corbusier's architectural symbolism and its background in Beaux Arts design'. Unpublished D Phil thesis, University of Maryland (1979), p.266.

10 J. Peter, *The Oral History of Modern Architecture* (New York: Harry N. Abrams, 1994), p.146.

11 Le Corbusier, *Sketchbooks Volume 3 1954–1957* (Cambridge, MA: MIT Press, 1981), sketch 549.

12 Trouin linked the fictional Abbey with La Sainte Baume. L. Montalte (E. Trouin pseud.), *Fallait-il Bâtir Le Mont-Saint-Michel?* (St Zachaire: Montalte, 1979), p.172.

13 F. Rabelais, *The Histories of Gargantua and Pantagruel* (London: Penguin, 1955), p.150.

14 Le Corbusier, *Oeuvre Complète Volume 5, 1946–1952* (Zurich: Les Editions d'Architecture, 1995), p.24. A much abbreviated version of this account of the scheme for La Sainte Baume appears in Flora Samuel, 'Awakening Place: La Sainte Baume' in S. Menin (ed.), *Constructing Place* (London: Routledge, 2003), pp.217–27.

15 K. Maurin, *Les Esclarmonde: la femme et la féminité dans l'imaginaire du Catharisme* (Toulouse: Editions Privat, 1995), p.62.

16 C. Saint-Palais, *Esclarmonde de Foix: Princesse Cathare* (Toulouse: Privat, 1956), p.121 in FLC.

17 Ibid., p.41.

18 In a note of 8 March 1955, while flying over the Jura region of France, Le Corbusier meditated on his Cathar ancestry: 'the Janret-truly "perfect" ones of Languedoc'. Le Corbusier, *Sketchbooks Volume 3*, p.26.

19 R. Abels and E. Harrison, 'The Participation of Women in Languedocian Catharism', *Mediaeval Studies* (1979), 4, pp.230–1.

20 Trouin, FLC 13.01.396–400, document not dated.

21 Le Corbusier, *Le Modulor* (Paris: Editions de l'Architecture d'Aujourd'hui, 1950), p.223. According to Antoine Moles it was a 'grand géomètre', Adon Hiram who helped to build the Temple of Solomon. Antoine Moles, *Histoire des Charpentiers* (Paris: Librairie Gründ, 1949), p.66, in FLC. See 1 Kings 12:18.

22 Letter Henriette Trouin to author, 09.10.1999.

23 Letter Trouin to Le Corbusier, 17.08.1953, FLC 13.01.76.

24 Letter Le Corbusier to Trouin, 14.09.1953, FLC 13.01.77.

25 Ouvrage: Oeuvre Complète, ed. Girsberger Tome V, FLC B1 6 111

26 M. McLeod, 'Urbanism and Utopia: Le Corbusier from Regional Syndicalism to Vichy', D Phil thesis, Princeton (1985), p.245.

27 A. V. Roche, *Provençal Regionalism* (Illinois: Northwestern University Studies, 1954), pp.76–7.

28 Ibid., p.77.

29 'Marseille a toujours exercé sur Le Corbusier un attrait fascinant'. Le Corbusier, *Oeuvre Complète Volume 5*, p.85.

30 *Marseille* magazine, 05.04.1957, FLC P5.02.120.

31 S. Haskins, *Mary Magdalene* (London: HarperCollins, 1993), p. 122.

32 Trouin wrote that the Compagnons du Tour de France, of which Moles was leader, were thinking about building a 'unité Corbu'. He also mentioned that Le Corbusier knew Moles. Letter Trouin to Le Corbusier, 08.02.1955, FLC 13.01.301.

33 On the frontispiece of this book are printed the words 'Exemplaire imprimé pour: Monsieur Charles Le Corbusier'. Perret contributed to the introduction. Moles, *Histoire des Charpentiers* in FLC. Moles, who lived in Marseilles, later tried to interest Le Corbusier in working on a scheme with him. Letter André Wogenscky to Antoine Moles, 03.01.1950, FLC G3 159.

34 Moles, *Histoire des Charpentiers*, p.114, in FLC.

35 For example M. Ghyka, *Nombre d'or: rites et rhythmes Pythagoriciens dans le development de la civilisation Occidental* (Paris: Gallimard, 1931), p.57 in FLC.

36 Ibid., pp. 26–7.

37 Le Corbusier, *Oeuvre Complète*, volume 5, pp.26–7. Le Corbusier retained control of the publication of the *Oeuvres Complètes* from their inception in 1929, apart from the volume completed after his death.

38 Ibid., p. 27.

39 Jacobus de Voragine, *The Golden Legend, Volume 1* translated by W. G. Ryan (Princeton: Princeton University Press, 1993), p.380. Originally written in 1275.

40 Ibid., p.375.

41 Letter Le Corbusier to Trouin, 09.03.1957, FLC 13 01 123. Le Corbusier suggested the use of 'black light' in his theatre to portray the life of the Magdalene, an idea that delighted Trouin.

42 Trouin, 'Plan D'Aups ou Plan-Plan D'Aups,' n.d., FLC 13 01 366.

43 Ibid.

44 Ibid., FLC 13.01.355.

45 Letter Trouin to Picasso, 23.02.1956, FLC P5.02.37.

46 Le Corbusier's own version, published in Paris in 1906 (originally published 1863), is signed Ch.E. Jeanneret in ink. On the frontispiece Le Corbusier wrote the page numbers of several passages that were of particular interest to him.

47 E. Schuré, *Les Grands Initiés* (Paris: Perrin, 1908), p.499 in FLC.

48 The Rev. Alban Butler, *The Lives of the Fathers, Martyrs and other Principal Saints, Volume 2* (London: H. Virtue and Co., 1922), pp.79–90.

49 E. Trouin, 'Appel au Monde en faveur du Plan d'Aups', n.d., FLC 13.01.348.

50 F. Samuel, 'The philosophical city of Rabelais and St Teresa; Le Corbusier and Edouard Trouin's scheme for St Baume', *Literature and Theology*, 13.02.1999, pp.111–26.

51 From introduction to Le Corbusier, *When the Cathedrals were White: A Journey to the Country of the Timid People* (New York: Reynal and Hitchcock, 1947), p.xvii.

52 Le Corbusier, *Precisions*, p.160.

53 According to Schuré the initiations of the Orphics took place in the depths of mountains. Schuré, *Les Grands Initiés*, p.246.

54 Le Corbusier, *Oeuvre Complète, Volume 5*, p.30.

55 Letter Trouin to Le Corbusier, 24.03.1950, FLC 13.01.456.

56 Le Corbusier, *Oeuvre Complète, Volume 5*, p.190.

57 These words were actually written about Le Corbusier's monastery at La Tourette, but would seem equally applicable here. Peter, *The Oral History of Modern Architecture*, p147.

58 Trouin, 'Un Appartement à la Cité de La Sainte Baume est non seulement esthetique,' n.d., FLC 13.01.43.

59 Le Corbusier, *The Radiant City* (London: Faber, 1967), p.186.

60 Trouin, 'Mémorial du P. Couturier Museon Madalenen [sic.].' Received by Le Corbusier on 18.05.1956, FLC 13.01.109.

61 Trouin, 'Table provisoire' for book entitled 'La Sainte Baume et Marie Madeleine,' n.d., FLC 13.01.398.

62 Letter Le Corbusier to Trouin, 08.10.1951, FLC 13.01. 68.

63 Letter Le Corbusier to Trouin, 09.03.1957, FLC 13.01. 123.

64 Trouin, 'Syndicat d'Initiative de La Sainte Baume Plan D'Aups (Var)' 08.02.1955, FLC 13.01.388.

65 Ibid.

66 This was the first of three volumes of Malraux's reflections on painting. A. Malraux, *Le Musée Imaginaire* (Paris: Gallimard, 1965). Originally published in 1947.

67 Trouin, 'Syndicat d'Initiative de La Sainte Baume Plan D'Aups (Var)' 08.02.1955, FLC 13.01.389.

68 Ibid.

69 Ibid.

70 Le Corbusier, 'Le Théatre Spontané' in André Villiers (ed.), *Architecture et Dramaturgie* (Paris: Editions d'Aujourd'hui, 1980). Originally published in 1950.

71 Le Corbusier, *Oeuvre Complète, Volume 6, 1952–1957* (Zurich: Les Editions d'Architecture, 1995), p.200.

72 On the frontispiece of his copy of Faure's *Equivalences* Le Corbusier wrote 'pour le musée Octobre 1956, p.17, 19, 30, 37, 47 voir'. Although it is not known which museum project he was referring to, the pages that he noted allude to cinema, performance and their effect upon the body. E. Faure, *Equivalences* (Paris: Robert Marin, 1951) in FLC.

73 Faure wrote in *Equivalences* that there was a 'mysterious accord between sensuality, sensibility and intelligence' which could be influenced through the orchestration of colour. Le Corbusier underlined these words in his own copy of Faure's work. Faure, *Equivalences*, p.18 in FLC.

74 Le Corbusier, *Precisions*, p.x. Taken from preface to second French edition dated 1960.

75 'Le Théâtre NO ancêtre de Kabuki'. Le Corbusier, *Sketchbooks Volume 2* (London: Thames and Hudson, 1981), sketch 357.

76 *L' Art Sacré*, 11–12 July/Aug 1954, special edition 'La leçon japonaise' included articles on the tea ceremony and Noh theatre, p.24.

77 Le Corbusier made a small sketch of the Noh theatre in a letter dated 18 February 1957, the only drawing that exists of the scheme in the archive in the FLC. Notes by Le Corbusier on La Sainte Baume dated 18.02.1957, FLC 13.01.120.

78 Letter Trouin to Le Corbusier, 26.11.1956, FLV 13.01.114.

79 Letter Trouin to Le Corbusier, Christmas 1955, FLC 13.01.100.

80 Letter Trouin to Le Corbusier, 22.07.1957, FLC 13.01.137.

81 Letter Trouin to Le Corbusier, 17.07.1959, FLC 13 01 179.

82 'Oui, le théâtre a été peint de couleurs vives'. Letter Henriette Trouin to author, 03.05.2000.

83 Letter Le Corbusier to Trouin, 21.01.1959, FLC 13.01.159.

84 Letter Trouin to Le Corbusier, 24.01.1959, FLC 13.01.163.

85 Letter Trouin to Le Corbusier, 27.11.1958, FLC 13.01.144.

86 Letter Trouin to Le Corbusier, 26.11.1956, FLC 13.01.114.

87 Letter Trouin to Le Corbusier, 01.01.1959, FLC 13.01.142.

88 Letter Trouin to Le Corbusier, 12.01.1959, FLC 13.01.151.

89 Trouin 'Mémorial du P. Couturier Museon Madalenen.' Received by Le Corbusier on 18.05.1956, FLC 13.01.109.

90 Letter Trouin to Le Corbusier, 12.01.1959, FLC 13.01.151.

91 Marion Delorme was a famous courtesan under Louis XIII, a beauty and an adventuress; she died in 1650. Victor Hugo wrote a flamboyant *drame romantique* about her (1831).

92 The French logical positivist philosopher Auguste Comte (1798–1857) met Clothilde de Vaux in 1845. Comte admired her writing greatly. He likened her to Dante's Beatrice. When she died in 1846 Comte was inconsolable. Presumably Trouin thought that Comte's response was too melodramatic.

93 This echoes Moore's comment that water (linked to woman) formed for Le Corbusier the 'primal matrix'. Moore, 'Le Corbusier and the *mecanique spirituelle*', p.297.

94 Letter Trouin to Le Corbusier, 29.01.1958, FLC 13.01.143.

95 Ibid.

96 E. R. Dodds, *The Greeks and the Irrational* (Berkeley: University of California Press, 1951), pp.80–81.

97 Letter Henriette Trouin to author, 22.10.1999.

98 Letter Trouin to Le Corbusier, 15.07.1951, FLC 13.01.61.

99 Le Corbusier, *Sketchbooks Volume 1, 1914–1948* (London: Thames and Hudson, 1981), sketch 622.

100 Trouin 'Mémorial du P. Couturier Museon Madalenen [sic.].' Received by Le Corbusier on 18.05.1956, FLC 13.01.109.

101 For a discussion of the house of the Muses see T. E. Winton, 'When the Old Mirror is not yet Published' in Alberto Perez Gomez (ed.), *Chora 2* (Montreal: McGill-Queen's University Press, 1996), p.272.

102 'And they produce a host of books written by Musaeus and Orpheus, who were the children of the Moon and the Muses'. Plato, *The Republic II*, in Scott Buchanan (ed.), *The Portable Plato* (Harmondsworth: Penguin, 1997), p.334.

103 W.K.C. Guthrie, *Orpheus and Greek Religion* (London: Methuen, 1935), p.191.

104 'Architecture and music are sisters, both proportion time and space.' Le Corbusier, *Le Corbusier Talks with Students* (New York: Princeton University Press, 1999), p.53.

105 Letter from Trouin to Le Corbusier, 27.11.1950, FLC 13.01.51. See FLC drawings 17748 and 17749.

106 Mogens Krustrup, 'The women of Algiers', *Skala*, 24/25, 1991, p.41.

107 V. Scully, *The Earth, the Temple and the Gods* (New Haven, CT: Yale University Press, 1962), p.11.

108 Letter Trouin to Le Corbusier, 02.04.1945, FLC 13.01.03.

109 M. L. Gothein, *A History of Garden Art, Volume 1* (London: Dent, 1928), p.88.

110 See Le Corbusier's sketch *Les Îles sont des corps de femmes*. Catalogue for the exhibition *Le Corbusier, Painter and Architect* (Arkitekturtidsskrift: Nordjyllands, 1995), p.186.

111 Letter Trouin to Le Corbusier, 11.11.1950, FLC 13.01. 45.

112 'the faraway pagan celebrations of all times:
the Sun the moon
Sowing time
Harvest = rites [of] Mother Earth.' Le Corbusier, *Sketchbooks Volume* 2, sketch 504.

113 Trouin, 'Table provisoire' for book entitled 'La Sainte Baume et Marie Madeleine,' n.d., FLC 13.01.397. Le Corbusier described the landscape around Marseilles as an example of a Homeric landscape which is to be seen at Delphi. Le Corbusier, *Modulor 2* (London: Faber and Faber, 1955), p.304.

114 Scully, *The Earth, the Temple and the Gods*, p.109.

115 R. Graves, *Greek Myths*, vol. 1. (New York: Penguin Books,1955), p.80.

116 Le Corbusier, *My Work* (London: Architectural Press, 1960), p.38.

117 Trouin, 'Rapport du Secrétaire Général (Edouard Trouin) sur nos projets en cours', 08.02.1955, FLC 13. 01.381.

118 Trouin [Montalte pseud.], *La Basilique Universelle de la Paix et du Pardon*, FLC 13.01.402.

119 A. Wogenscky, *Les Mains de Le Corbusier* (Paris: Édition de Grenelle), p.18.

120 Ibid.

121 Peter, *The Oral History of Modern Architecture*, p.146.

122 Le Corbusier, *The Chapel at Ronchamp* (London: Architectural Press, 1957), p.6.

123 M. Krustrup, *Porte Email* (Copenhagen: Arkitektens Forlag, 1991).

124 Le Corbusier, *Oeuvre Complète, Volume* 6, *1952–1957*, p.52.

125 Le Corbusier, *The Decorative Art of Today* (London: Architectural Press, 1987), p.167.

126 Peter, *The Oral History of Modern Architecture*, p.146.

127 Letter Le Corbusier to O. Messiaen, 21.05.1955 in J. Jenger, *Le Corbusier Choix de Lettres* (Basel: Birkhauser, 2002), p.386.

128 Le Corbusier notes on Ronchamp, FLC B1.2.229.

129 Le Corbusier, *Modulor* (London: Faber, 1954), p.32.

130 Le Corbusier, *Espace Indicible* (Boulogne-sur-Seine: Editions de L'Architecture d'Aujourd'hui, 1947).

131 Le Corbusier, *Modulor*, p.32.

132 Le Corbusier, *Modulor 2*, p.27.

133 Ibid., p.71.

134 C. Pearson, 'Integrations of Art and Architecture in the work of Le Corbusier. Theory and Practice from Ornamentalism to the "Synthesis of the Major Arts"'. Unpublished PhD thesis, Stanford University (1995), p.140.

135 J. Coll, 'Structure and Play in Le Corbusier's Art Works', *AA Files* 31 (1996), pp. 3–15.

136 L. Hervé, *Le Corbusier The Artist/Writer* (Neuchâtel: Editions du Grifon, 1970), p.28.

137 Le Corbusier, *Le Poème de l'angle droit*, p.89.

138 J. Labasant, 'Le Corbusier's Notre Dame du Haut at Ronchamp', *Architectural Record* 118, 4 (1955), p. 170.

139 Le Corbusier sketched a crab shell when writing notes on Ronchamp. 24.07.56, FLC B1.2.146.

140 D. Lyon, A. Denis and O. Boissière, *Le Corbusier Alive* (Paris:Terrail, 2001), p.137.

141 Peter, *The Oral History of Modern Architecture*, p.146.

142 In conversation with Saporta, one of Le Corbusier's assistants, Moore discovered that in order to refine the acoustics for the main auditorium for his League of Nations Competition scheme Le Corbusier made a foil tray the same shape in plan as the auditorium, filled it with water and watched the behaviour of waves as they moved across the tray. Moore, 'Le Corbusier and the *mecanique spirituelle*', pp.183–4.

143 Transcription from Rabelais in Le Corbusier, *Sketchbooks Volume* 3, sketch 80.

144 Le Corbusier, *Oeuvre Complète, Volume* 6 (Zurich: Les Editions d'Architecture, 1995), p.20.

145 M. Warner, *Alone of all her Sex The Myth and Cult of the Virgin Mary* (London: Weidenfeld & Nicolson, 1976), p.37.

146 J. Kristeva, 'Stabat Mater' in S. Rubin Sulieman (ed.), *The Female Body* (Cambridge, MA: Harvard University Press, 1986), p.108.

147 Hervé, *Le Corbusier The Artist/Writer*, p.25.

148 Le Corbusier, *Oeuvre Complète,Volume* 5, p.72.

149 J. Bloomer, '. . . And Venustas', *AA Files*, 25 (1993), p.3.

150 Le Corbusier, *Towards a New Architecture*, p.146.

151 S. Giedion, *Space, Time and Architecture*, fifth edition (Cambridge, MA: Harvard University Press), p.577.

152 J. Alford, 'Creativity and Intelligibility in Le Corbusier's chapel at Ronchamp', *Journal of Aesthetics and Art History*, March 1958, vol. XVI,3, pp.293–305.

153 Belot, *Manuel du Pelerin*, p.22 in FLC.

154 Le Corbusier, *Sketchbooks Volume* 4, *1957–1964* (Cambridge, MA: MIT Press, 1982), sketch 366.

155 Le Corbusier, *Sketchbooks Volume* 3, sketch 150.

156 Ibid., sketch 241.

157 Ibid., sketch 492.

158 Le Corbusier, *The Radiant City*, p.152.

159 M. Malvern, *Venus in Sackcloth* (Carbondale, Ill.: Southern Illinois University Press, 1975), p.39.

160 Le Corbusier, *Oeuvre Complète, Volume* 5, p.24. The 'Trois Maries' is a familiar concept in Provence in the South of France.

161 Flora Samuel, 'Le Corbusier, Women, Nature,' *Issues in Art and Architecture*, 5, 2 (1998), pp. 4–20.

162 Le Corbusier, *The Chapel at Ronchamp*, p.46.

163 J. Coll, 'Le Corbusier. Taureaux: an analysis of the thinking process in the last series of Le Corbusier's plastic work', *Art History* 18, 4 (1995), p. 547.

164 R. Evans, *The Projective Cast* (Cambridge, MA: MIT Press, 1995), p.284.

165 Letter Le Corbusier to his mother, 27.06.1955 in Jenger, *Le Corbusier Choix de Lettres*, p.388.

166 M. Krustrup, 'Les Illustrations de Le Corbusier pour l'Illiade' in G. Viatte (ed.), *Le Corbusier et la Mediterranée* (Marseilles: L'Université de Provence, 1991), p.107.

167 Le Corbusier, *Oeuvre Complète, Volume* 6, p.21.

168 Le Corbusier, *The Chapel at Ronchamp*, pp.131–3.

169 Peter, *The Oral History of Modern Architecture*, p.146.

170 Ibid.

171 Le Corbusier, *Modulor*, p.224.

172 For the Catholic Church the shell is the symbol of pilgrimage.

173 Le Corbusier, *The Radiant City*, p.8.

174 Le Corbusier, *Le Poème de l'angle droit* (Paris: Editions Connivance, 1989), E3, Caracteres.

175 On the frontispiece of his edition of Rabelais' *Gargantua and Pantagruel* in the Fondation Le Corbusier records, in a note dated 1961, as if for posterity, he recorded that his brother Albert introduced him to the concept of the four alchemical metals in 1905. He repeats the message inside on page 52.

176 Le Corbusier, *The Chapel at Ronchamp*, p.47.

177 Krustrup, 'Les Illustrations de Le Corbusier pour l'Illiade', p.113.

178 Haskins describes the Magdalene's transition into a Venus figure in Italy during the first half of the sixteenth century as part of Marcilio Ficino's (1433–99) attempt to merge the work of Plato and the Neoplatonists with both pagan philosophy and Christian religion. Haskins, *Mary Magdalene* (London: HarperCollins, 1993) pp.236–7.

179 Ibid., pp.131–3.

180 Le Corbusier, *Towards a New Architecture*, p.126.

181 Le Corbusier, *Modulor 2*, p.255.

182 Le Corbusier was Bauchant's first great supporter. Le Corbusier and De Fayet, 'Bauchant', *L'Esprit Nouveau*, 17 (1922).

183 A. Rüegg (ed.), *Le Corbusier Photographs by René Burri: Moments in the Life of a Great Architect* (Basel: Birkhäuser, 1999), p.18.

184 Haskins, *Mary Magdalen*, p.135.

185 Le Corbusier, *Sketchbooks Volume 3*, sketch 722.

186 Haskins, *Mary Magdalene*, p.365.

187 According to some heretical accounts Mary Magdalene became Christ's lover, the container of his body as well as his word.

188 Warner, *Alone of all her Sex*, p.334. The discovery of the Naag Hammadi Gospels, the Gospel of Mary and the Dead Sea Scrolls in 1947 would create still greater interest in this subject.

189 Coll, 'Le Corbusier's Taureaux', p.548.

190 According to Guthrie there were links between Dionysus and the Minotaur. Guthrie, *Orpheus and Greek Religion*, p.115.

191 Le Corbusier, *Sketchbooks Volume 4*, sketch 62.

192 'Pasiphae and the Bull' occupy part of a film sequence planned by Le Corbusier. Le Corbusier, *Sketchbooks Volume 3*, sketch 457. He also planned a work entitled 'Naissance du Minotaure': Le Corbusier, *Sketchbooks Volume 4*, sketch 830.

193 See ibid., sketch 1003, for evidence of his interest in labyrinths.

194 André Gide, *Thésée* (Paris: Gallimard, 1946), p.54.

195 Translated from ibid., p. 62.

7 Sexual Harmony and the Urbanism of Le Corbusier

Me: It has to do with a woman and a man and some children in the harmony of the home = aid and liberation of the Woman.[1]

Le Corbusier frequently wrote of the imbalance between people and things that had been caused by machine age times. He was particularly interested in what he called the 'sexual question',[2] the ways in which the daily grind of city life eroded the relationships between men and women. In his opinion: 'City planning, which is bound up with the essential elements in the profound actions of society, opens up indiscreet windows.'[3] In this chapter I will focus upon the ways in which Le Corbusier wanted to improve the relationships between men and women through his urbanistic schemes.[4]

Le Corbusier's vision of the city was based upon the ideas of biology, upon his studies of the homes of insects and other natural structures. Each city unit was built of an agglomeration of cells, the 'primordial cell',[5] man and woman, the family, providing the 'basis of society'.[6] In his vision 'everyone lives as if in his own small house' within the larger unit.[7] It was therefore vitally important to perfect the individual unit as 'in Nature, the smallest cell, determines the validity, the health of the whole'. He thought of the building as being in 'a state of equilibrium' in which conditions needed to be 'favourable to the group, while at the same time allowing sufficient freedom to its members'.[8] It was important therefore to provide each individual with a space in which they were free to live their lives undisturbed. In his opinion:

Basic individual liberty has to be guaranteed by an enclosure, a case. Vessel, or container which is of course nothing else than a ROOM. The room should be perfect. It should be complete, satisfy-ing all individual needs and encouraging personal activity, reading, drawing, sewing, weaving, pottering about, thinking, meditating etc.[9]

Note that Le Corbusier is not solely talking of activities associated with men, nor does he suggest who will be undertaking these activities: 'Monsieur will have his *cell*, Madame also. Mademoiselle also' in Le Corbusier's new vision of the home.[10]

In the previous chapter I described how Le Corbusier wanted to manipulate the physical responses of visitors to La Sainte Baume and Ronchamp in order to bring about a change in their thinking. He was profoundly interested in the issues of both physical and mental health and the means by which they could be affected by the surroundings,[11] wanting to create homes that would have a beneficent influence on the relationships of those who lived within them. He seems to have believed in the old alchemical idea that a transformation could be brought about within a person as a result of experiments in the material world, the two being intimately linked. He made a clear statement of his aims in *Precisions*:

My task . . . concerns especially re-establishing or establishing harmony between man and their environment. A live organism (man) and nature (the environment), this immense vase containing the sun, the moon, the stars, indefinable unknowns, waves, the round earth with its axis inclined on the elliptic producing the seasons, the temperature of the body, the circulation of blood, the nervous system, the respiratory system, the digestive system, the day, the night, the solar cycle of twenty-four hours, its implacable but varied and beneficent alteration, etc.[12]

He perceived that the cosmos was in a state of dynamic equilibrium linked holistically together. As well as establishing harmony between people and the environment, he wanted to establish harmony between men and women, a vital stage in his grandiose plan.

Having set out Le Corbusier's concerns about urbanism and the way in which it impacted on people's relationships with one another I will make a detailed analysis of the ideas behind his scheme for the Radiant City: it was at his own home, the penthouse apartment at 24 Rue Nungesser et Coli that he first put certain of his Radiant City principles into practice. I will then move on to a discussion of his schemes for mass housing, focusing in particular on the Unité in Marseilles, the first built Unité scheme. My aim is to show that, in addition to producing an architecture in which feminine and masculine aspects existed in balance, Le Corbusier felt it vital to involve women in the process of community building.

The design of the home was, for Le Corbusier, essentially a spiritual activity. It is for this reason that the chapter will end with a discussion of the links that Le Corbusier made between domestic and sacred space. My suggestion is that, for Le Corbusier, the same 'radiant spirit' that inhabited La Sainte Baume and Ronchamp also dwelt in his mass housing block, the Unité. It would, through its very presence, promote good relations between men and women.

Sex and planning

Towards the end of his life Le Corbusier reflected on the U.S.A., 'women, psychoanalysis everywhere, an act without resonance, without goal'.[13] The subject of his rumination, sex or architecture, is left unclear, both being intertwined in his conception of things. The link that he makes between urbanism and sexuality is made more explicit in When the Cathedrals were White than in any other book (perhaps because he had just embarked on a revivifying affair with Tjader Harris).

Many of the following observations on the problems of city life are draw from Le Corbusier's experience of North America:

Relations of men and women. engineers at work, 'hard labor' in the business community, the urban crime of frightfully extended city regions. Life injured every day by the unbalance of machine age times. I begin to put my reflections together: the core of the family is affected. Americans who live in cities often say: 'We are victims of an inferiority complex . . .' Thus those thousand-foot skyscrapers!

His jocular allusions to the relationship between skyscraper size and American sexual prowess disguise a profound concern for the difficulties encountered by real men and women in their relationship to one another. He consciously employs a Rabelaisian level of wit to convey issues of great seriousness. Bacon writes that Le Corbusier felt American culture to be a 'victim of its own agent of repression through what he metaphorically called "salpêtre" (saltpeter), an antiaphrodisiac. Broadway and burlesque as well as the freely passionate forces within the African-American community, especially music and dance, not only kept the white intelligentsia from recognising the physical decay of Harlem slums, but also diverted and deflated its sexual energy'.[14] He describes an episode that takes place in a hotel lobby which vividly brings this connection between jazz, the primitive, harmony and sex to light; what he called 'musical copulation'.[15] Here a number of Europeans are listening to 'syncopated music, in a minor key' producing in the men, in particular, a 'nostalgia for things one will never have'. There is a sexual tension in the air:[16] 'The Frenchwomen are absorbed in gossip. The 2 men are frustrated: they are mere accountants. They beat the rhythm on their knees with their fingers like idiots'.[17] They are constrained by custom and culture, but the music creates a yearning inside them for some other existence. Le Corbusier made the heartfelt plea:

As long as mechanized civilisation doesn't find a new moral to put men on their feet again and men and women together the way they should be, the black's song will unnerve us. It's only a question of time. Oh sociologist of minimum housing, why don't you study the stages of the minimum heart.[18]

For Le Corbusier architecture would play an important role in improving the deteriorating relations that he perceived between the sexes.

The world is bored

Le Corbusier wrote of the experience of being a husband in one of America's more privileged homes:

> You see your wife again at eight o'clock in the evening. – 'Hello, hello . . .' Well, she has been alone for twelve hours of the day. She has her life also, but with a quite different kind of time. She has seen her friends, she has read books, she has gone to lectures, to exhibitions; her mind is furnished with things different from those that have been going around in her husband's head – which continue to go around. The husband is a little uncomfortable. How to pick up the thread? How are such different voltages to go together in unity? They are not in harmony. In the USA women are inclined to take an interest in things of the spirit. Her life, which she organizes by herself, is expensive. A lot of money is needed. The economy of the USA, devoted to waste, pours out torrents of dollars, but you can't put many of them in your pocket. Seven hours of the day serve no useful purpose: four spent in sterile business activity and three in transportation. I have the feeling that in general these men and women, in spite of all their good will, have difficulty in communicating with each other. So it is every day throughout life. As a result the husband is intimidated, thwarted. The wife dominates. A great need of something other than business fills men's hearts, and contact is impossible because the voltages are different. Every day there is a kind of distance between them, a kind of trench. There are demands, the woman makes a kind of claim. For the man, the woman is like a dream difficult to take hold of. He showers her with attentions . . . he is in a sort of perpetual arrears . . . worn out. [19]

Woman, in this case, has the leisure to develop her mind, to fill it with new ideas while the husband is ground down by the everyday reality of supporting his cultured wife. They are thus on very different wavelengths and she holds him in contempt.

Le Corbusier noted a comment made by the editor of 'one of the smartest fashionable magazines' in the USA that 'The men are tired of everything and the women are tired of the men'.[20] According to Claire Duchen men were often seen as being 'peripheral to the wife's concerns as they were represented on the pages of women's magazines' in France at that time. This can be seen from a proliferation of humorous articles on the ineptitude of husbands in the home that appeared in contemporary journals.[21] The repeated message was that women and men felt somehow at odds with one another.

Annotations to his copy of René Allendy's book *Capitalisme et Sexualité* reveal the extent of Le Corbusier's intense interest in marriage and what it meant. He was in agreement with Allendy that the Christian marriage made no concessions to the needs of the flesh.[22] He was particularly interested in the apparent move towards monogamy in more 'civilised' societies,[23] yet he noted that the more monogamy became the established norm, the greater became the demand for mistresses and prostitutes because of 'an erotic need for variety'.[24] Allendy believed that prostitutes should be revered as 'artists of love', an idea that interested Le Corbusier who agreed that they should be given back the value and dignity they were accorded in ancient times when they were held sacred and housed within temples.[25]

His annotations to the book make it evident that Le Corbusier agreed with Allendy's idea that social constraints had taken the pleasure away from sex. Women in particular had suffered in this respect.

> Everywhere we have seen the fact that social life puts a restraint on the sensual aspirations of an individual human, but this restraint is even stronger amongst women who have always been treated as objects of conquest, and who have not, until recently, had the opportunity to realise freely their sentimental affinities. It is not surprising that a similar regime of sexual constraint has been maintained, during the entire history of humanity, a form of atrophy in the sensual lives of women. Clinical surveys tell us that more than 50% of women are frigid.[26]

It has been seen that for Le Corbusier 'the act of making love' was a fundamental law of nature, bringing man and woman together in 'harmony'.[27]

Such a process would be hindered by a loss of libido in women.

Le Corbusier perceived a real conflict between economic need and sexual need.[28] In the American city there was 'no question of "making love" (well)', leaving man 'screwed' as he 'frets over his carrots'.[29]

> The world is bored
> Men are bored
> Women [are bored]
> Gynecium/kitchen[30]
> Art
> Daily and conjugal
> Because acts no longer emanate from themselves but they are [place] in service on command.[31]

What was needed, in his opinion, was a return to the fundamental joys of life:

> modern society, – very much occupied by its daily difficulties, has forgotten this:
> One man
> One woman
> One child
> Sleep in their bed;
> They awake, they go to their work
> Then they come back to sleep in their bed.
> When such a state of affairs is brought to the attention, it will immediately be solved.[32]

Le Corbusier wrote of they way in which man in early times 'lived like a snail in his shell . . . The family life unfolded itself in a normal way. The father watched over his children in the cradle and later on in the workshop.'[33] The father had a greater role in the day-to-day life of the home and a greater degree of participation in the upbringing of his children. 'New joys await us, real spiritual joys . . . Let us create a home that will interest men as well as women' he urged.[34]

Crushing duties in the home

The problems that Le Corbusier perceived between men and women were not solely caused by a man's long absence from home and consequent alienation from his wife, but were also caused by what he called her 'crushing duties' in the home, 'garden, floors, linens, children, every day, including Sunday'.[35] Whilst labour saving household devices began to enter the market in the 1940s, very few people could afford them at a time when there was not enough food and power supplies were erratic.[36] Claire Laubier reports, for example, that in a survey of housing conditions in Rouen taken in 1949, more than half the flats were without running water, there were no bathrooms or inside lavatories and women frequently had to fetch water from the local fountain and wash in the river, a situation that persisted well into the 1950s.[37] In attempting to alleviate the work of the housewife Le Corbusier was thus responding to a very real need amongst women at that time.

Duchen notes that it was at this point that journalists began to write of the economic value of woman's work in the home.[38] 'A woman, a man, and a few children, elements of the harmony of the hearth. But, today, the mother of the family is crushed by housework'[39] wrote Le Corbusier; 'A hard lot hers and such a common one that she deserves all our consideration'.[40] For this reason he planned to provide communal services in the Unité to free the housewife from domestic drudgery.[41] He advocated that the working day, including the working day of the woman in the home,[42] should be reduced to five hours, thus freeing up time for relaxation and the more serious work of developing relationships with other people and with nature. In a letter to his mother he stated that 'it is absolutely imperative that women are liberated from the domestic drama (which results in problems for men)'. He felt that he had not succeeded in doing this with his design for her house at Le Lac or with his own apartment at 24 Rue Nungesser et Coli, but that the Unité at Marseilles would provide 'the solution to modern life'. Evidently the latter building was designed with a far greater consideration for issues of cleaning.[43] Similarly Trouin wrote that the Permanent City at La Sainte Baume would be 'conceived to resolve domestic problems'[44] leaving women free to take a more active role in the spiritual life of the community, thus encouraging a more balanced relationship between the sexes.

The gospels of both Luke[45] and John[46] contain the story of Martha and Mary, with whom the Magdalene has often been associated. In Luke's version an exhausted Christ takes refuge in the house of 'a certain woman named Martha' who has a sister, who sits at his feet, and listens to him talking. According to the account in the Bible, Martha is annoyed because Mary does not help her to prepare the house for their guest. Jesus reminds Martha that, although her own role is important, Mary's 'good part' is equally necessary. Le Corbusier seems to have taken a particular interest in this story as he underlined Jesus' words 'Martha, Martha you worry about many things when it is only necessary to worry about one thing' in his copy of Ernest Renan's *La Vie de Jésus*.[47] The story of Martha and Mary tells of the tensions between the life of the body and the life of the spirit, the resolution of the two being of central importance to Le Corbusier's work. At a more practical level it also tells of the necessity to balance the spiritual with the domestic.

It seems that Le Corbusier began to think about the ways in which communal living would make the burden of housework less onerous whilst travelling across the Atlantic to America. He observed how, on a liner, using communal resources, he only needed 'a fortieth of a cook', an admirably economical state of affairs. Assuming the traditional mantle of lady of the house he wrote: 'I am not concerned by my cook, I don't have anything to do with him. I give him neither orders nor money to go to the market.'[48]

Le Corbusier repeatedly wrote of the importance of including 'communal services' in the home. He referred to these as 'the machinery of domestic life (lightening the housewife's burden: food supply, domestic help, preparation of meals)'.[49] At the Unité there were to be 'more than twenty communal services intended not only to do away with the domestic drudgery of the housewife, but also to bring into the darkness of the hostile machine age a certainty of the joy of living and a concrete chance to found a home and bring up a family'.[50]

In *The Radiant City* Le Corbusier includes a picture from a women's magazine to suggest 'new social customs, an escape from hypocrisy and certain conventions'. In it a woman can be seen stirring the contents of a saucepan while chatting to friends (two female, two male) sitting around her. In the foreground a dining table can be seen (Fig. 7.1).[51] The kitchen would once again be positioned at the centre

Figure 7.1   Image taken from a women's magazine and included by Le Corbusier in *The Radiant City*.

of the home, cooking itself becoming a communal activity to be celebrated and seen. 'Don't forget,' wrote Le Corbusier of the wife of his 'radiant' farmer, 'she is a woman of our modern world also'.[52]

In a document entitled 'Woman and the Radiant City' Le Corbusier confirmed his belief that women played a vital role in the health and happiness of urban life:

> Woman and the Radiant City
> Woman centre of the Hearth [foyer]
> Hearth [foyer] = City
> Happy hearth = happiness[53]

Given her importance, it would be necessary to give adequate consideration to the needs of women in any urbanistic scheme.

The Radiant City

In his book *La Ville Radieuse*, translated as *The Radiant City*, Le Corbusier set out the characteristics of the city plan that would dominate his thinking for the rest of his life. It would be zoned, built off the ground on pilotis and would conform to a modular grid (Fig. 7.2). It would be built along arterial routes, capable of limitless expansion, its population accommodated in vast new apartment blocks within a garden setting. In a diagram showing the 'biological organization of the

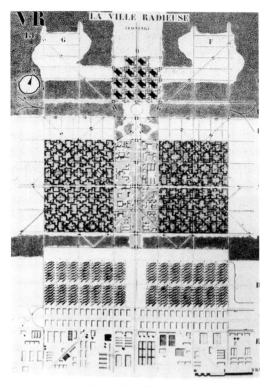

Figure 7.2   Plan of the Radiant City.

For the Rosicrucian Joséphin Péladan, whose influence on Le Corbusier was discussed in Chapter 4, the androgyne could be symbolised by such early forms of architectural expression as the menhir (a tall upright standing stone) and the cromlech (a megalithic tomb). It was also manifested in Greek temples; architecture could give this mystical concept tangible form.[56] It appears that, like Péladan, Le Corbusier believed that architecture and town planning could be used to make manifest the concept of the mystical androgyne, described in the writings of Plato.[57]

Adhering to old stereotypes[58] Le Corbusier defined 'male' architecture as 'strong objectivity of forms, under the intense light of a Mediterranean sun', while 'female' architecture was described in terms of 'limitless subjectivity rising against a clouded sky',[59] in other words, more nebulous.[60] His architecture became a marriage of these two opposites, in alchemical terms, a highly charged and erotic interplay intended to work upon the inhabitant through what he called 'a psychophysiology' of the feelings.[61] The plan of the Radiant City was developed through 'the interplay of two elements, one male and one female'.[62] In the discussion of alchemy in Chapter 4, evidence was provided to suggest that the idea of the philosopher's stone, the union of opposites, could be expressed through geometry. This idea, it will be argued, was central to Le Corbusier's notion of radiance.

The idea of the Radiant City was developed during the early 1930s, during the period when Le Corbusier was most involved in the Syndicalist movement. After the stock market crash in America there was a depression in France as in much of the rest of the world. During this period Le Corbusier, who is often portrayed as an apolitical being, looked to syndicalism as an alternative to capitalism and parliamentary democracy.[64] From 1931 to 1936 he acted as both a contributor and editor for two different syndicalist journals *Plans* and *Prélude*. It was in these journals that he first outlined his plans for the Radiant City.[65]

The concept of the Radiant City received its full expression in the book of the same name published in 1935. Shortly before his death Le Corbusier was to reflect on this city plan:

city' the business centre can be seen at the head of the city, with the body beneath made up of the residential zones, the 'green city' where housing blocks were to be placed within a garden setting. At the base are the factories and the heavy industry that form the economic base of the settlement. Le Corbusier was forced to change this layout quite radically when he applied his theories to specific sites, such as Stockholm (1933), where he attempted to 'enhance' and 'underline' the history of the city, and also to take advantage of the 'natural riches' of the site.[54]

It has been seen that Le Corbusier wrote of his plan for the Radiant City in terms of a balance between masculine and feminine elements.

This prodigious spectacle has been produced by the interplay of two elements, one male, one female: sun and water. Two contradictory elements that both need the other to exist . . .[55]

Radiant is a word of Mediterranean France. Its partner is 'ineffable' . . . taken up from youth with the phenomenon of the play of proportions, I had sometimes seen them bring about a shining, the illumination of a space rendered limitless and I had placed at the head of a book these beaming words : ineffable space . . .

Therefore, radiant, therefore Ineffable, this total potential with banal materials to make our cities, our homes, our houses and our countrysides, the modern world 'radiant'. Radiant on earth! The challenge is worth answering when today Sputnik is going to the moon.[66]

The word radiant 'radieuse' was exemplified by that perfect conjunction of sun and sea, the Mediterranean; it was thus a word with particular significance for Le Corbusier's schemes in Provence.[67]

It is necessary to focus upon Le Corbusier's use of this word in order to gain a better understanding of the Radiant City as a place where men and women would live together in harmony. He commented wryly that, at the time of the scheme's inception, one of his associates asked him: '"What does V. R. stand for?" I answered, "Ville Radieuse." He asked me, "Why don't you call it something more solid, like Locomotive, something that works?".'[68] In *Talks with Students* Le Corbusier wrote that the word radiant had 'a meaning that surpasses a merely functional connotation'. For him it had 'the attribute of consciousness', adding that 'in these perilous times, consciousness itself is at stake, more important than economics or technology'.[69] A radiant building would influence everything around it, like the Parthenon, which Le Corbusier described thus:

Effect of a work of art (architecture, statue or painting) on its surroundings: waves, outcries, turmoil (the Parthenon on the Acropolis at Athens), lines spurting, radiating out as if produced by an explosion: the surroundings, both immediate and more distant, are stirred and shaken, dominated or caressed by it. Reaction of the surroundings: the walls of a room and its dimension, the city square with its differently accentuated façades, the planes and slopes of the landscape, yes, even the bare horizons of the plain and the twisted outlines of the

mountain, the whole environment brings its weight to bear upon the place where there is a work of art, expression of the will of man; it impresses upon that place its depths or peaks, its textures, hard or flaccid, its violence and its gentleness. A kind of harmony is created, exact like a mathematical exercise, a true manifestation of the acoustics of plastic matter. It is not out of place, in this context, to bring in music, one of the subtlest phenomena of all, bringer of joy, (harmony) or of oppression (cacophony).[70]

Radiant architecture would impose its influence upon the surroundings. Radiant architecture would be connected with other edifices, both old and new, built in the same spirit and with the same sensitivity to geometry. Furthermore, architecture could be 'made radiant' through the use of the Modulor.[71]

Le Corbusier's artworks and his collection of 'objects that provoke a poetic reaction' would share this quality of radiance. However, Christopher Pearson writes that 'in Le Corbusier's theory, the work of art was only effective in radiating its metaphysical presence when placed in an isolated position of dominance, at some remove from distracting elements'.[72]

In a later work, *New World of Space*, published in 1948, Le Corbusier described the phenomenon of radiance in a chapter entitled 'Ineffable Space':

The flower, the plant, the tree, the mountain stand forth, existing in a setting. If they one day command attention because of their satisfying and independent forms, it is because they are seen to be isolated from their context and extending influences all around them. We pause, struck by such interrelation in nature, and we gaze, moved by this harmonious orchestration of space, and we realise that we are looking at the reflection of light.[73]

The flower, like its environment, is structured according to the mathematical laws of nature. It conforms to the same rules. It is in dialogue with the rest of nature, yet it remains an independent entity. For Le Corbusier, to see a flower in relationship with nature was to see the 'reflection of light'. From his reading of Henri Provensal, he would be aware of the links that the theologians of the Middle Ages made between God and light; it is therefore probable that he believed that the experience of radiance would bring man closer to the divine order at the heart of things.[74]

The notion of radiance also implies the presence of energy. Certainly, electricity was a very important theme in Le Corbusier's work, as can be deduced from his plans for The Electronic Poem for the Brussels World Fair of 1958. At that time atomic bombs were increasingly seen as a real and terrifying threat,[75] so the discussion of electricity and energy would have had a certain poignancy. Le Corbusier included an image of an atomic bomb within sequence 5 of Le Poème Electronique entitled 'How time moulds civilisation'. These followed on from images of the aeroplanes and of radar dishes receiving messages from space, all forms of interconnection.[76]

Like his symbol of the 24 hour day that formed the basis for his Basilica at La Sainte Baume, the electricity wave is cyclical; it represents a flow of energy from positive to negative and back again. Electricity could for this reason be used as a powerful and modern way in which to represent the oppositions central to the architect's ideas. The cross and arrow symbols that occur in 'outil', the final square of The Poem of the Right Angle, have been linked by Daphne Becket-Chary to the sexual symbols for man and woman, but they are also evocative of the positive and negative signs in electricity.[77]

Le Corbusier made a connection between the power of physical and spiritual attraction and energy. Reference should be made to a passage in When the Cathedrals were White in which he referred to the differences in 'voltage' between men and women as a problem of town planning.[78] For Le Corbusier the relationships between people and, indeed, things could be represented by electricity.[79] For this reason cities represented 'magnetic fields'.[80] 'The wave of architecture like a wave of electricity surrounds the earth and there are antennas everywhere. How old we still are in a new world! How squalid' he wrote in impassioned terms.[81] The word radiant encompassed a vision of the world in which both people and the material world were interconnected totally through the powers of geometry, electricity and love.

24 Rue Nungesser et Coli: an increment of the Radiant City

Le Corbusier would use the opportunity of building his own home, the penthouse at 24 Rue Nungesser et Coli (Fig. 7.3), as a chance to make manifest his Radiant City philosophy. Here he would create a dwelling for the man and woman of the 'machine age', mirroring and reinforcing the interplay of the masculine and feminine life within the apartment and, ultimately, the interplay of the idealised masculine and feminine within the inhabitants themselves.[82]

Built in 1933, Le Corbusier's penthouse was set into the projected plan for the Radiant City, envisaged around a balance between masculine and feminine elements. Although superficially simple the apartment is, like much of Le Corbusier's work, fantastically rich in meaning, 'a veritable world which reveals itself to those whom it may concern'.[83]

Figure 7.3   Exterior of Le Corbusier's Porte Molitor apartment block, 24 Rue Nungesser et Coli.

The fact that Le Corbusier worked closely with photographers in order to orchestrate images of his buildings that were satisfactory, both in aesthetic and symbolic terms, was briefly mentioned in the last chapter. Beatriz Colomina notes that not only did Le Corbusier paint on photographs but he often erased their details and re-framed them.[84] José Quetglas points out that, particularly in the case of Le Corbusier's earlier buildings, the photographic image does not actually correspond to the reality of what was created on site.[85] Le Corbusier used photography to convey a further level of meaning; it is therefore necessary to discuss the apartment at 24 Rue Nungesser et Coli as portrayed in Volume 3 of Le Corbusier's *Oeuvre Complète*, because these photographs will give us the clearest picture of his intentions.[86] My suggestion is that he may have manipulated these images in order to express a balance of what he deemed to be masculine and feminine elements.

Much energy has been expended by historians in an attempt to analyse the meaning of the peculiar objects that are carefully organised in the kitchen of the Villa Savoye in the famous photographs (1929) that appear earlier in this volume of the *Oeuvre Complète* (Fig. 7.4).[87] According to Arthur Rüegg, during the early part of his career Le Corbusier had a 'passion' for analysing and organising into new groupings objects that he discovered while out collecting. His aim was 'to recognize "series," to create "unities" that transcend time and space, to bring into palpitating life the sight of those things on which man has inscribed his presence'.[88] Rüegg observes that in order to achieve these new unities Le Corbusier 'cut across temporal sequences, thematic connections, and spatial separations'.[89] It is my suggestion that he had a similar agenda when organising objects around his own home, especially when they were to be captured on camera.[90]

The three photographs that I will analyse here are not the only images of the apartment in the *Oeuvre Complète*. I concentrate on these images because, being first in a sequence, they provide an important introduction to the apartment and because they seem to be so closely related. It should, however, be mentioned that several of the other photographs of the apartment appear to be composed with a similar degree of artifice.[91]

I shall now examine the possibility that the apartment, like the Radiant City, may have been designed in terms of a balance of such idealised masculine and feminine elements. In many of Le Corbusier's buildings there is a clear relationship between square and circular forms. The Salvation Army building in Paris (Fig. 7.5) and the Villas Savoye and Cook provide obvious examples. At Rue Nungesser et Coli, a far more constrained site, it can be seen in small details like the cladding – square blocks inset with a circular motif – and the line of columns that starts from a central position on the front and rear elevations, but which forms a distinctly unorthodox curve en route through the centre of the building (Fig. 7.6).

Occupying the two top storeys of the Porte Molitor building, Le Corbusier's home is set between two raw unplastered party walls. One side is devoted to his studio, the other to his shared space with Yvonne, living, dining, kitchen and bedroom. Upon

Figure 7.4   Photograph of the kitchen in the Villa Savoye taken from Le Corbusier's *Oeuvre Complète*.

Figure 7.5   Exterior of Le Corbusier's Salvation Army building, Paris from Le Corbusier's *Oeuvre Complète*.

entering the apartment the bulging wall opposite the door immediately deflects the eye away from the private studio beyond and in towards the spiral staircase which occupies the first photograph in the *Oeuvre Complète*. The curve of the treads wind in circular form from the darkness of the hall (Fig. 7.7), through the square aperture and up to the dazzling sunlight of the roof garden above (Fig. 7.8). It is the spiral route to enlightenment, a favoured Romantic theme, a combination of the orthogonal and the curved, light and dark, masculine and feminine. For Le Corbusier the roof garden was a space with enormous symbolic potential, representing the marriage of nature and culture, an appropriate destination for a spiritual *promenade architecturale*.

Next, in the second image, we are given a view of the roof garden from the top of the stairs. The composition, a binary opposition of near and far, is reminiscent of Piero della Francesca's *Flagellation of Christ*, a painting that fascinated Le Corbusier (Fig. 7.9). Traces of this organisation can be seen in all Le Corbusier's photos of the apartment. Thomas Schumacher writes:

> . . . the genre [of the Annunciation] . . . almost invariably uses a split screen; the angel is on the left and the Virgin is on the right. And while the figures of these compositions consistently oppose

each other, creating a binary tension, the frame often holds the same tension. Left/right, inside and outside, then/now, near/far, all are in opposition, expressing the hinge of History that Christian doctrine attaches to this event.[92]

He notes that Le Corbusier uses such a format so frequently that it must have been intentional and suggests that it is quite possible that it held some symbolic significance for him. Schumacher's comments provide further evidence of Le Corbusier's highly controlled manipulation of imagery to express a union of opposites.

On the left hand side of the roof garden photograph the lush foliage appears in the foreground framed in a right-angle of steel. The middle ground is occupied by a deep orthogonal black hole, which leads down to the spiral staircase. Arranged around a circular table, empty curved steel garden chairs can be seen in the roof garden beyond. At first this seems normal enough, but on closer inspection it is possible to discern that each chair is somehow doubled up. Each chair looks like two chairs not stacked, not next to each other, but somehow superimposed onto one other. One chair and its double have their backs to us. The other chair and its double, on the opposite side of the round table, face us.

B 3267   7ᵉᵐᵉ ÉTAGE

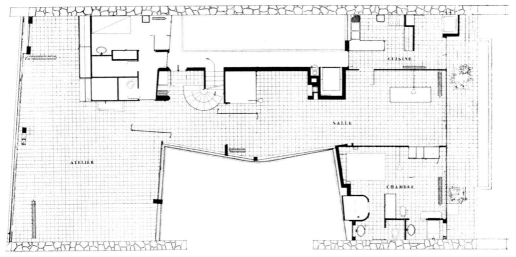

Figure 7.6   Main plan of Le Corbusier's penthouse apartment at 24 Rue Nungesser et Coli.

Figure 7.7 Photograph of the circular stair up to the roof garden, 24 Rue Nungesser et Coli from Le Corbusier's *Oeuvre Complète*.

If, as in Surrealist usage, we take each chair to indicate the presence or rather absence of a person, it seems that, by doubling the chairs, Le Corbusier is indicating the presence of a character with two sides, like the dual headed hermaphrodite of his sketches. Significantly, a 1933 sketch by Le Corbusier, contemporary with the apartment, shows two women, two chairs and the shadows of the chairs, suggesting

Figure 7.8 Photograph of the roof garden from the top of the stair, 24 Rue Nungesser et Coli from Le Corbusier's *Oeuvre Complète*.

yet again that a person, like the chair, has two sides (Fig. 7.10).

Taking his cue from alchemy, Carl Jung writes that the 'most important symbols of wholeness' are 'geometrical structures containing elements of the circle and the quaternity'. These can take the form of 'four objects or persons related to one another in meaning or by the way they are arranged'.[93] In these terms the round table and chairs in the roof garden form a symbol of wholeness or mandala. To suggest that Le Corbusier was using the chairs and table to represent a balance of opposites within himself and his wife might seem a little far-fetched until we turn to the next page in the *Oeuvre Complète*.

In the same position on the next double page layout is another photograph (Fig. 7.11), identical in size and identical in compositional terms to the roof garden photo. The orientation of the two shots is identical with respect to the views of Paris beyond and the direction of the sun is the same, coming down at a steep angle from the left, cutting the image into Corbusier's 'regulating lines'. The only thing that is different is the subject matter: the second photo is an image of the dining space seen from the living room. However, if we examine it in terms of Le Corbusier's symbolism, it can be seen that the symbolic content of the two photographs is also very similar.

In the living room photo Le Corbusier and Yvonne, his wife, can be seen in the distance, through the dining space, standing on the balcony. The position of the couple corresponds to the position of the

Figure 7.9 Piero della Francesca's *Flagellation of Christ* (1469).

two double chairs on the previous page. Indeed, both Le Corbusier and Yvonne are flanked by two chairs, one dark and one light, as if to reinforce this message. Le Corbusier stands with his back to us looking over his right shoulder while next to him, in contrast, Yvonne faces inwards. She appears to be looking over her shoulder at the same thing as Le Corbusier. They are opposite, but share the same view. He is dressed from head to foot in a dark colour; she is dressed from head to foot in white. As with the chairs, Le Corbusier is playing games of contrast, a contrast in balance which, in terms of his Radiant City project, is analogous to the relationship between the genders.

If we were to draw two diagonal lines across the roof garden photo they would meet on the two superimposed chairs that face us. If we were to draw similar lines on the dining room photo we would find, perhaps unsurprisingly, that at the centre of the photo and at the centre of this cosmos is Le Corbusier himself, his back turned to us as he looks out to the horizon.

The role of 'objects that evoke a poetic reaction' has already been discussed in terms of Le Corbusier's art work in Chapter 5. A number of these objects were placed on display in his own home, creating his own private museum:

Figure 7.10   Le Corbusier, sketch of two women and two chairs, 1933.

> Museum = the cherished respected adored word
> Because to learn to know facing each other =the actors
> Objects = men/ a man a woman you me us everyone
> The objects: the great object = nature[94]

Here objects as well as people are enlisted in the cause of creating tiny unities. In the foreground of the living room photo is a rectangular niche containing three very organic and anthropomorphic 'primitive' objects. They are on the same level as the figures of Yvonne and Le Corbusier, and seem to be of the same stature. To the left of the niche, lit by the sun, is a rotund pot, highly reminiscent of an ancient fertility goddess. She is in distinct contrast with the dark figure of Le Corbusier to the left of the balcony, yet she seems to be connected to him, perhaps as an expression of his other side. The shady priapic

Figure 7.11   Photograph of the dining space seen from the living room of Le Corbusier's penthouse, 24 Rue Nungesser et Coli from the Oeuvre Complète.

statuette on the right appears to have a similar correspondence with the figure of Yvonne. If this is indeed the case, Le Corbusier is linking himself and his wife back to an archetype of ancient primitive sexuality. It has been noted that Le Corbusier was highly superstitious, believing certain primitive fetish objects within his possession to have distinct powers.[95] In the niche above his fireplace Le Corbusier has created a unity like that between himself and Yvonne.

The sunlight falling on the feminine pot evokes the Apollonian light of reason, while the darkness that falls on the little phallus is distinctly chthonic and feminine. Each object forms a tiny marriage of opposites by itself. Although indistinct, the object in the middle is highly reminiscent of one of Le Corbusier's paintings of two lovers whose source is the image of the coming together of the masculine and the feminine in alchemical texts.

The theme of this *cuniunctio* is reiterated in the orthogonal aperture of the black fireplace where feminine darkness is framed by a masculine geometry and in the black and white fur of the organic animal skin in front of it, which lies, in turn, on the cold industrial tiles of the floor.[96] Then we notice the contrast between these shiny tiles and the warm cavernous shadowy round vaults of the ceiling above. The possibilities of this type of interpretation are endless. Light and dark, vertical and horizontal, geometric and organic, the contrasts permeate Le Corbusier's work of this period. As he wrote of the Unité in Marseilles, 'I will create beauty by contrast, I will find the opposite element, I will establish a dialogue between the rough and the finished, between precision and accident, between the lifeless and the intense and in this way I will encourage people to observe and reflect'.[97]

Although contrast is a technique used by many architects, it is my contention that, in this case, Le Corbusier uses it in a systematic way to suggest the coming together of the masculine and the feminine in the way that he mentions at the outset of *The Radiant City*. The penthouse at Rue Nungesser et Coli was built at a time when Le Corbusier was playing games of opposition and gender in a highly artificial way, seemingly because he believed that such games would impact beneficially upon the lives of those

who lived within his buildings. He drew attention to this intention through his manipulation of photography. As we have seen, his view of what constitutes a masculine or a feminine architecture is highly stereotypical. It is questionable whether Le Corbusier really thought that men and women could live within the straitjacket of such definitions.

A similar game would be played in his 1935 design for the French Pavilion for the Brussels International Fair, the name of the pavilion, Foyer de la Famille Française, evoking those family values so cherished in right wing Catholic circles. The room for the daughter of the family was not designed by Le Corbusier. This is unfortunate, as it would have been instructive to compare it with the study and gymnasium that he, his cousin Pierre and Charlotte Perriand designed for 'a young man'. Here, significantly, they shunned the use of 'masculine' steel and glass in favour of a more organic approach reflecting, as Romy Golan puts it, 'the needs of the human body' (Fig. 7.12).[98] Given that Le Corbusier himself evidently associated the organic with the female it is significant that the young man's room should be thus detailed. It is my belief that he felt such an environment would have a beneficial and balancing effect on the youth whom it was designed to contain.

One person at least was not prepared to conform to Le Corbusier's idealised vision. Yvonne Le Corbusier herself complained bitterly of the amount of glass in the apartment: 'all this light is killing me!'[99] she said, a damning indictment, in Le Corbusier's terms, of an architecture where light and

Figure 7.12   Le Corbusier and Charlotte Perriand's design for a Room for a Young Man, French Pavilion for the Brussels International Fair, 1935.

dark, masculine and feminine should exist in a balance.

Evidently Yvonne was attracted to the trappings of a more conventional marriage and home than that which her husband envisaged for her. When Le Corbusier put what Jencks calls 'a beautifully sculptural "object-type"', in other words a bidet, next to their bed she covered it up in disgust.[100] On one occasion Le Corbusier wrote in his sketchbook: 'A great event today: we brought upstairs, with great exertion, a large, homespun couch. All of a sudden everything took on an air of great comfort and calm, "like other people's houses". Yvonne was ravished. In addition, we could also serve ourselves coffee sitting on a sofa. It's like this one acquires by a long journey the rights to enter into bourgeois society'.[101]

Francesca Berry has identified a strong tendency in French women's magazines at that time to utilise the interior as 'a material metaphor for self'.[102] Certainly Le Corbusier believed in a strong link between architecture and psychological health. It is possible that he felt that he could change his wife into his perfect vision of modern woman by introducing her into this pristine new environment. In reality it seems that the opposite was the case: Le Corbusier seems to have been the one who changed. The apartment went through a gradual transformation from the 'open-hard edged interior' of the 1930s to its final form in the 1950s, what John Winter describes as an 'enclosed chunky-wood apartment',[103] a profound change in Le Corbusier's approach to architecture from the overly simplistic, dualistic thinking that I have illustrated here into something which was altogether more complex and subtle.

It is notable that although Le Corbusier would make a case for each individual member of the house having a space to call their own, to think and read and potter, in the case of his own home no such space appears to exist for Yvonne, unless the whole apartment (excluding Le Corbusier's studio) is considered to be hers.[104] Yvonne is pictured at work in the kitchen, 'the sanctuary in the home'.[105] Whilst this might be her own territory as she evidently enjoyed cooking,[106] it would not seem to meet Le Corbusier's own criteria for such a space (Fig. 7.13).

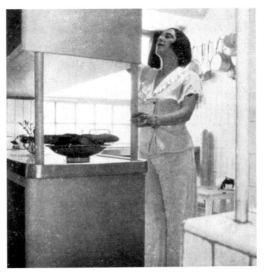

Figure 7.13   Yvonne Le Corbusier in the kitchen of Le Corbusier's penthouse at 24 Rue Nungesser et Coli, from the *Oeuvre complète*.

The Unité, Marseilles

It has been seen that Le Corbusier believed the design of the dwelling to have a pivotal role in alleviating the problems that he saw developing in the relationships between women and men. It seems very likely therefore that he designed the Unité with that very specific intention in mind, its name 'unity' a clear expression of what he hoped to achieve there. Le Corbusier described the Unité d'Habitation built on the Boulevard Michelet (Fig. 7.14) as the fruit of twenty-five years of study that began with the monastic architecture of the Middle Ages.[107] He saw it as a 'prototype . . . a solution to a universal problem' marking a new beginning in architecture and capable of infinite reproduction. In it would be assembled a 'natural social grouping' in a 'harmonious unit'.[108] Its foundation stone was eventually laid on 14 October 1947, after a long struggle with the authorities. It would take five years to build.

Life in this 'vertical garden city', built to Modulor proportions, would bring its inhabitants back into contact with nature and one another (Fig. 7.15);[109] simultaneously its cellular structure would bring into relief the connection between mass housing and the organisms of biology (Fig. 7.16).[110] Moulded out of

Figure 7.15   Le Corbusier, collage of exterior of Unité as vertical garden city.

Figure 7.14   Exterior of Le Corbusier's Unité, Marseilles from the *Oeuvre Complète*.

beton brut the huge horizontal housing block is supported on rough cast pilotis. Interlocking duplex units are set within its cellular frame, each with a double height balcony allowing spectacular views of nature (Fig. 7.17). Accessed from a colourful interior street, each prefabricated apartment or 'bottle' would slide into the overall structure, the wine rack, 'one fire, one hearth, one family' (Fig. 7.18).[111]

Le Corbusier wrote of a 'conscious organisation of disinterested human activities' that would need to take place alongside an urban redevelopment programme. These were 'the bringing up of children, education, body, spirit, heart. Total participation. Individual activity and collective activities. Goals assigned for human existence. True pleasures.'[112] It was his belief that 'supreme joys' could be earned 'by a spiritual or "maternal" participation in working for the collective good'.[113] It was for this reason that Le Corbusier planned to create on the roof of the building:

a running track, 300m long;
an open-air and a covered gymnasium;
a club;
a nursery installation laid out as a roof garden (water and sun therapy, games, etc.);
a mothers' room;
social life: sunbathing and refreshments.[114]

Communal facilities are housed at the base and within internal streets that run through the block and on the

roof where the nursery, gymnasium and theatre space form part of a spectacular roofscape. Tiles, in blue and green, stud the gymnasium walls evoking the hues of nature.

Le Corbusier's ambition was to create a building that would foster a sense of harmonious unity amongst its inhabitants.[115] This is evident from a list of objectives that he wrote for the residents' association in the Unité:

(a) the creation and development of bands of friendship between the inhabitants;
(b) the organization of collective activities (social, cultural, artistic and recreational);
(c) the defence, in all spheres, of the interests of its members, on all occasions when the interests in question were linked with the standard of living in the Unité;
(d) the participation of the inhabitants of the Unité in the determination of the material and moral administration of the Unité and its dependencies in an atmosphere of mutual understanding with all people who may be directly or indirectly interested.[116]

The building was conceived around a philosophy of mutual understanding and respect.

Within the Unité, families could dwell as independent units in privacy whilst, at the same time, being able to participate in the collective life of the building. Le Corbusier took great care over the design

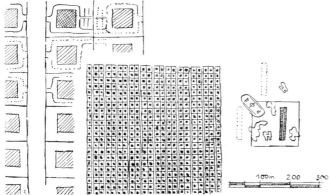

Figure 7.16   Le Corbusier sketch of underlying cellular diagram for the Unité block from the *Oeuvre Complète*.

Figure 7.17   Duplex cell within Unité from Le Corbusier's *Oeuvre Complète*.

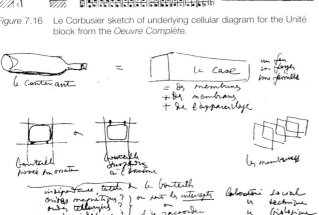

Figure 7.18
Diagram showing the way in which the bottle would inhabit the Unité frame from Le Corbusier's *Oeuvre Complète*.

of the individual units giving the optimum in both flexibility (through the use of pivoting walls) and privacy (for example through the use of sound-proofing). With carefully planned facilities he hoped to accommodate play space for children and isolate in peace the marital bed.[117] In the words of his assistant André Wogenscky, using an 'infinity of tact' he designed 'an envelope around man and woman . . . encompassing all their gestures, their movements and their acts . . . their thoughts'.[118]

Believing it to be important for the health of the community as a whole, Le Corbusier made a number of provisions that would vastly improve the life of its female inhabitants.

The Unité at Marseilles made it possible to create 26 communal services so as to free the housewife

from domestic drudgery and to further the bringing up of children. Women have their place in the realisation of this task. They can draw up the right programme for it, but they can also put it into practice.[119]

Le Corbusier wrote that at the opening of the Unité, one after another women came up to embrace him and thank him for the building. One heavily pregnant woman even asked him to be godfather to her child.[120] He believed that 'a soul immediately appeared in the building' when the mothers made each other's acquaintance at the nursery;[121] collectively they would play a vital role in the creation of the community there.

As he grew older Le Corbusier placed more and more emphasis upon the importance of the task of education,[122] his last book on kindergartens, *Les Maternelles*, being devoted to the subject. This may be why he seems to have been so friendly with Lilette Ougier,[123] the headmistress of the nursery school in the Unité (Fig. 7.19), whom he consulted extensively on the design[124] for the nursery at Unité at Nantes Rezé (1953–55) which is, according to its residents, a very successful building. At a celebration to mark the thirtieth anniversary of the Unité in Marseilles, Perriand returned there for a visit. She discovered to her dismay that Ougier, who had been so faithful to Corbusian ideals, teaching her young charges 'to draw pictures of wonderful flat-roofed radiant houses', had finally retired and now the children were copying pictures of a traditional house with a pitched roof. Perriand responded 'Farewell radiant life . . . it is all over'.[125]

The spiritual home incarnate

It had been Le Corbusier's intention that the Unité would, like Ronchamp, act as a radiant beacon, attracting and exuding beneficent influence into the surroundings. 'Let us describe then the Home of Man, the visible home that should be the spiritual home incarnate' wrote Le Corbusier and François de Pierrefeu, one of his syndicalist colleagues, in the introduction to a volume which they worked upon together during the Second World War.[126] The theme of the dwelling as a sacred space runs through Le Corbusier's work from the earliest times,[127] the 'dwelling' being the 'temple of the family',[128] its life revolving around that of the woman. Returning once

more to the language of chivalry, Le Corbusier observed that 'In her kitchen [the woman] receives the homage and tribute of her serfs and servants who – far from her castle (kitchen) take on an immense labour for her benefit'.[129] 'The fire the "hearth". One has come in from outside . . . one finds the ancient fire, the hearth of tradition. The mistress of the house is preparing a meal by the stove' (Fig. 7.20).[130]

According to de Pierrefeu the four 'essential' functions of houses were 'to dwell, circulate, work and improve oneself following the rule of the sun'.[131] The intention was that by providing them with an effective architecture, the building's inhabitants would be initiated into the mysteries of how to live. Le Corbusier asked:

> Knowing how to live is the fundamental question before modern society, everywhere, in the whole world. An ingenuous question and one that could be considered childish. How to live? Do you know reader? Do you know how to live soundly, strongly, gaily, free of the hundred stupidities established by habit, custom and urban disorganisation?[132]

He noted that it would be necessary to 'select suitable groups to live in the experimental buildings' of the Unité Marseille-Michelet and to teach them the 'know-how of dwelling'.[133] Although not an egalitarian move, he recognised that he needed a population who could enter into the spirit of his buildings, who could understand what he was trying to achieve. These people would be receptive to the intentions of

Figure 7.19   Children at play on the roof garden of the Unité, Marseilles.

Figure 7.20   Nineteenth century etching of the hearth taken from Le Corbusier's book *The Marseilles Block*.

the architect and would learn from the building. Like the oracle of the Holy Bottle, the Unité would be a place of initiation into a new form of being.

It may seem presumptuous to suggest that Le Corbusier thought of the Unité in religious terms, but such a connection seems to have been obvious to the priests of the L'Art Sacré movement. For them the Unité was firmly linked with the scheme for La Sainte Baume and, indeed, with the Ronchamp.[134] It is important to note the way that the Unité block at Marseilles is depicted in L'Homme et L'Architecture, a publication over which Le Corbusier had a supervisory role.[135] Here the vast columns that support the structure of the Unité block frame images of mysterious gods in a darkened underground world like the one evoked in Rabelais (Fig.7.21).

At the entrance to the Unité, Le Corbusier placed a large block of stone, to Modulor proportions, which was designed to help the visitor understand the key issues at stake in the building. 'Symbolically the entire construction rests upon it', he wrote.[136] On one side is carved a symbol, Le Corbusier's symbol of the 24 hour day. On the other side the symbol of Modulor man can be seen. This carved block of stone evokes those ancient ideas that formed the spiritual foundation of the scheme. Le Corbusier referred to the space beneath the pilotis as the 'main hall' and the 'place of honour' indicating that it was, for him, very special.[137] The dark underworld of the Unité and the dazzling upper world of the rooftop garden form part of a route of initiation like that experienced by Panurge as he travelled through the bowels of the earth and then up into the light. As at La Sainte Baume and Ronchamp, the architecture of the building, its

tactile surfaces and forms, its colours, its dramatic lighting and its proportions, echoing those of nature, would work upon the body and spirit instilling within those who lived in it an appreciation of the power of harmony and thus enabling them to create harmony in their relationships with one another. His experiments in his own apartment, 24 Rue Nungesser et Coli, provided the prototype for the type of thinking that we see in operation here.

Le Corbusier's painted work was dominated by the idea of a primal feminine divinity to whom he gave a sculptural presence in the undulating forms of Ronchamp. Uterine symbolism is also present in the Unité, Marseilles where the rooftop gymnasium is housed in a space that is evidently derived in form from an upturned boat, evoking those that populate his paintings, as well as those associated with feminine divinities in a number of different cultural contexts (Fig.7.22). In the context of Marseilles, the boat that has come to ground here must surely be that of Mary Magdalene and the other Marys.[138]

Within the pages of Le Modulor, Le Corbusier made a point of drawing attention to the fact that it was possible to see the mountains of La Sainte Baume from the roof of the Unité.[139] The undulating sculptures[140] of the nursery play space echo in form the landscape of La Sainte Baume beyond.[141] Indeed, there is a profound affinity between the two schemes. A solitary

Figure 7.22 Gymnasium on the roof of the Unité. Photograph from Le Corbusier's *Oeuvre Complète*.

Figure 7.21 Photograph of early model of area under the pilotis of the Unité, from Le Corbusier's special edition of *L'Homme et l'Architecture*.

column stands amongst these artificial mountains evoking the ruins of an ancient Greek temple, conceivably that of Delphi, the source of the ideas upon which the Unité was built (Fig. 7.23).

Le Corbusier was known to refer to his buildings as though they were living beings to which he had given 'birth'. Stephen Gardiner notes one occasion on which Le Corbusier rushed up and hugged one of the columns of the Unité.[142] In the *Oeuvre Complète* he alludes to it as a person. Analogies can clearly be drawn between figures in his paintings and some of the forms in his later buildings. Although it might be an exaggeration to suggest that Le Corbusier thought of his buildings as being in some way alive, acting upon us through what he called a 'psychophysiology of the feelings', the implication is that they are not entirely passive. The relationship between Ronchamp and the body of woman was discussed in the last chapter. I would argue that the Unité too shares something of its anthropomorphic character: it appears to stand on two stolid legs like the women in Le Corbusier's paintings (Fig.7.24). Like Ronchamp, it too is a bulging and anthropomorphic vase, a primal feminine deity. The building was designed to appeal to the senses at the most rudimentary level, hence its gruff maternal bearing.

Conclusion

Le Corbusier perceived that society was breaking down as men and women became more and more estranged from one another. It was his belief that architecture could be put to the service of resurrecting such flagging relationships. At a simple level, reducing travel, providing communal services and modern household conveniences would give men and women more time and leisure to be together. Le Corbusier referred to the eleven hours of leisure that each person would have in his Radiant City as 'the true working day' of mankind.

Simultaneously Le Corbusier aimed to create a subtle web of favourable influence around the family home that would aid men and women in their relationships with one another. This occurs with some artifice in the apartment at 24 Rue Nungesser et Coli, but with greater subtlety in his later buildings. A

Figure 7.23   Artificial mountains and column on roof of Unité taken from Le Corbusier's *Oeuvre Complète*.

Figure 7.24   End elevation of Unité under construction.

radiant building would give and receive energy, the energy of number, of electricity and of love. As at La Sainte Baume, the inhabitant of the Unité would be initiated into the powers of harmony, achieved most notably through geometrical proportion, but also in other ways such as contrasting materials, colour, light and symbolism. Built in emulation of nature the building would draw the attention of its inhabitants to what Le Corbusier believed to be nature's laws. The union of opposites, man and woman, itself a law of nature, would be facilitated by the presence of this harmonious framework, the whole presided over by a beneficent feminine presence.

Notes

1 Le Corbusier, *Sketchbooks Volume 3, 1954–1957* (Cambridge, MA: MIT Press, 1982), sketch 521.
2 Le Corbusier, *When the Cathedrals were White: A Journey to the Country of the Timid People* (New York: Reynal and Hitchcock, 1947), p.104. See also his comments on the problem of a population explosion in India. 'The sexual problem is key'. For Le Corbusier there was 'hypocrisy on this issue'. He planned to include a chapter on this subject in his book 'Fin d'une Monde'. Le Corbusier, *Sketchbooks Volume 2* (London: Thames and Hudson, 1981), sketch 685.
3 Le Corbusier, *When the Cathedrals were White: A Journey to the Country of the Timid People*, p.105.
4 Le Corbusier noted that at the CIAM meeting in Hoddesdon in 1951, Jose Luis Sert had posited a 'new theme . . . The Core'. This, like the cell, was for Le Corbusier about 'sociability' the 'friendly and fruitful relationships among men (+ women)'. Le Corbusier, *Sketchbooks Volume 2, 1950–1954* (London: Thames and Hudson, 1981), sketch 494.
5 Le Corbusier, *Poésie sur Alger* (Paris: Editions Connivances, 1989), p.12.
6 Le Corbusier, *Towards a New Architecture* (London: Architectural Press, 1982), p.25.
7 Ibid., p.130.
8 Le Corbusier, *The Marseilles Block* (London: Harville, 1953), p.17.
9 Ibid., p.18.
10 Le Corbusier, *Precisions on the Present State of Architecture and City Planning* (Cambridge, MA: MIT Press, 1990), p.130.
11 'Only the architect can strike a balance between man and his environment (man = a psycho-physiology; his environment = the universe, nature and cosmos)'. Le Corbusier, *Modulor* (London: Faber, 1954), p.111.
12 Le Corbusier. *Precisions*, p.vii.
13 Le Corbusier, *The Final Testament of Père Corbu: a Translation and Interpretation of Mise au Point by Ivan Zaknic* (New Haven, CT: Yale University Press, 1997), p.87.
14 Mardges Bacon, *Le Corbusier in America* (Cambridge, MA: MIT Press, 2001), p.214.
15 Le Corbusier, *Sketchbooks Volume 1, 1914–1948* (London: Thames and Hudson, 1981), sketches 616–20.
16 Ibid.
17 Ibid.
18 Ibid.
19 Le Corbusier, *When the Cathedrals were White*, p.155.
20 Ibid., p.149.
21 C. Duchen, *Women's Rights and Women's Lives in France* (London: Routledge, 1994), p.79.
22 R. Allendy, *Capitalisme et Sexualité: le conflits des instincts et les problèmes actuels* (Paris: Denoel), p185 and p.200 in Fondation Le Corbusier (hereafter referred to as FLC).
23 Ibid., p.181.
24 Ibid., p.183.
25 See annotations. Ibid., pp.227–9.
26 Ibid., p.207. Underlined by Le Corbusier.
27 Le Corbusier, *Precisions*, p.29.
28 See Le Corbusier's heavy annotations to Allendy, *Capitalisme et Sexualité*, p.25 in FLC.
29 Le Corbusier, *Sketchbooks Volume 2, 1950–1954*, sketch 452.
30 The Gynecium was in ancient Rome the part of the house that was the territory of women.
31 Le Corbusier, *Sketchbooks Volume 2*, sketch 502.
32 Le Corbusier, *My Work* (London: Architectural Press, 1960), p.300.
33 Ibid., p.253.
34 Le Corbusier, *Precisions*, p.106.
35 Le Corbusier, *Sketchbooks Volume 2*, sketch 452.
36 C. Laubier, *The Condition of Women in France: 1945 to the Present* (London: Routledge, 1990), p.2.
37 Ibid.
38 C. Duchen, *Women's Rights and Women's Lives in France* (London: Routledge, 1994), p.85.
39 Le Corbusier, *Oeuvre Complète, Volume 6, 1952–1957* (Zurich: Les Editions d'Architecture, 1995), p.176.
40 Le Corbusier, *The Marseilles Block*, p.17.
41 Ibid., p.26.
42 Le Corbusier, *The Radiant City* (London: Faber, 1967), p.112.
43 Letter Le Corbusier to his mother, 17.06.1948, FLC R2.4.123.
44 Trouin, 'Table provisoire' for book entitled 'La Sainte Baume et Marie Madeleine,' n.d., FLC 13.01.400.
45 Luke 10: 38–42.
46 John 11: 1.
47 E. Renan, *La Vie de Jesus* (Paris: Calmann-Levy, 1906), p.184 in FLC. Le Corbusier also referred to the story of Martha and Mary in a letter to his mother of 10.11.1931, in J. Jenger, *Le Corbusier Choix de Lettres* (Basel: Birkhauser, 2002), p.215.
48 Le Corbusier, *Precisions*, p.88.
49 Le Corbusier, *Modulor*, p.110.
50 Ibid., p123.

51 Le Corbusier, *The Radiant City*, p.115.

52 Le Corbusier, *My Work*, p.112.

53 Le Corbusier, 'La Femme et la Ville Radieuse', 06.05.1933, FLC B2.11.31.

54 Le Corbusier, *The Radiant City*, pp.297–303.

55 Ibid., p.78.

56 R. Pincus Witten, *Occult Symbolism in France: Joséphin Peladan and the Salons de la Rose-Croix* (New York: Garland, 1976), p.58.

57 Ibid.

58 See 'On Difference: Masculine and Feminine' in A. Forty, *Words and Buildings* (London: Thames and Hudson, 2000), pp.42–61 for a discussion of the enduring tendency to see architecture in terms of gender.

59 Le Corbusier, *Modulor*, p.224.

60 Pearson writes of the way in which Le Corbusier distributed gendered artworks within his clients' houses, for example in the Villas Stein and Mandrot. 'At the Mandrot villa . . . the association of the female form with passivity and nature and the male form with a more active dominance of its surroundings is more typical of Le Corbusier's masculinist symbology'. C.E.M. Pearson, 'Integrations of Art and Architecture in the Work of Le Corbusier. Theory and Practice from Ornamentalism to the "Synthesis of the Major Arts"'. Unpublished PhD thesis, Stanford University (1995), p.139.

61 Le Corbusier, *The Modulor*, p.113.

62 Le Corbusier, *The Radiant City* p.78.

63 See also Pearson's discussion of the term 'irradiation'. Pearson, 'Integrations of Art and Architecture in the Work of Le Corbusier', p.90.

64 M. McLeod, 'Urbanism and Utopia: Le Corbusier from Regional Syndicalism to Vichy', DPhil, Princeton (1985), p.iv.

65 J. Jennings, *Syndicalism in France: A Study of Ideas* (London: Macmillan, 1990), p.203.

66 Le Corbusier, 'Où est-on 26 ans après la Charte d'Athènes,' May-June 1962, 18 pp. Typed ms. (unpublished, intended for M.P. Delouvrier's book *Le District de Paris*), p.14, FLC A3.01.365.

67 Pearson has written of the significance of the word radiant in terms of sound. Christopher Pearson, 'Le Corbusier and the Acoustical Trope', *Journal of the Society of Architectural Historians*, 56, 2 (1997), pp.168–83.

68 J. Peter, *The Oral History of Modern Architecture* (New York: Harry N. Abrams, 1994), p.143.

69 Le Corbusier, *Le Corbusier Talks with Students* (New York: Princeton University Press, 1999), p.27.

70 Le Corbusier, *Modulor 2* (London: Faber, 1955), p.26.

71 Ibid., p.306.

72 Pearson, 'Integrations of Art and Architecture in the Work of Le Corbusier', p.91.

73 Le Corbusier, *New World of Space* (New York: Reynal and Hitchcock, 1948), p.7.

74 H. Provensal, *L'Art de Demain* (Paris: Perrin, 1904), p.182 in FLC.

75 The bomb was dropped on Hiroshima on 6 August 1945. The Cuban missiles crisis was to take place in 1962.

76 Le Corbusier, *Le Poème electronique* (Paris: Les Cahiers Forces Vives aux Éditions de Minuit, 1958), pages not numbered.

77 D. Becket-Chary, '*Le Corbusier's Poem of the Right Angle*'. Unpublished MPhil thesis, Cambridge (1990).

78 Chapter entitled 'The Family Divided', Le Corbusier, *When the Cathedrals were White*, p.154.

79 See Le Corbusier's annotations to Allendy, *Capitalisme et Sexualité*, pp.33–4 in FLC.

80 Le Corbusier, *The Radiant City*, p.135.

81 Le Corbusier, *Precisions*, p.17.

82 See F. Samuel, 'Animus, Anima and the Architecture of Le Corbusier', *Harvest*, 48/2 (2003), pp.42–60 for a Jungian interpretation of this argument.

83 Le Corbusier. *The New World of Space* (New York: Reynal and Hitchcock, 1948), p.8.

84 D. Naegele, 'An Interview with Lucien Hervé', *Parametro*, 206, pp.71–83. See also B. Colomina, 'Le Corbusier and Photography', *Assemblage*, 4 (1987), pp.12–13.

85 J. Quetglas, 'Journeys on my Counterpane', *Arquitectura*, 264–5 (1987), p.110.

86 Le Corbusier and Pierre Jeanneret, *Oeuvre Complète Volume 3, 1934–38* (Zurich: Les Editions d'Architecture, 1995), pp.144–53.

87 Colomina, for example, notes that the trail of objects left by Le Corbusier in his images of the Villa Savoye as a trace of somebody who has just left the room are all 'male'. Such an interpretation would not seem to apply to the enigmatic fish, pot and electric fan that appear in the kitchen, the pot in particular being traditionally 'feminine' in character. B. Colomina, 'The split wall: Domestic Voyeurism' in B. Colomina (ed.), *Sexuality and Space* (New York: Princeton University Press, 1992), p.100.

88 A. Rüegg, 'Marcel Levaillant and "La Question du Mobilier"', in S. Von Moos and A. Rüegg (eds), *Le Corbusier before Le Corbusier* (New Haven, CT: Yale University Press, 2002), p.128.

89 Ibid.

90 In 1935 Le Corbusier used his home as a gallery for an exhibition 'Les Arts dits Primitifs'.

91 For another interpretation of the apartment see S. Menin and F. Samuel, *Nature and Space: Aalto and Le Corbusier* (London: Routledge, 2003), pp.126–30.

92 T. Schumacher, 'Deep Space Shallow Space', *Architectural Review*, vol. CLXXXI, No. 1079, 1987, pp.37–43.

93 C.G. Jung, 'The Fish in Alchemy'. *C.W.9.* part II: 193–238 (London: Routledge & Kegan Paul, 1951), para 351.

94 Le Corbusier, *Sketchbooks Volume 4, 1957–1964* (Cambridge, MA: MIT Press, 1982), sketch 731.

95 C. Kagal, 'Le Corbusier: The acrobat of architecture interview with Balkrishna Doshi, 1986', *Architecture and Urbanism*, no. 322, July 97, p.48.

96 Pearson writes of Le Corbusier's habit of 'superim-posing organic forms over an organising grid'. Pearson, 'Integrations of Art and Architecture in the Work of Le Corbusier', p.312.

97 Le Corbusier, *Oeuvre Complète*, Vol. 5, p.190.

98 R. Golan, *Modernity and Nostalgia: Art and Politics in France between the Wars* (London: Yale University Press, 1995), p.96.

99 C. Jencks, *Le Corbusier and the Tragic View of Architecture* (London: Allen Lane, 1973), p.100.

100 C. Jencks, *Le Corbusier and the Continual Revolution in Architecture* (New York: Monacelli Press, 2000), p.191.

101 Ibid., p.77.

102 F. Berry, 'Femina 1901–1938', AHRB Centre for Domestic Interior Symposium, Victoria & Albert Museum, London, 7 February 2003.

103 J. Winter, 'Le Corbusier's Technological Dilemma' in R. Walden (ed.), *The Open Hand* (Cambridge, MA: MIT Press, 1982), p.334.

104 Constant notes that despite the 'radical' appearance of the Pavillon d'Esprit Nouveau, suggestive of a new way of life, Le Corbusier's buildings contained a number of spaces 'associated with a bourgeois lifestyle'. This included a maid's room, a 'man's study (complete with globe) adjoining the dining room and a lady's boudoir (with its traditional divan) off the bedroom'. She continues: 'rejecting the conventional self-contained form for the latter pair of gendered spaces, Le Corbusier situated them within a spatial continuum; the boudoir occupies a mezzanine that overlooks the living room, and the study takes up the protected corner of the multipurpose living room. Each space thus affords its occupant exposure to the activities within the dwelling unit as a whole.' C. Constant, *Eileen Gray* (London: Phaidon, 2000), p.61.

105 Le Corbusier, *Precisions*, p.222.

106 L. Montalte (E. Trouin pseud.), *Fallait-il Bâtir Le Mont-Saint-Michel?* (St Zachaire: Montalte, 1979), p.147.

107 Notes made in the summer of 1955. Le Corbusier, *Sketchbooks Volume 3*, sketch 520.

108 Le Corbusier Special Number *L'Homme et l'Architecture*, 12–13 (1947), p.5.

109 Le Corbusier, *La Ville Radieuse*, p.83.

110 Le Corbusier wrote of the work of the entymologist Jean-Henri Fabre who had made a number of obser-vations about the social relationship between ants. 'We realised that natural phenomena have an organisation, and we opened our eyes. 1900. An outpouring. Truly, a fine moment!' Le Corbusier, *The Decorative Art of Today* (London: Architectural Press, 1987), p.13.

111 Le Corbusier, *Oeuvre Complète Volume 5* (Zurich: Les Editions d'Architecture, 1995), p.186.

112 Le Corbusier, *The Radiant City*, p.85.

113 Ibid., p.86.

114 Le Corbusier, *Modulor*, p146.

115 Le Corbusier, *L'Homme et l'Architecture*, p.5.

116 Le Corbusier, *Oeuvre Complète Volume 5*, p.190.

117 Le Corbusier, *Sketchbooks Volume 2*, sketch 913.

118 A. Wogenscky, *Les Mains de Le Corbusier* (Paris: Grenelle, n.d.), p.32.

119 From an article originally published in Le Point in 1948 and cited in Le Corbusier, *Modulor 2*, p.162.

120 Letter Le Corbusier to his mother, 15.10.1952 in Jenger, *Le Corbusier Choix de Lettres*. p.361.

121 Le Corbusier, *Sketchbooks Volume 2*, sketch 857.

122 Le Corbusier quotes M. André Sive, an architect from Paris: 'I should like the Modulor to be made obliga-tory in the building of schools, so that the sense of plastic harmony might be introduced into the minds of children. That is an essential condition of a future in which building would, once more, become the very expression of civilisation.' Le Corbusier, *Modulor 2*, p.105.

123 J. Heilbuth to L. Ougier, 23.12.1958, FLC 91.14.499.

124 Letter Le Corbusier to L. Ougier, 03.07.1959, FLC E2.17.376.

125 C. Perriand, *Une Vie de crèation* (Paris: Editions Odile Jacob), p.242 cited in G.H. Marcus, *Le Corbusier: Inside the Machine for Living* (New York: Monacelli Press, 2000), p.160.

126 Le Corbusier and François de Pierrefeu, *The Home of Man* (London: Architectural Press, 1958), p.12.

127 Le Corbusier discussed what he calls 'the cult of the home' which has stayed the same for centuries, primarily represented by 'the roof' and then 'the other household gods' in Le Corbusier, *Towards a New Architecture*, pp.18–19.

128 Le Corbusier, *The Final Testament of Père Corbu*, p.93.

129 Le Corbusier, *Oeuvre Complète Volume 5*, p.94.

130 Ibid.

131 Le Corbusier and de Pierrefeu, *The Home of Man*, p.21.

132 Le Corbusier, *When the Cathedrals were White*, p.xvii.

133 Le Corbusier, *The Marseilles Block*, p.34.

134 A-M. Cocagnac (1955), *L'Art Sacré*, Sep-Oct, Vols 1–2.

135 Le Corbusier Special Number *L'Homme et l'Architecture*, 12–13 (1947), p.5.

136 Le Corbusier, *Modulor*, p.140.

137 Ibid.

138 According to Trouin Le Corbusier's scheme for the 'bar-que', one of the later versions of the Permanent City at La Sainte Baume, was based on the boat of the Marys. Montalte, *Fallait-il Bâtir Le Mont-Saint-Michel?*, p.147.

139 Le Corbusier, *Le Modulor*, p.150.

140 Pearson writes of the way in which Le Corbusier posi-tioned a small figure of a reclining nude in the window of the Villa Mandrot to 'serve to echo the form of the distant hills'. Pearson, 'Integrations of Art and Architecture in the Work of Le Corbusier', p.139.

141 Le Corbusier, *Oeuvre Complète Volume 5*, pp.174–200.

142 Stephen Gardiner, *Le Corbusier* (London: Fontana, 1974).

Conclusion

Being a man of his time, Le Corbusier's attitude to the feminine was complex and his behaviour towards women contradictory, but at a fundamental level he does seem to have believed in the principle of equality as an ideal to which we should all aspire. Many commentators have noted his interest in the idea of balancing contradictory elements, the union of opposites, used both as a design tool and a personal philosophy. It was a principle which he brought to bear on a wide range of disparate subjects, including the relationship between the sexes.

If being a feminist involves advocating the extended recognition of women's achievements, then Le Corbusier was a feminist. Certainly, his ideas coincided with those of the feminist agenda in early twentieth century France, particularly with regard to the freedom of the body and its resultant effect in liberating the mind. When he did work with women, he worked with them as equals. He saw woman as an instigator of change with a particularly important role in bringing about the new order that he so desired. He recognised her growing economic strength and her increasing influence upon the evolution of culture. He acknowledged her new role in the world of work. Whilst he could be criticised for consigning married women and those with children to the home, he recognised the full importance of their work, seeing the married couple as a team operating together. The best place for women is still a hotly debated issue for which there is no easy answer. Le Corbusier is to be commended for recognising it as an issue at all.

Le Corbusier had a strong sense of women's worth instilled into him by his mother. He may have been referring to her when he wrote of his own 'ideal' being a 'magnificent and dominating type of woman'.[1] However, as a young man, mixing in dandyish circles, his attitude to them seems to have become more fashionably· ambivalent.[2] Jenger considers the possibility that the nature of his rela-

tionship with Yvonne may have been characteristic of his dealings with women in general. In his opinion certain statements with which Le Corbusier peppered his letters leave hardly any doubt on this matter.[3] 'It is nice to pamper women, these idiotic and yet so beautiful women.'[4] 'Let's not dwell on women's whims, innocence or ignorance.'[5] 'Once more, I realise ladies go for it . . . with sublime selfishness.'[6] The first quotation is from a letter to Ritter, a homosexual, written before Le Corbusier had launched into his affair with Yvonne, when his knowledge of women may have been minimal.

Early in his career Le Corbusier wrote of the 'male abilities' which he believed to be 'considerations of *ensemble*, organisation, sense of unity, balance, proportion, harmony'.[7] The context of this quote, a discussion of women's handiwork, suggests that these were qualities that he believed were absent in women.[8] 'Men – intelligent, cold and calm – are needed to build the house and lay out the town' wrote Le Corbusier in the late 1920s.[9] Toward the end of his life he made a note in his sketchbook that a certain Louis Bonnier had accused him of being a misogynist in 1922, suggesting that this was certainly an issue that concerned him.[10] Interestingly, Le Corbusier's references to women increased in warmth and respect as he grew older and his work changed in character from the cold white buildings such as the Villa Savoye to more warm and earthy creations such the Maison du Petite Weekend. In *When the Cathedrals were White* he wrote of the fact that in medieval times 'Women were not well thought of because they had loved gaiety, etc . . .'[11] suggesting in his tone that this was an injustice. It was at this point, in the early 1930s, that he began to see women as an important force for change.

While Le Corbusier's view of women seems to have changed over time I consider that Jacques Gubler is essentially correct in suggesting that he believed that woman was 'a creature of nature'.[12] This should not necessarily be seen as a pejorative statement given that Le Corbusier made it his life's work to reconnect to this realm. However, it does herald the presence of the old nature versus culture argument that has hovered continually on the fringes of this account of the architect's life and work.[13] For generations feminists have considered the association of women with nature to be one of the fundamental reasons for their secondary status within culture. In her classic essay 'Is Female to Male as Nature is to Culture?', Sherry Ortner describes the way that, in our society, nature and culture are seen as separate entities.[14] Women inhabit neither realm fully; they live on the periphery, neither one nor the other. In Camille Paglia's terms the shaping of nature is synonymous with the shaping of the feminine and art is 'order', ruled by men in an attempt to control the dark and messy forces of the feminine.[15] Undoubtedly there is some truth in this statement as far as Le Corbusier is concerned, but again it depends on the status afforded to those 'dark and messy forces'.[16] In Le Corbusier's ideal vision in which all things exist in balance, nature and culture would be of equal status. However, given the reality of the times in which he lived and his own psychological limitations, such a synthesis eluded him.

This said, all Le Corbusier's actions were governed by a desire for a state of Orphic unity, in which all things would be interconnected through number and through love. To this end the ideal of the Platonic androgyne seems to have been one to which he aspired both in his work and in his relationships. He perceived that it was vital to explore possible ways in which men and women could be encouraged into a state of balanced relationship. This could not be done without making changes to the lives of both sexes, granting both equal respect. This idea of sexual balance, which he perceived to be a natural law, had a tremendous impact upon his theories.

Whether Le Corbusier saw each individual as a balance of masculine and feminine elements is not clear. Whilst we know of at least two instances of him dressing up as a woman, we do not know whether this was done as an earnest exercise in testing out a woman's perception, or purely for fun. Either way he certainly seems to have taken an increasingly ironic view of masculinity.[17] Le Corbusier divided his days in two, devoting half to the subjective work of the imagination in his artist's studio and half to rational action within his office. He believed that this synthesis between reason and passion would result in inspiration.[18] We know that Le Corbusier associated 'female architecture' with the 'subjective', the meandering path. It may be that, during those long mornings in his penthouse studio, he was in fact 'battling' with his inner feminine. Certainly the female form dominates his work as an artist.

It was seen in Chapter 4 that, for the Surrealists, it was the task of the artist to access the inner feminine to allow the creative process to take place. The Surrealists used the imagery of the womb as a metaphor for the act of artistic creation.[19] Similarly Le Corbusier was fond of using procreative imagery when talking about his own creative processes, referring, for example, to the design of Ronchamp as a process of 'spontaneous birth'.[20] It may be that in doing so he was drawing upon the ideas of Plato who wrote of 'poets and artists' as 'souls that are pregnant . . . with wisdom and virtue'. It was his opinion that children produced in this way would be 'fairer and more immortal [sic] than mortal offspring'.[21] Men have in this way both co-opted and denigrated women's role in the act of procreation for centuries.

Julia Kristeva has commented on the fact that it is not so much the 'feminine' that occupies a peripheral role in our culture, rather it is the biological woman, the procreative body that is edited out.[22] Certainly Le Corbusier himself betrays some ambivalence about this particular female role. It has been seen that unlike for many of his counterparts, *maternité* does not figure large in his painted work, perhaps because it plays such a small role in his own life story.

Maternité was undoubtedly an issue for Le Corbusier, though not I suspect, as Kristeva suggests, because it reminds man of his own mortality, a subject about which the architect seems to have been remarkably sanguine, seeing it as a return to nature. The roots for this ambivalence may lie in the ideas of the Cathars who believed the body to be base matter, preventing the soul from achieving unification with the Holy Spirit. The impact of Catharism on Le Corbusier's work cannot be underestimated. He repeatedly made his own sense of connection with this beleaguered group very clear. Reproduction was frowned upon by the Cathars as it only served to perpetuate the reign of base matter. While Le Corbusier may have wished to avoid the issue of maternity in his own life he was happy to accommodate it in the life of others, taking particular care with the provision of facilities for families with children.

For Le Corbusier Yvonne was the catalyst in his creative life, bringing him both stability and inspiration. An anarchic figure, she provided a vital mercurial element, forcing him to address both the spiritual and bodily aspects of his being. However, his relationship with her does not seem to have been easy. He found it necessary to have affairs with other women, calling into question the veracity of his vision of himself and his wife as a unified whole. Significantly *The Poem*, in which Yvonne plays such a central role, was written after his relationships with Baker and Tjader Harris. It may be that through its pages he wished to reassert Yvonne's true importance to him. Certainly he seems to have felt guilty at his treatment of her and helpless at the increasing hold her illness took.

Through Le Corbusier's later paintings the figure of Yvonne is transformed into an archaic goddess, a figure of archetypal femininity. She is Ariadne to Le Corbusier's Theseus, Mary Magdalene to his Jesus. In the series of *Icône* paintings she holds in her cupped hands the candle, the divine light. Through her association with water, with waves, sound and balance, she is that primal datum through which man arrives at a better understanding of the world. Together they inhabit the cosmic realm of the gods. Like the idealised woman of the Surrealists, with whom she could be mistaken, she is, as Whitney Chadwick puts it, a '. . . muse, the image of man's inspiration and his salvation . . . an externalised source of creative energy and a personification of the female Other.' Unlike the idealised woman of the Surrealists she is a passionate intellectual combining elements of extreme wisdom with bodily instinct, the essence of the 'right angle'. It is she who is celebrated in the chapel of Notre Dame du Haut Ronchamp and indeed in all of Le Corbusier's late work. My suggestion is that Le Corbusier's muse figure was rather more complex and subtle than those envisaged by certain of his contemporaries.

It has been seen that Le Corbusier seems to have adhered to the Teilhardien idea that woman played a vital part in helping man to gain contact with the earth and hence the divine. He approaches the subject from a man's point of view. His own point of view. Whether his ideas are equally applicable to women is not clear. His theories appear to have many of the same flaws as that, rather better known, model of C.G. Jung, who saw women as being inherently feminine and subjective with a guiding masculine animus element. Men meanwhile are essentially masculine and intellectual with a feminine muse, the anima, the suggestion being that women were intellectually inferior to men. My feeling is that Le Corbusier does not, in reality, seem to have adhered to such a view, operating, as has been seen in the course of this discussion, with women as intellectual equals, even to the extent that he chose to collaborate with a female mathematician on the Modulor.

Being a man who wanted to see all phenomena as part of a wider cosmic pattern, Le Corbusier was fond of casting the women whom he loved in archetypal roles. The question is whether he was then less able to see these women for who they really were. Le Corbusier himself was troubled by the tensions between the reality of womanhood and the different roles woman was made to play, for example in contemporary American society.

Do the women instinctively feel, through the creative conceptions of dress designers, that they will shine like goddesses/ I sense that men, held at a certain distance by the hard labour of their normal life, would thus satisfy the obscure need of their spirits for adoration.

Nevertheless, I have met here two women of this type, one all goodness, the other like Pallas Athena.

Shall I be plunging into the ridiculous if I make the supposition that the people are creating feminine fetishes? For ordinary purposes and for daily use, the little blonds of the movies. To finish off, the vamp – an American invention. Caravaggio and inferiority complexes. Separation, independent lives, lack of contact. All kinds of strange phenomena. Tendency towards pathos. Prose in everyday life, inevitably, except in unusual cases. Consequence: idols on pedestals, fervor – magnificent wax manikins.[23]

When this passage is examined closely it becomes apparent that he is not objecting to the creation of 'feminine fetishes', something with which he was deeply familiar. His objection was to their 'ordinary' use in 'everyday life'. Women were to be worshipped, but not on this basis.

Dust from the Parthenon, the temple of the Virgin, was buried with Le Corbusier when he died in his beloved Mediterranean sea in 1965.[24] In his speech in memory of his friend, André Malraux, minister of cultural affairs, spoke of 'the pensive goddess' who slowly lowered her 'lance over' Le Corbusier's 'silent shroud'.[25] From birth to death Le Corbusier inhabited a world in which the female and the feminine were paramount. The 'pensive goddess' was to play a primary role in his life and work until its very end.

Notes

1 Le Corbusier, *When the Cathedrals were White: A Journey to the Country of the Timid People* (New York: Reynal and Hitchcock, 1947), p.166.

2 It seems that early in life Le Corbusier was rather ambivalent about women and their charms. This diffidence is expressed for example through his description of the women and men at a party. 'Carmen d'Assilca; I like her name, Budry and a host of other forgotten names, for the most part I don't have the hots.' Le Corbusier, *Sketchbooks Volume 1* (London: Thames and Hudson, 1981), sketch 139.

3 J. Jenger, *Le Corbusier Choix de Lettres* (Basel: Birkhauser, 2002), p.23.

4 Le Corbusier to William Ritter, 05.10.1918, Fondation Le Corbusier (hereafter referred to as FLC) R3.19.29.

5 Letter Le Corbusier to Marcel Levaillant, 04.12.1923, FLC H3.7.86.

6 Letter Le Corbusier to Madame Chastanet-Cros, 27.04.1963, FLC E1.15.130.

7 Le Corbusier, *The Decorative Art of Today* (London: Architectural Press, 1987), p.134.

8 Perry writes of 'traditional . . . divisions of art into intellectual "masculine" genres, as against "feminine" or more decorative, superficial forms of artistic expres-

sion'. Such associations are in her belief 'shifting and constantly renegotiated in the critical writings which surround the work of the . . . avant-garde during the first three decades of the twentieth century'. G. Perry, *Women Artists and the Parisian Avant-Garde* (Manchester: Manchester University Press, 1995), p.6.

9 Le Corbusier, *Towards a New Architecture* (London: Architectural Press, 1982), p.119.

10 Le Corbusier, *Sketchbooks Volume 4, 1957–1964* (Cambridge, MA: MIT Press, 1982), sketch 679.

11 Le Corbusier, *When the Cathedrals were White*, p.122.

12 G. Baker and J. Gubler, *Le Corbusier: Early Works by Charles-Edouard Jeanneret Gris* (London: Academy, 1987), p.116.

13 The same applies to the age-old analogy that Le Corbusier makes between man and sun and woman and moon. The sun, dominant in our modern minds, appears to be the stronger.

14 S. B. Ortner, 'Is Female to Male as Nature is to Culture?' in M. Z. Rosaldo and L. Lamphere (eds), *Women, Culture and Society* (Stanford: Stanford University Press, 1974).

15 C. Paglia, *Sexual Personae* (London: Penguin, 1990), p.1.

16 Hagan addresses this issue more extensively in S. Hagan, *Taking Shape: A New Contract between Architecture and Nature* (London: Architectural Press, 2001).

17 For a discussion of 'the increasingly ironicized conception of male artistic identity' from the turn of the twentieth century onward see A. Jones, 'Clothes Make the Man: The Male Artist as a Performative Function', *The Oxford Art Journal*, 18, 2, 1995, pp.18–33.

18 Le Corbusier, *Precisions on the Present State of Architecture and City Planning* (Cambridge, MA: MIT Press, 1991), p.82.

19 Ibid., p.47.

20 D. Pauly, 'The Chapel at Ronchamp' *AD Profile* 60, 55, 7/8 (1985), p.33. See Diana Agrest, 'Architecture from Without: Body, Logic and Sex', *Assemblage* 7 (1988), pp.28–41 for a discussion of the male sex's usurpation of woman's reproductive role.

21 Plato, *Symposium*, in S. Buchanan (ed.), *The Portable Plato* (Harmondsworth: Penguin, 1997), p.168.

22 J. Kristeva quoted in V. Burgin, 'Geometry and Abjection', *AA Files*, 15 (1987), p.39.

23 Le Corbusier, *When the Cathedrals were White*, p.166.

24 J. Glancey, *Swimming toward the Sun: a Look at the Architect Le Corbusier and the Cathars*, BBC Radio 3, 29 September 2002.

25 Le Corbusier, *Oeuvre Complète Volume 7, 1957–1965* (Zurich: Les Editions d'Architecture, 1995), p.188.

Selected Bibliography

Agrest, D., 'Architecture from Without: Body, Logic and Sex', *Assemblage 7* (1988), pp.28–41.

Ahrentzen, S. and Groat, L., 'Rethinking Architectural Education: Patriarchal Conventions and Alternative Visions from the Perspectives of Women Faculty', *Journal of Architectural and Planning Research*, 9:2, summer 1992, pp.95–111.

Allendy, R., *Capitalisme et Sexualité: le conflits des instincts et les problèmes actuels* (Paris: Denoel, 1931) in FLC.

Auslander, L.,'The Gendering of Consumer Practices in Nineteenth Century France', in V. de Grazia (ed.), *The Sex of Things* (Berkeley: University of California Press, 1960), pp.79–118.

Bacon, M., *Le Corbusier in America* (Cambridge, MA: MIT Press 2001).

Baker, G. and Gubler, J., *Le Corbusier: Early Works by Charles-Edouard Jeanneret Gris* (London: Academy, 1987).

Baker, J.C. and Chase, C., *Josephine* (New York: Random House, 1993).

Banham, R., *The New Brutalism, Ethic or Aesthetic* (London: Architectural Press, 1966).

Benstock, S., *Women of the Left Bank* (London: Virago, 1994).

Benton, T., *The Villas of Le Corbusier* (London: Yale University Press, 1987).

Benton, T. (ed.), *Le Corbusier Architect of the Century* (London: Arts Council, 1987), p.239.

Billeter, E., *Le Corbusier Secret* (Laussanne: Musée Cantonal des Beaux Arts, 1987).

Billy, A., 'La Sainte-Baume contre Lourdes!', *Le Figaro*, 9 December 1948, front page.

Billy, A., 'Sainte Baume,' *Le Figaro*, 16 December 1948, p.2.

Bozdoğan, S., 'Journey to the East: Ways of Looking at the Orient and the Question of Representation', *Journal of Architectural Education*, 41, 4 (1989), pp.38–45.

Breton, A., *Arcane 17* (Paris: Jean-Jacques Pauvert, 1971), p.66. Originally published 1947.

Bristow, J., *Sexuality: the New Critical Idiom* (London: Routledge, 1997).

Brookes, H.A., *Le Corbusier's Formative Years* (London: University of Chicago Press, 1997).

Buchanan, S. (ed.), *The Portable Plato* (Harmondsworth: Penguin, 1997).

Cali, F., *The Architecture of Truth: The Cistercian Abbey of la Thoronet in Provence* (London: Thames and Hudson, 1957).

Carl, P., 'Le Corbusier's Penthouse in Paris: 24 Rue Nungesser et Coli', *Daidalos*, 28 (1988), pp.65–75.

Carl, P., 'Architecture and time: a prolegomena', *AA Files*, 22 (1991), pp.48–65.

Carl, P., 'Ornament and time: a prolegomena', *AA Files*, 23 (1992), pp.49–64.

Celik, Z., 'Le Corbusier, Orientalism, Colonialism', *Assemblage*, 17 (1992), pp.61–77.

Chadwick, W., 'Eros or Thanatos – The Surrealist Cult of Love Reexamined,' *Art Forum*, 14 (1975), pp.46–56.

Chadwick, W., *Women Artists and the Surrealist Movement* (London: Thames and Hudson, 1985).

Chadwick, W. and de Courtivron, I., *Significant Others: Creativity and Intimate Partnership* (London: Thames and Hudson, 1993).

Christ-Janer, A. and Mix Foley, M., *Modern Church Architecture* (London: McGraw Hill, 1962).

Coll, J., 'Le Corbusier. Taureaux: An Analysis of the thinking process in the last series of Le Corbusier's Plastic work', *Art History*, 18, 4 (1995), p.537–68.

Coll, J., 'Structure and Play in Le Corbusier's Art Works' *AA Files*, 31 (1996), pp.4–14.

Colli, L.M., 'Le Corbusier e il colore; I Claviers Salubra,' *Storia dell'arte*, 43 (1981), pp.271–91.

Colli, L.M., 'La Couleur qui cache, la couleur qui signale: l'ordonnance et la crainte dans la poètique corbuséenne des couleurs' in *Le Corbusier et La Couleur* (Paris: Fondation Le Corbusier, 1992), pp.21–34.

Constant, C., *Eileen Gray* (London: Phaidon, 2000).

Coombs, R., 'Le Corbusier and Vernacular Architecture: A Newly Discovered Drawing for the Bergerie at Sainte Baume', *Minutes of the 83rd ACSA Meeting* (1995), p.149.

Deepwell, K. (ed.), *Women Artists and Modernism* (Manchester: Manchester University Press, 1998).

Devoucoux du Buysson, P., *Le Guide du Pèlerin à la grotte de sainte Marie Madeleine* (La Sainte Baume: La Fraternité Sainte Marie Madeleine, 1998).

Dupont, R., 'Près de Marseille Dans les forêts millenaires de la Sainte-Baume la "cathédrale engloutie" surgira pour devenir la basilique de la Paix', *L'Aube* (2 June 1948), front page.

Eliel, C.S. (ed.), *L'Esprit Nouveau: Purism in Paris* (New York: Harry N. Abrams, 2001).

Evans, A.B., *Jean Cocteau and His films of Orphic Identity* (London: Associated University Press, 1977).

Fagan-King, J., 'United on the Threshold of the Twentieth Century Mystical Ideal', *Art History*, 11, 1 (1988), pp.89–113.

Faure, É., *Fonction du Cinéma: de la cinéplastique à son destin social* (Paris: Éditions Gonthier, 1995), p.12. Originally published 1953.

Fellin-Yeh, S., 'Dandies, Marginality and Modernism: Georgia O'Keefe, Marcel Duchamp and Other Cross-dressers', *Oxford Art Journal*, 18, 2 (1995), p.33.

Fer, B., 'What's in a Line? Gender and Modernity', *Oxford Art Journal*, 13, 1, 1990, pp.77–88.

Feurstein, G., *Androgynos: The Male-Female in Art and Architecture* (Stuttgart: Axel Menges, 1997).

Forty, A., *Words and Buildings* (London: Thames and Hudson, 2000).

Fowlie, W. (ed.), *The Journals of Jean Cocteau* (London: Museum Press, 1957), p.81.

Franck, D., *The Bohemians* (London: Weidenfeld & Nicolson, 2001).

Friedman, A.T., *Women and the Making of the Modern House* (New York: Harry N. Abrams, 1998).

Friedman, A.T., 'Frank Lloyd Wright and Feminism: Mamah Borthwick's Letters to Ellen Key', *Journal of the Society of Architectural Historians*, 61, 2 (2002), pp.140–51.

Ghyka, M., *Nombre d'or: rites et rhythmes Pythagoriciens dans le development de la civilisation Occidental* (Paris: Gallimard, 1931).

Ghyka, M., *Esthetique des proportions dans le nature et dans les arts* (Paris: Gallimard, 1927).

Gimpel, J., *Les Bâtisseurs de Cathédrales* (Paris: Éditions Seuil, 1959).

Glancey, J., *Swimming toward the Sun: a Look at the Architect Le Corbusier and the Cathars*, BBC Radio 3, 29 September 2002.

Golan, R., *Modernity and Nostalgia: Art and Politics in France between the Wars* (London: Yale University Press, 1995).

Gresleri, G., 'Prima da Ronchamp La Sainte Baume: Terra e cielo, ombra e luce,' *Parametro*, 207 (1995), pp. 34–43.

Griffin, F., and Millet M., 'Shadey Aesthetics', *Journal of Architectural Education*, 37/3,4 (1991), pp.43–60.

Gronberg, T., *Design on Modernity: Exhibiting the City in 1920s Paris* (Manchester: Manchester University Press, 1998).

Guthrie, W.K.C., *Orpheus and Greek Religion* (London: Methuen, 1935).

Hagan, S., *Taking Shape: A New Contract between Architecture and Nature* (London: Architectural Press, 2001).

Haskins, S., *Mary Magdalene* (London: HarperCollins, 1993).

Hicken, A., *Apollinaire, Cubism and Orphism* (Aldershot: Ashgate, 2002).

Hooper, B., 'Urban Space, Modernity, and Masculinist Desire: The Utopian longings of Le Corbusier' in Bingaman, A., Sanders, L. and Zorahc, R., *Embodied Utopias: Gender, Social Change, and the Modern Metropolis* (London: Routledge, 2002).

Ingersoll, R., *A Marriage of Contours* (Princeton: Princeton Architectural Press, 1990).

Jencks, C., *Le Corbusier and the Tragic View of Architecture* (London: Allen Lane, 1973).

Jencks, C., *Le Corbusier and the Continual Revolution in Architecture* (New York: Monacelli Press, 2000).

Jenger, J. *Le Corbusier Choix de Lettres* (Basel: Birkhauser, 2002).

Jones, A., '"Clothes Make the Man": The Male Artist as a Performative Function', *Oxford Art Journal*, 18, 2 (1995), pp.18–33.

Jung, C.G., *Alchemical Studies, Collected Works* 13 (London: Routledge & Kegan Paul, 1951).

Kagal, C., 'Le Corbusier: the Acrobat of Architecture. Interview with Balkrishna Doshi, 1986', *Architecture and Urbanism*, 322 (1997), pp.168–83.

Kime Scott, B. (ed.), *The Gender of Modernism* (Bloomington: Indiana University Press, 1990).

Krustrup. M., *L'Illiade Dessins* (Copenhagen: Borgen, 1986).

Krustrup, M., 'Poème de l'Angle Droit', *Arkitekten*, 92 (1990), pp.422–32.

Krustrup, M., *Porte Email* (Copenhagen: Arkitektens Forlag, 1991).

Krustrup, M., *Persona in Le Corbusier, Painter and Architect* (Arkitekturtidsskrift: Nordjyllands, 1995).

Krustrup, M., 'The women of Algiers', *Skala*, 24/25, 1991, pp.36–41.

Lahiji, N., 'The Gift of the Open Hand: Le Corbusier's Reading of Georges Bataille's La Part Maudite,' *Journal of Architectural Education*, 50, 1 (1996), pp. 50–67.

Lapunzina, A., 'The pyramid and the wall: an unknown project of Le Corbusier in Venezuela', *arq*, 5, 3 (2001), pp.255–67.

Laubier, C., *The Condition of Women in France: 1945 to the Present* (London: Routledge, 1990).

Le Corbusier, *Towards a New Architecture* (London: Architectural Press, 1982). Originally published as *Vers une Architecture* (Paris: Crès, 1923).

Le Corbusier, *The Decorative Art of Today* (London: The Architectural Press, 1987. Originally published as Le Corbusier, *L'Art décoratif d'aujourd'hui* (Paris: Editions Crès, 1925).

Le Corbusier, *The City of Tomorrow* (London: Architectural Press, 1946). Originally published as *Urbanisme* (Paris: Crès, 1924).

Le Corbusier, *Precisions on the Present State of Architecture and City Planning* (Cambridge, MA: MIT Press, 1991). Originally published as *Précisions sur un état présent de l'architecture et de l'urbanisme* (Paris: Crès, 1930).

Le Corbusier, *Une Maison – un palais, A la recherche d'une unité architecturale* (Paris: Crès, 1928).

Le Corbusier, *The Radiant City* (London: Faber, 1967), p.i. Originally published as Le Corbusier, *La Ville Radieuse* (Paris: Éditions de l'Architecture d'Aujourd'hui, 1935).

Le Corbusier and Pierre Jeanneret, *Oeuvre Complète Volume 2, 1929–34* (Zurich: Les Editions d'Architecture, 1995). Originally published in 1935.

Le Corbusier and Pierre Jeanneret, *Oeuvre Complète Volume 1, 1910–1929* (Zurich: Les Editions d'Architecture, 1995). Originally published in 1937.

Le Corbusier and Pierre Jeanneret, *Oeuvre Complète Volume 3, 1934–38* (Zurich: Les Editions d'Architecture, 1995). Originally published in 1938.

Le Corbusier, *Le Corbusier Talks with Students* (New York: Orion, 1961), p.34. Originally published as *Entretien avec les étudiants des écoles d'architecture* (Paris: Denoel 1943).

Le Corbusier, *When the Cathedrals were White: A Journey to the Country of the Timid People* (New York: Reynal and Hitchcock,

1947). Originally published as *Quand les cathédrales étaient blanches* (Paris: Plon, 1937).

Le Corbusier, *Oeuvre Complète Volume 4, 1938–1946* (Zurich: Les Editions d'Architecture, 1995). Originally published in 1946.

Le Corbusier, *A New World of Space* (New York: Reynal and Hitchcock, 1948).

Le Corbusier, *Poésie sur Alger* (Paris: Editions Connivances, 1989). Originally published in 1950.

Le Corbusier, *Modulor* (London: Faber, 1954). Originally published as *Le Modulor* (Paris: Editions d'Architecture d'Aujourd hui, 1950).

Le Corbusier, 'Le Théatre Spontané' in André Villiers (ed.), *Architecture et Dramaturgie* (Paris: Editions d'Aujourd'hui, 1980). Originally published in 1950.

Le Corbusier, *Oeuvre Complète Volume 5, 1946–1952* (Zurich: Les Editions d'Architecture, 1995). Originally published in 1953.

Le Corbusier, *Modulor 2* (London: Faber, 1955). Originally published as *Le Modulor II* (Paris: Editions d'Architecture d'Aujourd'hui, 1955).

Le Corbusier, *Le Poème de l'angle droit* (Paris: Editions Connivance, 1989). Originally published in 1955.

Le Corbusier, *Oeuvre Complète Volume 6, 1952–1957* (Zurich: Les Editions d'Architecture, 1995). Originally published in 1957.

Le Corbusier, *The Chapel at Ronchamp* (London: Architectural Press, 1957).

Le Corbusier, *Le Poème Electronique* (Paris: Les Cahiers Forces Vives aux Éditions de Minuit, 1958).

Le Corbusier, *Oeuvre Complète Volume 7, 1957–1965* (Zurich: Les Editions d'Architecture, 1995). Originally published in 1965.

Le Corbusier, *Journey to the East* (Cambridge, MA: MIT Press, 1987). Le Corbusier, *Le Voyage d'Orient* (Paris: Parenthèses, 1887). Originally published in 1966.

Le Corbusier, *The Final Testament of Père Corbu: a Translation and Interpretation of Mise au Point by Ivan Zaknic* (New Haven, CT: Yale University Press, 1997), p.91. Originally published as *Mise au Point* (Paris: Editions Forces-Vives), 1966.

Le Corbusier, *Sketchbooks Volume 1* (London: Thames and Hudson, 1981).

Le Corbusier, *Sketchbooks Volume 2* (London: Thames and Hudson, 1981).

Le Corbusier, *Sketchbooks Volume 3, 1954–1957* (Cambridge, MA: MIT Press, 1982).

Le Corbusier, *Sketchbooks Volume 4, 1957–1964* (Cambridge, MA: MIT Press, 1982).

Léger, F., *Functions of Painting* (New York: Viking, 1965).

Loach, J., 'Studio as Laboratory', *Architectural Review*, Special Issue, 181, 1079 (1987), pp. 73–7.

Loach, J., 'Le Corbusier and the Creative use of Mathematics', *British Journal of the History of Science*, 31 (1998), pp.185–215.

Lowman, J., 'Le Corbusier 1900–1925: The Years of Transition.' Doctoral Dissertation, University of London, (1979).

McCorquodale, D., Ruedi, K., Wigglesworth, S. (eds), *Desiring Practices: Architecture, Gender and the Interdisciplinary* (London: Black Dog, 1996).

McLeod, M., 'Charlotte Perriand, Her First Decade as a Designer', *AA Files*, 15, (1987), pp.3–13.

McLeod, M., 'Urbanism and Utopia: Le Corbusier from Regional Syndicalism to Vichy', DPhil thesis, Princeton, (1985).

McLeod, M., 'Undresssing Architecture: Fashion, Gender, Modernity' in Fausch, D., Singley, P. and Efrat, Z., *Architecture in Fashion* (Princeton: Princeton Architectural Press, 1994), pp.38–123.

Maisch, I., *Mary Magdalene: The Image of Woman through the Centuries* (Collegeville, Minnesota: Liturgical Press, 1998).

Mâle, E., *Religious Art in France: the Twelfth Century*, (Princeton: Bollingen, 1973). Originally published as *L'Art religieux du XIIe siècle en France. Etude sur l'origine de l'iconographie du Moyen Age* (Paris: Armand Colin, 1922).

Mâle, E., *The Gothic Image* (London: Fontana, 1961). Originally published as *L'Art Religieux du XIII° Siècle en France* (Paris: Armand Colin, 1910).

Marcus, G.H., *Le Corbusier: Inside the Machine for Living* (New York: Monacelli Press, 2000), p.85.

Menin, S. and Samuel, F., *Nature and Space: Aalto and Le Corbusier* (London: Routledge, 2003).

Mitchell, C., 'Style/Ecriture. On the classical ethos, women's sculptural practice and pre-First-World-War feminism', *Art History* (February 2002), pp.1–22.

Mitchell, C., 'Facing horror: women's work, sculptural practice and the Great War', in Mainz, V. and Pollock, G. (eds), *Work and the Image II* (Aldershot: Ashgate, 2000), pp.33–60.

Moles, A., *Histoire des Charpentiers* (Paris: Librairie Gründ, 1949).

Montalte, L. (E. Trouin pseud.), *Fallait-il Bâtir Le Mont-Saint-Michel?* (St Zachaire: Montalte, 1979).

Moore, R.A., 'Le Corbusier and the *mecanique spirituelle*: An investigation into Le Corbusier's architectural symbolism and its background in Beaux Arts design'. D Phil thesis, University of Maryland (1979).

Moore, R.A., 'Alchemical and mythical themes in the Poem of the Right Angle 1947–65', *Oppositions* 19/20 (winter/spring 1980), pp.110–39.

Pauly, D., 'The Chapel at Ronchamp' *AD Profile 60*, 55, 7/8 (1985), pp.30–37.

Pearson, C.E.M., 'Integrations of Art and Architecture in the Work of Le Corbusier. Theory and Practice from Ornamentalism to the "Synthesis of the Major Arts"'. PhD thesis, Stanford University (1995).

Peter, J., *The Oral History of Modern Architecture* (New York: Harry N. Abrams, 1994).

Petit, J., *Le Corbusier Lui-même* (Paris: Forces Vives, 1970).

Perry, G., *Women Artists and the Parisian Avant-Garde* (Manchester: Manchester University Press, 1995).

Pevsner, N., *Pioneers of Modern Design* (Harmondsworth: Pelican, 1975).

Pico della Mirandola, G., *On the Dignity of Man* (Indianapolis: Hackett, 1998). Originally written in 1486.

Pincus Witten, R., *Occult Symbolism in France: Joséphin Péladan and the Salons de la Rose-Croix* (New York: Garland, 1976).

Pollock, M., 'Modernity and the Spaces of Feminism' in F. Frasina (ed.), *Art in Modern Culture* (London: Phaidon, 1992), pp.110–35.

Pottecher, F., 'Que le Fauve soit libre dans sa cage', *L'Architecture d'Aujourd'Hui*, 252 (1987), pp.58–66.

Praz, M., *The Romantic Agony* (Oxford: Oxford University Press, 1979). Originally published in English 1933.

Price, M., 'The missing *méchanicienne*: gender, production and order in Léger's machine aesthetic' in Mainz, V. and Pollock, G. (eds), *Work and the Image II* (Aldershot: Ashgate, 2000), pp.91–112.

Provensal, H., *L'Art de Demain* (Paris: Perrin, 1904).

Rabelais, F., *Oeuvres Complètes* (Paris: Gallimard, 1951).

Réau, L., *Iconographie de l'art Chrétien Volume 1* (Paris: Presses Universitaires de France, 1955).

Réau, L., *Iconographie de l'art Chrétien Volume 2* (Paris: Presses Universitaires de France, 1957).

Renan, E., *La Vie de Jesus* (Paris: Calmann-Levy, 1906).

Roberts, M.L., 'Sampson and Delilah Revisited', *American Historical Review*, June 1993, pp.657–84.

Roche, A.V., *Provençal Regionalism* (Illinois: Northwestern University Studies, 1954).

Roller, T., *Les Catacombes de Rome. Histoire de l'art et des croyances religieuses pendant le premiers siècles du Christianisme, Volume II* (Paris: Morel, 1881).

Rougemont, D. de, *Passion and Society* (London: Faber and Faber, 1958), p.294. Originally published as Denis de Rougement, *L'Amour et L'Occident* (Paris: Plon, 1940).

Rüegg, A. ed., *Le Corbusier Photographs by René Burri: Moments in the Life of a Great Architect* (Basel: Birkhäuser, 1999).

Rüegg, A. ed., *Polychromie architecturale* (Basel: Birkhäuser, 1997).

Saint Palais, C., *Esclarmonde de Foix: Princesse Cathare* (Toulouse: Privat, 1956).

Samuel, F., 'Le Corbusier, Women, Nature and Culture', *Issues in Art and Architecture* 5, 2 (1998), pp. 4–20.

Samuel, F., 'A Profane Annunciation; The Representation of Sexuality in the Architecture of Ronchamp', *Journal of Architectural Education*, 53, 2 (1999), pp.74–90.

Samuel, F., 'Le Corbusier, Teilhard de Chardin and the Planetisation of Mankind', *Journal of Architecture*, 4 (1999), pp.149–65.

Samuel, F., 'The Philosophical City of Rabelais and St Teresa; Le Corbusier and Edouard Trouin's scheme for St Baume', *Literature and Theology* 13, 2 (1999), pp.111–26.

Samuel, F., 'The Representation of Mary in Le Corbusier's Chapel at Ronchamp', *Church History*, 68, 2 (1999), pp.398–417.

Samuel, F., 'Le Corbusier, Teilhard de Chardin and *La Planétisation humaine*: spiritual ideas at the heart of modernism', *French Cultural Studies*, 11, 2 (2000), pp.181–200.

Samuel, F., 'Le Corbusier, Rabelais and Oracle of the Holy Bottle', *Word and Image: a Journal of verbal/visual enquiry*, 16 (2000), pp.1–13.

Samuel, F., 'Animus, Anima and the Architecture of Le Corbusier', *Harvest*, 48/2 (2003), pp.42–60.

Schumacher, T., 'Deep Space Shallow Space', *Architectural Review*, vol. CLXXXI, no. 1079 (1987), p.41.

Schuré, E., *Les Grands Initiés: Esquisse secrete des religions* (Paris: Perrin, 1908).

Scott, W., *Hermetica* (Oxford: Clarendon Press, 1924).

Scully, V., *The Earth, the Temple and the Gods* (New Haven, CT: Yale University Press, 1962).

Serenyi, P., 'Le Corbusier, Fourier and the Monastery of Ema', *Art Bulletin*, 49 (1967), p.297.

Shinar, M., 'Feminist Criticism of Urban Theory and Design, Case Study: Le Corbusier', *Journal of Urban and Cultural Studies*, 2,2 (1992), pp.29–39.

Silver, K., *Esprit de Corps: The Art of the Parisian Avant-Garde and the First World War, 1914–1925* (Princeton: Princeton University Press, 1989).

Spate, V., *Orphism: the Evolution of Non-figurative Painting in Paris in 1910–14* (Oxford: Clarendon Press, 1979).

Sperling, H. and Simon, M., trans., *The Zohar* (London: Soncino Press, 1933).

Swietlicki, C., *Spanish Christian Cabala* (Columbia: University of Missouri Press), 1986.

Teresa of Jesus, Saint, *The Way of Perfection* (London: Thomas Baker, 1911).

Teresa of Jesus, Saint, *The Interior Castle* (London: Thomas Baker, 1912). Originally written in 1577.

Thomas, L., *André Gide, the Ethic of the Artist* (London: Secker & Warburg, 1950).

Treib, M., *Space Calculated in Seconds* (Princeton: Princeton University Press, 1996).

Turner, P., *The Education of an Architect* (New York: Garland, 1977).

Ven Herck, K. (ed.), 'First Interlude: on the nuances of historical emancipation', *Journal of Architecture*, 7 (Autumn 2002), pp.245–7.

Viatte, G., *Le Corbusier et la Meditérranée* (Marseilles: L'Université de Provence, 1991).

Vogt, A. M., Le Corbusier, *The Noble Savage: Towards an Archaeology of Modernism* (Cambridge, MA: MIT Press, 1998).

Von Moos, S. & Rüegg, A. (eds), *Le Corbusier before Le Corbusier* (New Haven, CT: Yale University Press, 2002).

Voragine, Jacobus de, *The Golden Legend*, vol. 1 translated by William Granger Ryan (Princeton: Princeton University Press, 1993).

Walden, R. ed., *The Open Hand* (Cambridge, MA: MIT Press, 1982).

Weber, H., ed., *Le Corbusier the Artist* (Zurich: Editions Heidi Weber, 1988).

Wigley, M., *White Walls, Designer Dresses: The Fashioning of Modern Architecture* (Cambridge, MA: MIT Press, 1995).

Wogenscky, A., *Les Mains de Le Corbusier* (Paris: Éditions de Grenelle, n.d.).

Index

Page references for illustrations are in *italics*; those for notes are followed by n
All works are by Le Corbusier unless otherwise attributed